Ratio in Relatione

Ratio in Relatione

The Function of Structural Paradigms and Their
Influence on Rational Choice and the Search for Truth

ANTHONY HOLLOWELL

☙PICKWICK *Publications* • Eugene, Oregon

RATIO IN RELATIONE
The Function of Structural Paradigms and Their Influence on Rational Choice and the Search for Truth

Copyright © 2020 Anthony Hollowell. All rights reserved. Except for brief quotations in critical publications or reviews, no part of this book may be reproduced in any manner without prior written permission from the publisher. Write: Permissions, Wipf and Stock Publishers, 199 W. 8th Ave., Suite 3, Eugene, OR 97401.

Pickwick Publications
An Imprint of Wipf and Stock Publishers
199 W. 8th Ave., Suite 3
Eugene, OR 97401

www.wipfandstock.com

PAPERBACK ISBN: 978-1-7252-6194-5
HARDCOVER ISBN: 978-1-7252-6193-8
EBOOK ISBN: 978-1-7252-6195-2

Cataloguing-in-Publication data:

Names: Hollowell, Anthony, author.

Title: Ratio in relatione : the function of structural paradigms and their influence on rational choice and the search for truth / Anthony Hollowell.

Description: Eugene, OR : Pickwick Publications, 2020 | Includes bibliographical references.

Identifiers: ISBN 978-1-7252-6194-5 (paperback) | ISBN 978-1-7252-6193-8 (hardcover) | ISBN 978-1-7252-6195-2 (ebook)

Subjects: LCSH: Theological anthropology. | Theological anthropology—Christianity. | Reason. | Philosophy and religion. | Civilization—Philosophy. | Guardini, Romano, 1885–1968—Criticism and interpretation. | Tocqueville, Alexis de, 1805–1859—Criticism and interpretation.

Classification: BT701.3 .H65 2020 (paperback) | BT701.3 .H65 (ebook)

Revised Standard Version of the Bible—Second Catholic Edition (Ignatius Edition) Copyright © 2006 National Council of the Churches of Christ in the United States of America. Used by permission. All rights reserved worldwide.

10/23/20

Vidimus et approbamus ad normam Statutorum Academiae Alfonsianae
Prof. Martin McKeever, C.Ss.R., Prof. Theol. Moralis systematicae
Prof. Martín Carbajo-Nuñez, O.F.M., Prof. Theol. Moralis systematicae
Prof. Alfonso Vincenzo Amarante, C.Ss.R., Praeses Academiae Alfonsianae
Roma, 30/5/2019

Nihil Obstat
Prof. Vincenzo Buonomo
Rector Magnificus
Pont. Universitatis Lateranensis
Roma, 3/6/2019

Imprimatur
✝Mons. Giuseppe Tonello
Cancelliere
Vicariato di Roma
Roma, 4/6/2019

Contents

Introduction | ix

CHAPTER 1: *RATIO ET RELATIO* | 1

CHAPTER 2: THE DEMOCRATIC MIND | 28

CHAPTER 3: THE TECHNOCRATIC MIND | 77

CHAPTER 4: *RATIO IN RELATIONE* | 115

CONCLUSION | 182

Bibliography | 187

Introduction

THE FIRST COMMAND GOD gave to human beings was to "be fruitful and multiply, and fill the earth and subdue it; and have dominion . . . over every living thing that moves upon the earth."¹ God does not first tell Adam and Eve to follow the ten commandments; rather, he commands them to exercise a fruitful dominion over the whole earth, subduing it according to the freedom of man. Such freedom was never meant to be haphazard or directionless, for it was ordered to the very specific end of dominion; to guide human freedom towards this end, man was endowed with human reason which seeks those truths which can guide him towards his proper fulfillment. This is why Pope John Paul II emphasized "the fundamental dependence of freedom on truth," for without the truth, man's freedom disintegrates into the directionless pursuit of stimuli and desires which often do not bring the fruit they promise.² Only a freedom anchored in truth is capable of being an authentic guide to human action and the moral life.

Because reason is used by the human person to attain truth and thus direct one's freedom by this truth, the nature of reason is of considerable consequence for both the practice of Catholic morality and the discipline of Catholic moral theology. All men have a rational faculty according to their nature as human beings, but this rational faculty is not universally identical in its expression within each human person, for a whole spectrum of ideas, intelligences, and even types of logic are present within various persons. Although the causes which contribute to this variation are not always apparent, one cause which we will examine throughout this thesis is the role of relationships.

Therefore, this thesis will attempt to think critically on the category of relation as it pertains to the faculty of reason. This is accomplished by completing a more general task in the first three chapters and is described

---

1. Genesis 1:28.
2. John Paul II, *Veritatis Splendor*, 34.

by the first words of the title, "Ratio in Relatione." These first three chapters identify relational factors which habituate the mind to specific patterns of logic, thereby demonstrating how the rational faculty of human nature is influenced by the relational dimension of the human person. After establishing this more general grounding, the thesis then concentrates on a more specific task that is described by the subtitle, "The function of structural paradigms and their influence on rational choice and the search for truth." The subtitle describes how the main authors in the first three chapters illustrate the role of relational structures within a culture which contribute to the creation of a distinct framework (or "paradigm") that influences rational choice and the search for truth. The influence of these relational structures on human reason is not limited to rational choice and the search for truth, but these particular expressions of reason naturally emerged as the most relevant connections for a thesis in moral theology.

By focusing on the relational dynamics of human reason, this thesis makes an epistemological claim which necessarily requires a philosophical grounding as much as a theological grounding, and this has several important consequences for the thesis as a whole. First and foremost, this means that the thesis is not rooted in extensive quotes from Scripture or from Magisterial teachings. Because we are seeking a philosophical truth as much as a theological truth, these theological sources of authority are only discreetly present, and even when they are present, they often only contribute to the discussion without necessarily substantiating the discussion.

Perhaps the biggest consequence of this decision to pursue an epistemological claim is that it led to the desire (if not the need) to consider multiple authors instead of a single author. Because the insights of Alexis de Tocqueville are profound and could provide enough content for several theses, he was initially considered as the primary thinker to be investigated in this thesis, but as the philosophical claim emerged as the main contribution of this thesis, it became apparent that an additional thinker could better illustrate any philosophical claims inherent in Tocqueville by either confirming, complementing, or diverging from his thought. If Tocqueville's insight into the role of relational structures in creating forms of logic could be substantiated, then these insights could be enriched and more adequately balanced by considering them in light of another thinker. Having made this decision, it was then decided to pursue some of the central claims of Romano Guardini as they relate to Tocqueville, and these two authors then function as two sets of lenses which provide insight into the central epistemological claim. Their vision is not identical, but their line of sight does converge, and although some stylistic and intellectual richness is lost by the complication of integrating a second main thinker into the thesis as a whole, their convergence provides some epistemological fruits which provide just compensation for what is lost.

Neither thinker has been richly exhausted in this thesis, but exhausting the primary thought of a single thinker was not the goal of this thesis; rather, we investigated an epistemological claim by considering some of the richest insights of two great minds of the modern age. Part of the inspiration for this methodology came from Tocqueville himself, whose usage of "democracy" and "aristocracy" function almost as two distinct persons whom he is continually comparing and contrasting to better understand what he sees in the political and social state of his day. Because Tocqueville and Guardini are just as complex as "democracy" and "aristocracy," their analogous epistemologies are more clearly seen, and more cogently defended, when in the presence of one another. By not concentrating exclusively on one thinker, we lose some of the richness of their individual thought, but our purpose from the beginning was to expose the richness of an idea and not necessarily the richness of a particular mind, and each thinker was used only in so far as he contributes to clarifying this central idea.

To introduce the primary themes important to this epistemological discussion, the thesis begins by examining the development of the mind of Augustine of Hippo. He is sometimes called the "first modern philosopher," and his development as a person and as a thinker provides many convenient parallels and illustrations for the role of *relatio* in the development of the rational faculty. Contrary to the claim of modern philosophers that every person must "think for himself," our personalist survey of Augustine's life shows that such a modern, individualistic epistemology does not adequately describe his own rational development, and by highlighting the mutual interaction between his relational development and his rational development, a basic framework emerges which reveals the role of *relatio* in forming the *ratio* of a human person. This only introduces us to these initial epistemological considerations, and after their introduction, the thought of Augustine will not appear again until the fourth chapter, at which point several parallels are drawn from both his life and teachings which enrich the thesis as a whole.

In the second chapter, we introduce the writings of Alexis de Tocqueville which provide a more substantial articulation of the role of relational structures in forming the logic of persons within a given culture. In order to explore his central claims which relate to this topic, we chose a methodology of exposition of his text *De la Démocratie en Amérique*. It was essential to use and include the French text in this exposition because several subtle but critical distinctions within his epistemology are lost when one relies only on the English translation. The first draft of this chapter tried to rely on the English translation, but it resulted in a confusing and unsatisfactory description of his thought; by maintaining the French in the footnotes of the current text, the reader is invited into encountering his thought with a greater depth and precision which only his French can provide. Ultimately, this chapter will demonstrate the role of a structural order called "equality of conditions" in creating a particular form of democratic logic, and the emergence of this logic is contrasted with a structural order like inequality of conditions which creates its own form of aristocratic logic.

In the third chapter, we will turn our attention to the role of relational structures in creating a technocratic logic. The inspiration for this theme originated from Pope Francis' encyclical *Laudato Si'*, which refers at multiple points to a type of logic which he calls the "technocratic paradigm." When Pope Francis is speaking about this form of logic, he relies heavily on quotes and footnotes from Romano Guardini's *The End of the Modern World*. Therefore, we chose to examine the thought of Romano Guardini more explicitly, examining the way in which the relational structure of modern culture has created a distinct way of thinking (or "logic") which is derived from this very structure.

One notable weakness in Guardini's writing which is not present in Tocqueville is that he is writing about a technocratic culture which he himself states is only in its embryonic form and not yet fully developed. This contrasts with Tocqueville, who was able to examine a social state in America in which equality of conditions was almost perfectly established, and this allowed him to make clean and consistent observations in a way which was not possible for Guardini. The transient nature of the technocratic culture gives Guardini's text more of a prophetic than academic grounding, and although his insights are rich for epistemology, we desired that his insights be grounded in something less abstract than prophecy. To that end, we included several other thinkers in this chapter who help describe more clearly what Guardini was only able to describe partially, and their voice was essential for substantiating the way in which relational structures of technology generate a specific form of logic within the technocratic culture under development. Although the homogeneity and consistency which we were able to achieve in the second chapter is notably missing from this third chapter, and although the involvement of several distinct voices besides Guardini provides a complication which weakens the chapter as a whole, these other voices were necessary for moving beyond the partial and hypothetical dimensions of Guardini's insights and showing how his prophecy has come to life and manifested itself more clearly in this present age. The inclusion of other voices besides Guardini is not a reflection of the inadequacy of his thought; it is only a reflection of an inherent complication involved in what he was trying to consider. He surely can be forgiven for not being able to articulate fully a future which could only be seen partially, and his academic credibility is only increased when one considers how his foresight has been substantiated by future thinkers, including recent popes. Another consequence of this variety of thinkers is that it did not allow us to use a methodology of exposition but rather a textual survey of several authors, and in order to make this survey clear and consistent, the entire chapter is presented in English without putting the original language in the footnotes. The original language of each thinker was consulted on points of particular interest, but unlike our treatment of Tocqueville, it was not necessary to provide Guardini's thought in German or Pope Francis's thought in Italian or Spanish.

In the fourth chapter, we seek to synthesize the specific way in which relational structures of a culture influence the rational faculty of human nature. To do this, we first compare and contrast the epistemological consequences of the relational structures of equality of conditions and technology, showing how Tocqueville and Guardini converge on the role of these structures in forming a particular pattern of thought or "logic." This then allows us to more adequately explore a term which first appears in the third chapter but is not ready for explanation until the fourth chapter, and that is the term "paradigm." This is a term which has undergone considerable philosophical development, and after introducing its connection to Thomas Kuhn and some of its principle characteristics, we then go on to argue that it is a term which is appropriate to apply to the role of relational structures in forming particular patterns of thought. Although neither Tocqueville nor Guardini use the term in their writings, we argue that it appropriately applies to what they were attempting to describe, for as relational structures change within a culture, various paradigms of thought arise which then condition so many expressions of human reason. After establishing the term's intimate connection to Tocqueville and Guardini, we then spend the remainder of the thesis exploring how cultural paradigms influence two rational activities of great concern to moral theology: rational choice and the search for truth.

Regarding language in this fourth chapter, we present the thoughts of all thinkers in an English translation, including Tocqueville. This provided an important and even necessary symmetry to the fourth chapter, for although the beauty and richness of Tocqueville's French is not fully preserved in the English translation, the consistency of the chapter as a whole was vital to maintain. This consistency and clarity was exceedingly difficult to preserve through the intermittent appearance of Tocqueville's French, so we rely on the residual clarity from the exposition of his texts in the second chapter to sustain the reader throughout the English translations in the fourth chapter. We have thoroughly footnoted the text should access to these French translations be desired.

If we were to describe the underlying motivation for this thesis as a whole, we would point to an interest in the process of *metanoia*. The moral relevance of this term is revealed in the first words of Christ as he begins his ministry in Galilee: "The time is fulfilled, and the kingdom of God is at hand; repent (*metanoiete*), and believe in the gospel."[3] The Greek roots of *metanoia* are *meta* and *nous*, and when taken together, they literally mean "to change one's mind," revealing how conversion is very much concerned with the mind, with human reason, and with our entire way of thinking. Saint Paul said something similar when he stated that Christians must "be transformed by the renewal of their mind (*nous*)," and that the true disciples of God are those who "have the mind (*nous*) of Christ."[4] Because true conversion, and thus authentic human freedom, is dependent on acquiring this Christian logic (a Christo-logos), we considered it worthwhile to investigate the way in which the relational dimension of human persons influences their logical framework. While we did not exhaust this topic, we nonetheless considered some relational factors of rational development which are not always readily seen, and attention to these relational factors is important for a comprehensive understanding of what is required for authentic *metanoia*.

---

3. Mark 1:15.
4. Romans 12:2; 1 Corinthians 2:16.

Chapter 1

Ratio et Relatio

ON THE DEVELOPMENT OF *RATIO* IN THE LIFE OF SAINT AUGUSTINE

THIS THESIS BEGINS BY introducing, not an idea, but a person.

Saint Augustine was born in the African city of Hippo to a Christian mother and a pagan father, and such religious differentiation between the parents was not without consequence. From the religious discipline of his mother, Augustine inherited the experience of attending Catholic masses, learning to recite basic prayers, and encountering the essential stories of Scripture. From the pagan discipline of his father, Augustine inherited a knowledge of the great pagan speeches of the classical world, an education dedicated to the pursuit of rhetoric and the crafting of words in order to convince, and a zealous desire to achieve status and recognition among his fellow men. These two contrasting yet complimentary foundations would be structural supports that would intertwine and interact in unexpected but fruitful ways throughout the entirety of his life.

His parents were mutually (if not equally) determined to provide their son with an excellent education which would allow him to rise above his inherited social status and obtain a reputation both for himself and for his family. Their son was not as interested in this education as his parents, for Augustine often despised and frequently ignored his studies, which subjected him to various beatings from his father.[1] These beatings actually became

---

1. Augustine, *Confessions* (1961), i, 9. All mentions of Augustine's *Confessions* will refer to this specific edition; the other two which appear in the bibliography were used

a source of his earliest religious devotion, for the fear of such beatings was a strong motivation to pray:

> I used to prattle away to you, and though I was small, my devotion was great when I begged you not to let me be beaten at school. Sometimes, for my own good, you did not grant my prayer, and then my elders and even my parents, who certainly wished me no harm, would laugh at the beating I got—and in those days beatings were my one great (burden).[2]

Both Monica and Patricius (the parents of Augustine) considered these beatings humorous, and so their son turned to a heavenly father whom he hoped would answer his prayers to be spared from this suffering and humiliation. This prayer was not always answered.

As Augustine progressed in his education, his father's ambition for his son progressed as well, and though his father's "determination was greater than his means," he nonetheless chose to do everything in his power to find these means and saved up the money to send him to Carthage.[3] Carthage was a superior educational environment, and thus Patricius was greatly respected by his contemporaries because of his willingness to sacrifice so much of his own wealth and comfort for the progress and social advancement of his son. The one person who was not impressed with such sacrificial parenting was Augustine, lamenting to God that "this same father of mine took no trouble at all to see how I was growing in your sight or whether I was chaste or not. He cared only that I should have a fertile tongue."[4] Once he arrived in Carthage, it did not take long for Augustine to seek after his father's desires, as "it was my ambition to be a good speaker, for the unhallowed and inane purpose of gratifying human vanity."[5] Augustine excelled at this discipline, winning various awards for superior speeches and attaining the respect of his classmates and teachers, but in the middle of such vain pursuits of human glory, the prescribed course of studies brought him to a book and a person whose writings would reorient the entirety of his life: Cicero's *Hortentius*.

This book by Cicero recommends the reader to engage in a study of philosophy, and it is difficult to overestimate the impact of such a book and such a person in the life of Augustine. He says that "it altered my outlook on life" and that "the only thing that pleased me in Cicero's book was his advice not simply to admire one or another of the schools of philosophy, but to love

---

as reference material for difficult/important passages.

2. Augustine, *Confessions*, i, 9.
3. Augustine, *Confessions*, ii, 3.
4. Augustine, *Confessions*, ii, 3.
5. Augustine, *Confessions*, iii, 4.

Wisdom itself, whatever it might be, and to search for it, pursue it, hold it, and embrace it firmly."[6] Instead of being captivated by the pursuit of a job or a career laid out by his parents and his society, Augustine was now captivated by the idea of pursuing Wisdom, and from this point onwards, it was not the mastery of a school of philosophy which was important but rather the attainment of Wisdom itself. Thus he says that "all my empty dreams suddenly lost their charm and my heart began to throb with a bewildering passion for the Wisdom of eternal truth."[7] This was a true conversion for Augustine, as his entire life was reoriented towards a "bewildering passion" for arriving at "eternal truth." After reading this book, his intellectual life would never be the same, and what happened with this book would become a recurring theme throughout his life, for it would not be the last time a book or a person reoriented his entire way of thinking.

Despite a swollen heart which had begun to throb for the ideas which he encountered in *Hortentius*, this text was deficient in one respect: it did not mention the name of Christ. Augustine explains:

> The only check to this blaze of enthusiasm (for Cicero's book) was that (it) made no mention of the name of Christ . . . for from the time when my mother fed me at the breast my infant heart had been suckled dutifully on his name . . . Deep inside my heart his name remained, and nothing could entirely captivate me, however learned, however neatly expressed, however true it might be, unless his name were in it.[8]

Once again, we see the religious prejudice which dominated much of his early thought, and so in his feverish resolve to pursue Wisdom, we should not be surprised to see that the first place he went to in order to attain Wisdom was the Bible. Yet he was greatly disappointed by what he found there because, in the words of Peter Brown,

> He had been brought up to expect a book to be "cultivated and polished": he had been carefully groomed to communicate with educated men in the only admissible way, in a Latin scrupulously modelled on the ancient authors. Slang and jargon were equally abhorrent to such a man; and the Latin Bible of Africa, translated some centuries before by humble, nameless writers, was full of both. What is more, what Augustine read in the Bible seemed to have little to do with the highly spiritual Wisdom that Cicero had told him to love. It was cluttered up with earthy and

---

6. Augustine, *Confessions*, iii, 4.
7. Augustine, *Confessions*, iii, 4.
8. Augustine, *Confessions*, iii, 4.

immoral stories from the Old Testament; and even in the New Testament, Christ, Wisdom Himself, was introduced by long, and contradictory, genealogies.[9]

Such contradictory and unpolished writing surely was not the source of Wisdom which Augustine's educated and polished mind had grown to admire, but even though he would later write that this first serious reading of Scripture was distorted by his own lack of simplicity, lack of insight, and his inflated self-esteem, such distasteful distortions led him to seek Wisdom elsewhere, commencing a long journey through various philosophical disciplines that would lead him back to nothing other than Scripture itself. It would only be after many years of journeying that he could finally learn something he was not taught in school: that "a statement is not necessarily true because it is wrapped in fine language or false because it is awkwardly expressed."[10]

The first philosophical sect which attracted Augustine's attention were the Manichees, and for a man who had just dedicated himself to the search for "eternal truth," the Manichees were a perfect match, for "'Truth and truth alone' was the motto which they repeated to me again and again."[11] Augustine was greatly enticed by this promise: "Truth! Truth! How the very marrow of my soul within me yearned for it as they dinned it in my ears over and over again!"[12] Not only did Augustine have an irresistible attraction to their promise to lead one to the truth, but he was also drawn to their methodology of arriving at this truth, which was one of "pure reason." In refuting the Manichees in later writings, Augustine would write about how this methodology of appealing to reason alone attracted him:

> What was it that for almost nine years drove me to disdain the religion that had been instilled in me as a child by my parents and to follow those people and listen attentively to them except that they said that we were held in fear by superstition and that faith was imposed on us before reason, whereas they did not put pressure on anyone to believe without first discussing the truth? Who would not be enticed by promises like that, especially if it was the mind of a young man yearning for the truth and made proud and outspoken by the debates in the classes of certain scholars? This is how they found me at that time, scornful of

---

9. Brown, *Augustine of Hippo*, 31.
10. Augustine, *Confessions*, v, 6.
11. Augustine, *Confessions*, iii, 6.
12. Augustine, *Confessions*, iii, 6.

"old wives tales" and keen to have and to imbibe the open, uncontaminated truth that they promised.[13]

Augustine had a strong desire to "imbibe the open, uncontaminated truth" exclusively by way of the exercise of human reason, and this desire was perfectly matched with a sect who was known to be "deaf to any appeal other than to reason."[14] For nine years, Augustine was to be a "hearer" of this sect, which was someone who could study their writings and teachings and attend various meetings and gatherings, all while pursuing the truth by a methodology which distinguished itself as one which was independent of any authority other than the self-evident truths which could be discovered by any rational person.

Here we get our first glimpse into the many parallels between the life of Saint Augustine and those who have grown up in a post-enlightenment age, an age which has many voices who also desire the truth by reason alone, and we will encounter some of these voices later in this chapter. But perhaps what is surprising for a post-enlightenment mind to discover in the Manichean philosophical tradition is that this methodology was applied, first and foremost, to truths about God. The first truths taught by the Manichees are referred to today as "religious truths," for they concerned themselves with the nature of God, the origin of evil, and the explanation of the created world. So by a strict process of "reason alone," the Manichees claimed that "(evil) came from an invasion of the good—the 'Kingdom of Light'—by a hostile force of evil, equal in power, eternal, totally separate—the 'Kingdom of Darkness.'"[15] The Manichees were a dualist sect, and this dualistic drama between Good and Evil was so central to the rest of their teaching that the Chinese Manichean catechism would write, "The first thing man must do is to distinguish the Two Principles (the Good from the Evil). He who would enter our religion must know that the Two Principles have natures absolutely distinct: how can one who is not alive to this distinction put into practice the doctrine?"[16] Augustine was someone who was fully capable of putting this doctrine into practice because he "was confident that he could uphold this fundamental tenet of his religion by reason alone."[17] Strictly adhering to this reliance on reason as the sole basis of truth, Augustine became a devoted follower of the Manicheans and would share this philosophical system (or was it a religious system?) with many of his closest friends.

13. Augustine, *Advantage of Believing*, i, 2.
14. Brown, *Augustine of Hippo*, 44.
15. Brown, *Augustine of Hippo*, 36.
16. Brown, *Augustine of Hippo*, 37.
17. Brown, *Augustine of Hippo*, 37.

Over time, this methodology began to produce mixed results, for he encountered other rational explanations of the world which conflicted with the core tenets of his philosophical system. The most influential were the scientific writings which explained the movement of bodies in the heavens, and these writings were so powerful that their principles could be used "to forecast the year, the month, the day, and the hour of eclipses of the sun and moon, and the degree of their totality. And these eclipses will take place just as they foretell."[18] Anything that could predict the movement of heavenly bodies with such accuracy must have been aligned with the truth, and yet their explanation of how and why this happened was radically different from the Manichean explanation. So Augustine was forced to conclude that "the theories of the scientists were the more likely to be true" than the theory of the Manichees, and this conclusion caused a period of intense questioning about core tenets of the Manichean tradition as a whole.[19] He awaited the arrival of the great Faustus, a Manichean bishop of international renown whom many recommended to Augustine as someone who could answer all of his unresolved questions, but when the moment finally came and Augustine was able to present his concerns to Faustus about these apparent contradictions, he discovered that Faustus could not answer his questions: "As soon as it became clear to me that Faustus was quite uninformed about the subjects in which I had expected him to be an expert, I began to lose hope that he could lift the veil and resolve the problems which perplexed me."[20] Such an experience with one of the most respected teachers among the Manicheans was to play a significant factor in his slow departure from this sect, eroding his confidence not only in Faustus but also in the many other teachers of the sect who relied on Faustus as the source of answers for these unanswered contradictions. Thus he would enter a period of transition, stating that

> all my endeavors to make progress in the sect, as I had intended, were abandoned. I did not cut myself off entirely from the Manichees, but as I could find nothing better than the beliefs which I had stumbled upon more or less by chance, I decided to be content with them for the time being, unless something preferable clearly presented itself to me.[21]

Augustine's hope in the Manichean tradition had deflated, but nothing as of yet was able to take its place.

18. Augustine, *Confessions*, v, 3.
19. Augustine, *Confessions*, v, 3.
20. Augustine, *Confessions*, v, 7.
21. Augustine, *Confessions*, v, 7.

One of the first things Augustine tried to do in this period of disillusionment was to "find some certain proof which would convict the Manichees of falsehood . . . but this I could not do."[22] Neither convinced by Manichean doctrines nor able to disprove them, Augustine's mind became frozen in a state of paralyzing doubt, naturally considering himself a sceptic who began "treating everything as a matter of doubt, as the Academics are generally supposed to do."[23] This period of intellectual doubt was an intense agony for Augustine, for he was someone who "wanted complete certainty on ultimate questions."[24] Unable to find this certainty in any philosophical system, he "was in despair of finding the truth."[25] Despairing of ever finding absolute certainty but nonetheless still searching for it, he would later write that "At that time, there was no one more open to being taught than I was . . ."[26]

It is precisely in this time of intellectual docility that Augustine was introduced to Ambrose of Milan, a man whose intellectual vibrancy was a natural match for his own. Augustine left Rome because he decided to accept a teaching post in Milan, and in this time of both physical and intellectual transition, he found himself listening to Ambrose explain the Scriptures: "every Sunday I listened as he preached the word of truth to the people, and I grew more and more certain that it was possible to unravel the tangle woven by those who had deceived both me and others with their cunning lies against the Holy Scriptures."[27] It is as if Ambrose was able to be everything for Augustine which Faustus was not, helping him to grow in certainty as opposed to despairing of certainty. He also began to reflect on his previous infatuation with absolute certainty by reason alone, writing that "I grew more and more ashamed that I had been misled and deluded by promises of certainty for so long, and had talked wildly, like an ignorant child, about so many unconfirmed theories as though they were beyond question."[28] Augustine came to understand how these "promises of certainty" had actually misled him into a non-rational confidence in their veracity, finding himself now in the ironic situation of not only questioning these "certainties" but also no longer believing them. Such disillusionment did nothing to quench

22. Augustine, *Confessions*, v, 14.

23. Augustine, *Confessions*, v, 14. He would say elsewhere that "I began to think that the philosophers known as the Academics were wiser than the rest, because they held that everything was a matter of doubt and asserted that man can know nothing for certain" (*Confessions*, v, 10).

24. Brown, *Augustine of Hippo*, 79.

25. Augustine, *Confessions*, vi, 1.

26. Augustine, cited in Brown, *Augustine of Hippo*, 71.

27. Augustine, *Confessions*, vi, 3.

28. Augustine, *Confessions*, vi, 4.

his thirst for certainty, for he says that "I wanted to be just as certain of (spiritual realities) which were hidden from my sight as that seven and three make ten, for I was not so far out of my wits as to suppose that not even this could be known. But I wanted to be equally sure about everything else, both material things . . . and spiritual things."[29] Augustine was a skeptic at this time, but his severity of doubt was not so great as to dismiss mathematical certainties. Was there any way he could find certainty about spiritual things which would be equivalent to his ability to find certainty about mathematical things?

The next great evolution of thought for Augustine came when he began to realize how much of his own thought was dependent on trust. This realization was described as a sort of revelation, for he says "then O Lord, you laid your most gentle, most merciful finger on my heart and set my thoughts in order" by revealing how

> I believed countless things which I had never seen or which had taken place when I was not there to see—so many events in the history of the world, so many facts about places and towns which I had never seen, and so much that I believed on the word of friends or doctors or various other people. Unless we took these things on trust, we should accomplish nothing in this life. Most of all it came home to me how firm and unshakeable was the faith which told me who my parents were, because I could never have known this unless I believed what I was told.[30]

Through this revelation, Augustine encountered a "firm and unshakeable" source of certainty, and it was "the *faith* which told me who my parents were." In such a moment of revelation, Augustine realized that it was faith which provides certainty to reason, and not the other way around, and this faith is received on the basis of some authority which requires belief in order to be certain. Augustine realized that he was certain about Manicheanism, not because of "reason alone," but because he made a prior commitment of belief in their authority, and thus he would later write, "You know, Honoratus, that the only reason we fell in with them is because they declared with awesome authority, quite removed from pure and simple reasoning, that if any persons chose to listen to them they would lead them to God and free them from all error."[31] Such a revelation about the role of authority in providing certainty was to have a significant impact on his assent to religious truths:

29. Augustine, *Confessions*, vi, 4.
30. Augustine, *Confessions*, vi, 5.
31. Augustine, *Advantage of Believing*, i, 2.

> In this way you made me understand that I ought not to find fault with those who believed your Bible, which you have established with such great authority amongst almost all the nations of the earth, but with those who did not believe it; and that I ought to pay no attention to people who asked me how I could be sure that the Scriptures were delivered to mankind by the Spirit of the one true God who can tell no lie. It was precisely this that I most needed to believe, because in all the conflicting books of philosophy which I had read, no misleading proposition, however contentious, had been able, even for one moment, to wrest from me my belief in your existence and in your right to govern human affairs.[32]

In this moment, Augustine realized that an appeal to the authority of Scriptures is not "unreasonable" but is actually in accord with reason; for Augustine, believing was no longer considered a violation of rational principles but instead a very reasonable thing to do. If belief in some authority could lead Augustine to logical certainty about the identity of his biological father, it was no longer absurd to suggest that belief in another authority could lead to logical certainty about the identity of his heavenly father. And in the quote above, he reveals the deepest *a priori* belief which was influencing him all along, which was his belief in God. Nothing was able to erode this belief: "My belief that you existed and that our well-being was in your hands was sometimes strong, sometimes weak, but I always held to it."[33] Holding on to this belief in a God whom he had learned about since birth, he was led to those Scriptures which spoke about this God and he began to approach them with a newfound reverence for their authority.

While engaging in this obedient study of Scripture, Augustine encountered his last significant philosophical school on his path to Wisdom, which was the school of the Platonists. Through the providential assistance of a man who "was bloated with the most outrageous pride," he was given "some books of the Platonists" which helped him overcome his greatest intellectual hurdle in his understanding of God.[34] For the entirety of his life, Augustine was only able to conceive of God as a material substance, but "by reading these books of the Platonists I had been prompted to look for truth as something incorporeal."[35] With such an intellectual development, the veracity of Scripture began to appear before his very eyes, as Augustine began to see

---

32. Augustine, *Confessions*, vi, 5.
33. Augustine, *Confessions*, vi, 5.
34. Augustine, *Confessions*, vii, 9.
35. Augustine, *Confessions*, vii, 20.

how the "Word who was God" is the same "Word become flesh"; that "before time began, he was" and thus he was not subject to change. God was no longer understood as a "monad" or a material substance; he was immaterial and still substantial; he was an incorporeal truth who had taken on flesh.

The influence of such a platonic idea led to the most significant intellectual discovery for Augustine. He says that "these books served to remind me to return to my own self" and within his self, he found a deeply profound truth:

> I entered, and with the eye of my soul, such as it was, I saw the Light that never changes casting its rays over the same eye of my soul, over my mind . . . What I saw was something quite, quite different from any light we know on earth. It shone above my mind . . . It was above me because it was itself the Light that made me, and I was below because I was made by it . . . And far off, I heard your voice saying *I am the God who IS*. I heard your voice, as we hear voices that speak to our hearts, and at once I had no cause to doubt. I might more easily have doubted I was alive than that Truth had being. For we catch sight of the Truth, as he is known through his creation.[36]

Augustine had just encountered, for the first time, the most important "self-evident" truth he would ever encounter, the truth that within him, there was a voice of Truth which was not an idea but a person; this was not a truth as a rational concept but Truth that had *being*. Instead of discovering within himself only his own mind, he discovered the presence of a Light which did not come from himself but "from above," a Light which was "over" and "above" his own mind and therefore not derived from his own cognition but was knowable to his own cognition, a Light which made him and formed him and even spoke words to him which are heard as clearly "as we hear voices that speak to our hearts." And in the presence of this Light, in the presence of this Truth who is a being and not just an idea, Augustine's own mind was finally cleared of all doubt about the Truth. The absolute certainty for which he had spent his life searching and looking was now attained, and he could no longer doubt this Truth any more than he could doubt that he was alive. His search for Wisdom, which had begun with reading *Hortentius*, had been completed by finding within himself the presence of a Wisdom that spoke to him saying, "I am the God who IS."

In the presence of such ultimate certainty, it may appear that the drama of Augustine's conversion was now over, for he finally found the Wisdom which he had been seeking since reading Cicero, and the next logical step

---

36. Augustine, *Confessions*, vii, 10.

was to conform his way of life to this Wisdom by being baptized and then committing himself to the moral life demanded of the followers of Christ; but mysteriously, Augustine was not able to make this next logical step. He says, "I did not ask for more certain proof of you, but only to be made more steadfast in you. But my worldly life all was confusion . . . I should have been glad to follow the right road, to follow our Saviour himself, but still I could not make up my mind to venture along the narrow path."[37] Augustine was no longer in need of rational certainty about the existence of God and what is needed to follow him, and yet he discovered that this rational certainty was insufficient for allowing him to "follow the right road" and change the ways of his "worldy life." Thus he states, "I could no longer claim that I had no clear perception of the truth—the excuse which I used to make to myself for postponing my renunciation of the world and my entry into your service—for by now I was quite certain of it. But I was still bound to earth and refused to serve in your army."[38] Augustine understands the great contradiction in which he was now immersed, for he was a man who insisted that he would always follow the truth wherever it would lead, and yet he found himself unwilling to go where this Truth was leading him. Thus he would lament how "in my weakness I recoiled and fell back into my old ways, carrying with me nothing but the memory of something that I loved and longed for, as though I had sensed the fragrance of the fare but was not yet able to eat it."[39] Augustine was morally paralyzed, unable to follow his mind to the food which he knew with certainty existed and was necessary to sustain him. He "found the pearl of great price," but he still held back.[40] He had an intellectual conversion of the utmost certainty, and yet his moral conversion was delayed.

In the face of such a contradictory situation, a series of questions naturally come to mind. Why was Augustine's will unable to follow his mind? What happened in his life to allow for his intellectual certainty to result in true moral conversion? How, exactly, did he ever attain a true *metanoia*, a conversion to the "way" of the gospel that demands not only intellectual conversion but also moral conversion? The answers to these paradoxical questions form the outer limits of this thesis, and we cannot discover their answer until we better understand how the rational faculty of human nature develops in response to the relational dimension of the human person. So, having just witnessed the development of Augustine's rational concepts, we

---

37. Augustine, *Confessions*, viii, 1.
38. Augustine, *Confessions*, viii, 5.
39. Augustine, *Confessions*, vii, 17.
40. Augustine, *Confessions*, viii, 1.

now look at the role of various relationships which influenced the development of these concepts.

RATIO IN RELATIONE IN THE LIFE OF SAINT AUGUSTINE

When we look at Augustine's life with an attention to relationships, we discover a plethora of relational experiences which deeply impress, mold, and develop his mind. In fact, it was impossible for us to trace the outline of his thought without necessarily involving several relationships which distinctly impacted his intellectual development, such as the role of his parents, Cicero, Faustus, and Ambrose. Each one of these relationships had a profound impact on his rational faculty, and while there are many others which could be mentioned, we will limit ourselves to identifying a few others which were the most influential.

From reading the *Confessions*, it becomes apparent that one of the most influential relationships on the mind of Augustine was his relationship with his mother. In many ways, her influence on his mind was more subtle and less apparent than the influence of someone like Ambrose, but it was no less real and consequential. We saw above how the absence of the name of Christ influenced Augustine's ability to accept the philosophy of Cicero, how he used Scripture to better understand the Platonists, and how he encountered Ambrose by listening to his sermons in a church. Behind each one of these ideas we can see the intellectual impact of his mother, for Monica was the one who taught him the name of Christ and how to reverence this name; she was the one who exposed him to Scripture and spoke to him of the stories within; she was the one who first brought him to church and mourned when he stopped coming to church. Even when not explicit, Monica's authority over the mind of Augustine is constantly unfolding in the *Confessions*.

Augustine stated above that the one idea of which he was never in doubt was the existence of God, an idea which was "sometimes strong, sometimes weak" but never abandoned, and he received this idea through the influence of his mother. He would exercise this belief when he prayed to avoid a beating, he would distort this belief when he was with the Manichees, and he would grow confused about this belief when he was with the Academics, but he would never abandon it. In much the same way that his mother was always following him ("for as mothers do, and far more than most, she loved to have me with her"), so too did this idea constantly follow

Augustine.⁴¹ To say that his belief in the existence of God came merely from superstition is contrary to everything revealed about his rigorous adherence to the truth wherever it may lead; but to say that his belief in the existence God came from the influence of his mother is harmonious with all that has been revealed in his *Confessions*.⁴² This is not to deny that he had other reasons for believing in the existence of God, but the first teacher of this idea, and the ever-abiding presence which was constantly bringing it back to his mind, was his mother.

Monica was influential in many indirect ways, but she also influenced his thinking in other direct ways. For example, she played a prominent role in a series of dialogues that were written by Augustine while leisurely exploring various philosophical disciplines with a group of friends, including his mother. In this conversation, Monica made various points which directed their communal thinking in a specific direction, the most notable being her conclusion about those who say that nothing can be attained with certainty and that everything must be held in doubt, even existence itself. Such a teaching was found in the school of the Academics, and when Augustine explained to his mother their central tenet of doubt, she famously replied, "These are epileptics (*caducarii*)."⁴³ By countering an entire philosophical school by labeling them epileptic, Augustine and his other colleagues were reduced to joy and laughter, and although Augustine himself would write a two-volume work which countered the arguments of the Academics with many more words, he would find no better refutation of their errors than this single word. From this instance, we get a brief glimpse into the way in which a single phrase or condemnatory tone from Monica could influence his own thought.

Another relationship of considerable import to the development of Augustine's mind is his relationship with Ambrose. The role of Ambrose has already been partially revealed, so we mention here only one relevant detail. Augustine says,

> For although I did not trouble to take what Ambrose said to heart, but only to listen to the manner in which he said it—this being the only paltry interest that remained to me now that I had lost hope that man could find the path that led to you—nevertheless his meaning, which I tried to ignore, found its way *into*

---

41. Augustine, *Confessions*, v, 8.

42. "What Augustine remembered in the Confessions was his inner life; and this inner life was dominated by one figure—his mother, Monica" (Brown, *Augustine of Hippo*, 17).

43. Augustine, *Happy Life*, ii, 16.

my mind together with his words, which I admired so much. *I could not keep the two apart*, and while I was all ears to seize upon his eloquence, I also began to sense the truth of what he said, though only gradually.[44]

Augustine first came to Ambrose because he admired the way people spoke about him and because of the way he spoke, but sitting in the presence of his words, Augustine's own rationality begins to develop. This was contrary to Augustine's experience of someone like Faustus, a person who Augustine acknowledged as supremely eloquent and a master with words but whose substance and content was unconvincing. Faustus delighted Augustine with his eloquence but wearied him with his incoherence, whereas Ambrose not only delighted Augustine but also slowly began to change his intelligence by way of this eloquence; Augustine would listen to Faustus and grow weary, but he would listen to Ambrose and become awake. In this way, Ambrose becomes what Augustine hoped Faustus would be, a man whose great rhetorical skill was matched also with a logical consistency capable of leading him to the truth. He would follow the path revealed by Ambrose all the way to the end.

Besides his relationship with Ambrose and Monica, the *Confessions* are full of intimate friendships which influence both his joy and his intellect, and throughout his life, "Augustine will never be alone."[45] Augustine writes about the way these friendships influenced both his life and his mind:

> We could talk and laugh together and exchange small acts of kindness. We could join in the pleasure that books can give. We could be grave or gay together. If we sometimes disagreed, it was without spite, as a man might differ with himself, and the rare occasions of dispute were the very spice to season our usual accord. Each of us had something to learn from the others and something to teach in return. If any were away, we missed them with regret and gladly welcomed them when they came home. Such things as these are heartfelt tokens of affection between friends. They are signs to be read on the face and in the eyes, spoken by the tongue and displayed in countless acts of kindness. They can kindle a blaze to melt our hearts and weld them into one.[46]

For Augustine, friends were not merely companions through life but were also a source of much-needed variation, a way not only to escape the

44. Augustine, *Confessions*, v, 14.
45. Brown, *Augustine of Hippo*, 50.
46. Augustine, *Confessions*, iv, 8.

boredoms of the self but also the intellectual limitations of the self. The idea that "each of us had something to learn from the others and something to teach in return" is something that would recur throughout the *Confessions*.

There was one important friendship which would leave an indelible mark on his mind even though this friendship was short in duration, for "before we had reached the end of the first year of a friendship that was sweeter to me than all the joys of life as I lived it then, you took him from this world."[47] This friend is never named, and although he died within a year of their mutual acquaintance, this friend would leave Augustine with a final intellectual gift before his death. Their friendship was founded on a mutual certainty in the Manichean philosophy and a mutual abhorrence of the superstitious practices of the Christians, being especially critical of the idea that a person needed to be baptized in order to be saved. They often laughed and ridiculed those who pursued something superstitious like baptism instead of relying on their own rational powers to become free, but while his friend lay unconscious in the final days of his illness, a priest was called and his friend was baptized. Augustine was sure his friend would be amused to discover that he had been baptized while he was unconscious, but he was not, for Augustine writes,

> As soon as I could talk to him—which was as soon as he could talk to me, for I never left his side since we were so dependent on each other—I tried to chaff him about his baptism, thinking that he too would make fun of it, since he had received it when he was quite incapable of thought or feeling. But by this time he had been told of it. He looked at me in horror as though I were an enemy, and in a strange, new-found attitude of self-reliance he warned me that if I wished to be his friend, I must never speak to him like that again. I was astonished and confused, but I did not tell him what I felt . . .[48]

In the presence of this complete reversal of mind by one who had been so similar to his own thought and so convergent with his philosophical outlook, Augustine was left "astonished and confused," and what had once been a matter of certainty for them both was now a point of bitter dispute. He would never get a chance to share these feelings of confusion with his friend, for he died only a few days after this incident, leaving Augustine to sort through this confusion himself. While this situation did not lead Augustine to embrace Christianity, it is a notable event in his intellectual journey which he records in the *Confessions* over twenty years after it happened.

47. Augustine, *Confessions*, iv, 4.
48. Augustine, *Confessions*, iv, 4.

Augustine had profound relationships not just with the living but also with the dead, admiring their thought by way of reading their books. Throughout his life, he is constantly reading books, talking about what he has read in these books, and even admires and watches the way other people read books. His young education is filled with plays and poems and the recitation of dramatic literature: Cicero's *Hortentius* fires him with a love for philosophy, books from Seneca teach him about the Stoic philosophical outlook, Aristotle's *Ten Categories* enlightens him with classical philosophy, he absorbs the writings of Manes and better understands the entire Manichean system, he reads the books of scientists who predict the movements of stars and sees how their computations conflict with the Manichean system, he dabbles in the works of the astrologists and learns how they try to predict the future based on the movement of the stars, he reads the works of Platonists and begins to conceive of truth as an incorporeal being, and last but not least, there is his lifelong and complicated relationship with the Bible. His entire life is permeated by a relationship with literature, and the role of this literature in forming his thought is well documented. Though he will converse with his friends about the content of these books, he nonetheless displays a remarkable capacity for self-interpretation, reflecting on "all those books, with their tangled problems, which I unraveled *without the help of any human tutor*" and stating that "I read and understood *by myself* all the books that I could find on the so-called liberal arts."[49] Augustine has an intimate and personal relationship with many people whose bodies are dead but whose ideas are still alive, and these ideas will profoundly change not just what he thinks but also how he thinks.

And then there is his relationship with beauty. Perhaps it is better to say that he had an *encounter* with beauty, but in calling it a relationship, we are signifying that this beauty was not found "within" Augustine but rather was mediated through an experience which was not "self-derived." In so far as a person's relational dimension allows for the self to encounter realities outside of itself, one's relationship with the created world is of great significance; if this is not true for all thinkers, then it certainly was for Augustine. His encounter with beauty was so influential for the development of his mind that it was the subject of his first book, *Beauty and Proportion*. This encounter with beauty was not only a stimulating sensory experience; it was also an intense intellectual experience, stirring up questions about its origin and essence: "I used to ask my friends, 'Do we love anything unless it is beautiful? What then is beauty and in what does it consist? What is it that

---

49. Augustine, *Confessions*, iv, 16.

CHAPTER 1: *RATIO ET RELATIO* 17

attracts us and wins over to the things we love?'"[50] For Augustine, beauty was not just something to admire but also something to contemplate, and it would take many years before he could understand that it was Wisdom herself who was the one speaking through beauty, eventually writing in his *Confessions* the following: "O sweetest light of the purified mind! Wisdom! You do not cease to suggest to us what you are. Your beckoning is all the beauty of creation."[51] For Augustine, beauty is a cryptic sign of the presence of Wisdom, a sign that points to a deeper reality of existence that is beyond the self:

> What is that light whose gentle beams now and again strike through to my heart, causing me to shudder in awe yet firing me with their warmth? I shudder to feel how different I am from it: yet in so far as I am like it, I am aglow with its fire. It is the light of Wisdom, Wisdom itself, which at times shines upon me, parting my clouds.[52]

For Augustine, Wisdom is an active agent and not just a passive idea, and the transformative presence of beauty is one of Wisdom's most prominent agencies, causing a soul to set aglow with its fire and stir the heart. Beauty, therefore, is just as active in the life of Augustine as one of his friends, and his attention to its presence throughout his life is one more important relationship which greatly influences how he thinks.

By examining Augustine's many relationships above, we have deepened our understanding of some of the important ways in which the development of his mind was not a "do-it-yourself" project. Augustine's life was permeated by a wide variety of relationships which provided an encounter with truths which lay beyond his own mind, a series of relational encounters which authoritatively influence not just what he thinks but also how he thinks. These relationships compete for his cognitive attention, and once this attention is gained, his mind is molded by what this relationship has to give. None of these relationships seem to control his mind, but they do influence it and direct it in significant ways (Augustine will speak of this as an experience of being "guided" or "directed"), so much so that we might say that his rational faculty was more directly influenced by his relationships than by rational principles found within himself.

Yet all these relationships eventually direct him to a very important moment in which he no longer looks outside himself but gazes inwards:

---

50. Augustine, *Confessions*, iv, 13.
51. Augustine, *On Free Choice of the Will*, 74.
52. Augustine, *Confessions*, xi, 9.

"these books served to remind me to return to my own self. Under your guidance, I entered into the depths of my soul . . . "[53] It was during this gazing inwards that Augustine had his profound experience of rational certitude recounted above, but instead of finding an absolutely certain rational principle, he found an absolutely certain divine presence; he did not find a logical equation but instead heard a voice which speaks; he did not find a "self-evident" truth but instead found a being who IS Truth; he did not see certitude with the light of his own reason but instead saw an Uncreated Light which is above his own reason. The many relationships which molded and formed his rationality sent him to look inward, and there he found, perhaps paradoxically, another relationship; but this was a primordial relationship, a relationship with some*one* and not just some*thing*, a person who commands and not just an idea that is known.

Once again, we have come to the outer limits of this thesis which can only be addressed at the end of our study, but we must point out why it is necessary to take this journey. If it is indeed the case that the human person is meant to be guided, not by a rational concept, but by a divine person, then the entire moral life is predicated on a relationship with this person. If we spend all our time trying to figure out what we are supposed to do by way of "reason alone," only to discover that we were meant to be guided in our actions by the command of a person, then we will have grounded our moral life on an *a priori* deficiency. Furthermore, Augustine's life foreshadows another significant moral dilemma connected to the search for rational certainty as a guide to the moral life, for even once it was obtained, Augustine found himself in the mysterious situation of not being able to follow where this truth was certainly leading. His problem was no longer a lack of certainty but a lack of the ability to act on this certainty. These are some of the moral considerations revealed by a brief survey of the development of Augustine's rational faculty, and as we will soon see, they are considerations which are imminently relevant to morality today.

INTO MODERNITY

Since the time of Augustine, there have been many other thinkers who share his desire for absolute certainty about the fundamental truths of human existence. René Descartes is one such thinker, and because his philosophical system is interwoven with the central claim of this thesis, we will now look at his own journey towards certitude and evaluate it in light of what has been articulated by Augustine.

53. Augustine, *Confessions*, vii, 10.

Descartes shares many of the same thoughts and desires as Augustine, most especially the desire for certitude: "I always had an extreme desire to learn to distinguish the true from the false, in order to see clearly in my actions and to proceed with assurance in this life."[54] Like Augustine, Descartes's search for truth is concerned with grounding his actions on a firm and immovable foundation, and only an intellect rooted in certainty can be a faithful guide to right action. Descartes does not want a moral life built on probabilities; he wants it built on certainty.

Descartes, like Augustine, is also a great admirer of the sciences, especially mathematics: "I delighted, above all, in mathematics, because of the certitude and the evidence of its reasonings."[55] Mathematics is revered by Descartes, not necessarily because of its conclusions, but because of its indisputable foundations and rigor of proof. If mathematics can have such indisputable foundations, then every other discipline ought to be rooted in truths which are equally indisputable, thus leading Descartes to decide "not to accept anything as true that were not to seem to me more clear and more certain than the demonstrations of the geometers had previously seemed."[56] For Descartes, the discipline of mathematics is the template for all truth, and any idea which cannot be upheld with this same rigor is an idea built on insufficient foundations.

Fueled by this great desire for certitude, Descartes embarked on an extensive educational formation. He says that he attended

> one of the most famous schools of Europe, where I thought that there must be learned men if there were any of them anywhere on earth. There I had learned all that which the others had been learning there; and, not being content with the sciences that one taught us, I had even read through all the books . . . on which I had been able to get my hands.[57]

Formed by some of the strongest minds in Europe, and supplementing these studies with his own extensive reading, Descartes considered his education sufficiently rigorous to attain the certitude which he so desired and which such an education promised. But he was greatly disappointed by the final result, for

> as soon as I had achieved the whole course of studies at the end of which one is accustomed to be admitted to the ranks of the

---

54. Descartes, *Discourse on the Method*, 23.
55. Descartes, *Discourse on the Method*, 21.
56. Descartes, *Discourse on the Method*, 63.
57. Descartes, *Discourse on the Method*, 17.

learned, I changed my opinion entirely. For I found myself embarrassed by so many doubts and errors that it seemed to me that, in trying to instruct myself, I had gained nothing, if not that I had discovered more and more my ignorance.[58]

Instead of finding certitude, this extensive education had only provided him with many "doubts and errors" which only seemed to reveal to him his ignorance instead of providing a firm grasp of truth. It is the presence of a great diversity of opinions which seems to have driven him to this despair, for he says, "considering how many different opinions there can be concerning one and the same matter, which be maintained by learned people, without there ever being able to be more than only one of them which be true, I held to be well-nigh false all that which was merely probable."[59] The indisputable certainty of mathematics which he had so much admired was not found in other disciplines, especially in those areas of knowledge which speak of ultimate truths like philosophy and theology, and this was a great disappointment for Descartes.

Like Augustine, Descartes became disillusioned by the search for certitude, but unlike Augustine, he tried to rectify this conflict by "resolving no longer to seek any other knowledge than that which could be found within myself."[60] When Augustine became disillusioned with the alleged certainty that the Manichees said they could provide, he continued looking outside of himself, saying that "At that time, there was no one more open to being taught than I was . . . "[61] But when Descartes becomes disillusioned with other thinkers of his time, he concludes that there is no teacher who can guide him to the certainty which he desires, and so he places all his hope in the only teacher he can now trust: himself. So "I made the resolution to study within myself . . . and to employ all the powers of my mind in choosing the paths that I should follow."[62] He continues to desire certitude, but because he can no longer trust those who provide divergent opinions on ultimate matters, "the powers of *my* mind" become the only teacher capable of leading him to the truth. He makes this more explicit when he says "I found myself constrained, as it were, to undertake to guide myself by myself," and that "My plan has never gone beyond trying to reform my own thoughts and building on a foundation that is totally my own."[63] In Augustine's crisis of

---

58. Descartes, *Discourse on the Method*, 17.
59. Descartes, *Discourse on the Method*, 21.
60. Descartes, *Discourse on the Method*, 23.
61. Augustine, cited in Brown, *Augustine of Hippo*, 71.
62. Descartes, *Discourse on the Method*, 23, 25.
63. Descartes, *Discourse on the Method*, 31.

certitude, he built an intellectual foundation on Scripture and the Platonists and allowed himself to be guided by Ambrose; in Descartes's crisis of certitude, he builds a foundation "that is totally my own" and allows himself to be guided only by his same self. This marks the definitive point of methodological divergence between two minds which share so much in common.

Once Descartes turns inside himself and begins to build on this foundation, he resolves to follow a specific methodology to attain certitude, the first principle being "never to accept anything as true that I did not evidently know to be such . . . and to include in my judgements nothing more than that which would present itself to my mind so clearly and so distinctly that I were to have no occasion to put it in doubt."[64] Descartes applied this methodology with the utmost rigor, realizing that there are many things he can doubt, such as whether or not he is awake or asleep, anything provided to him by his senses, and the existence of God (what if God were only an evil genius deceiving him?) But with all these formerly held beliefs rejected on account of his ability to have doubts about them, Descartes discovers that the very fact that he is thinking provides him with one metaphysical truth about which he cannot doubt:

> I took note that, while I wanted thus to think that everything was false, it necessarily had to be that I, who was thinking this, were something. And noticing this truth—I think, therefore I am—was so firm and so assured that all the most extravagant suppositions of the skeptics were not capable of shaking it, I judged that I could accept it, without scruple, as the first principle of the philosophy that I was seeking.[65]

Descartes has just discovered one absolutely certain truth which becomes the first principle of the philosophy that he had been seeking, which is the fact that he exists. This certain knowledge of his existence is predicated on the fact that he thinks because "if I had simply ceased to think, even if all the rest of that which I had ever imagined been true, I would have had no reason to believe that I had been."[66] Being absolutely certain that personal cognition implies personal existence, he has discovered one self-evident truth which he cannot doubt; he has discovered one truth which is just as certain as any rigorous proof found in mathematics.

Alongside this principle, and perhaps most immediate to it, Descartes also realizes something else very important, which is that this indubitable truth has consequences for how we understand the human person. He says,

64. Descartes, *Discourse on the Method*, 35.
65. Descartes, *Discourse on the Method*, 51.
66. Descartes, *Discourse on the Method*, 53.

> Seeing that I could feign that I had no body, and that there was no world, nor any place where I were; but that I could not feign, for that reason, that I was not at all; and seeing that, on the contrary, from the very fact that I thought of doubting the truth of the other things, it followed very evidently and very certainly that I was ... I knew from this that *I was a substance the whole essence or nature of which is only to think*, and which, in order to be, does not have need of any place, and does not depend on any material thing.[67]

Because he can doubt the existence of his body and senses and all the world, he concludes that these things do not form the essence of his substance. Thus, the essence of his human nature is "only to think," and this thinking mind "does not depend on any material thing." This allows him to conclude, "this 'I', that is to say the soul through which I am that which I am, *is entirely distinct from the body*."[68] For Descartes, the "I" is exclusively an immaterial, thinking self, making the essence of the human being a thinking being. This does not ignore the body, but it does conceive of the body as "entirely distinct" from the mind, and since the mind is the essence of the "I," then the body is not integral to the essence of the "I."

Descartes then proceeds from his indubitable truth to prove many other truths, such as the existence of God, the various laws of nature, and the dynamics of human movement and cognition, but our attention to his philosophy at this point only concerns this first and most fundamental principle of his philosophy. We are specifically interested in his assertions about the human mind, assigning it an authority which is rooted purely on the rational principles knowable to any self-reflective person. This methodology of arriving at truth, in which a person searches within themselves to find the basis of *all* truth, is of special interest to moral theology because it is a methodology which would seek to direct moral choices from within the human person. If a person can search within themselves to find all truth, then it follows that they will search within themselves to find moral truths. If one were to doubt whether such a methodology is relevant to moral theology today, we appeal to the following example for consideration.

In a recently printed advice column which is syndicated to over two hundred newspapers, a person asked for advice about the following moral dilemma:

> My boyfriend and I have been together for eleven months. We love each other and want to get married. The problem is, he

---

67. Descartes, *Discourse on the Method*, 53 (emphasis added).
68. Descartes, *Discourse on the Method*, 53 (emphasis added).

wants to have sex before we get married. I was raised to wait until marriage to have sex. I love him with all my heart, but I don't want to go against my parents and sleep with him. He says it's either sex or nothing at all.[69]

This person has just asked advice for a very important moral question, trying to resolve her conflict between what her boyfriend desires, what she desires, and the authority of her parents. This question touches on human sexuality, moral development, power, and authority, all which are of considerable import to the flourishing of the human person and thus require one's full attention. In response to such a serious moral question, the columnist wrote the following advice in answer to her question,

> The only orders you should ever heed on personal matters are the ones that come *straight from your own mind*. If you're old enough to get married, you're old enough to know: What do you want? What do you value? What do you think is right? And if you don't know the answers, then don't get married yet to anyone—not even to someone who conveniently agrees with your parents. Then all you get is a new parent and still *no mind of your own* . . .
>
> Figure this stuff out before you make any irreversible decisions. Take the next decade or two, if you need it. I'm serious. The test isn't timed, and the only wrong answers are the ones you don't bother to find. He is absolutely entitled to decide he won't marry someone he has never slept with. And you, likewise, are absolutely entitled to decide *your values* are more important to you than he is.[70]

Just as Descartes spent nine years searching his own mind for rational principles that could guide him, the columnist advises the young girl to take as much time as she needs to find out what her own mind values, even if it takes "the next decade or two," presumably because the only authority which should ever be consulted in making this moral decision is her own mind. If she were to just follow either the advice of her parents or the desires of her boyfriend, she will be in the morally impermissible situation of having "no mind of her own." We do not know if Descartes would agree with this conclusion of the columnist, but we can know for certain that he would approve of the logic, for it has appealed to the authority of one's own mind as the ultimate guide of all truth, including moral truths.

---

69. Hax, "Premarital Sex isn't the Issue," para. 1.
70. Hax, "Premarital Sex isn't the Issue," paras. 2–4.

This idea of Descartes became the founding principal of the Enlightenment, with Kant himself stating that the motto of the Enlightenment is "Have courage to use your own understanding!"[71] We can see from this columnist's advice that such an idea still permeates much of Western thought, and it's implications for morals is also equally clear, for if we conclude that a person's own reason is the basis of *all* truth, then this same logic will be the method by which we arrive at moral truths. There are some apparent difficulties of such a methodology, the first being practical, for must a person really spend a few decades of self-seeking in order to determine whether or not they should have sexual intercourse before marriage? If only the self can serve as an authoritative guide for moral decisions, then every person would seem bound to a lifelong search inward to determine what to do with their life, a life that has already passed in searching for truths that can only be found within their own mind.

Besides the practical difficulties of such a methodology, this thesis is going to examine its underlying principles, for such a methodology presupposes that the rational faculty is an isolated function which arises spontaneously from the self. But is it really true that each person has their *own* mind and their *own* rationality? What if, instead of my own reason, I actually possess a form of thinking and have a specific mind that develops according to realities outside of the self? What we really want to know is whether or not it is really true that I can "think for myself," and whether or not cognition is truly the essence of existence. Entire moral systems are built on our answers to these questions, and so these questions are the point of departure for this thesis. As we saw in the life of Saint Augustine, there are strong reasons to suggest that his mind was not a self-created project but rather relied on many relationships for its authentic development and arrival at what he considered to be *the* Truth. What is needed is a more detailed analysis of the presumption that the rational faculty is self-derived, and inspired by the example of Saint Augustine and seeing its importance for moral questions today, we will conduct that analysis in the following chapters. But before we do so, we must mention one theological idea which has prejudiced us in our investigation, and it has to do with the role of relationship in the Christian tradition.

TRINITARIAN MINDS

The revealed doctrine that is the most immediate source of our desire to explore the role of relationship in forming our rationality is the doctrine of the Trinity. It is a doctrine whose mystery is rooted "in the beginning," for

---

71. Kant, *What is Enlightenment?*, para. 1.

it is in the book of Genesis that an odd phenomenon occurs: God speaks in the plural about himself. As early as the first chapter, God says "Let *us* make man in *our* image," and "behold, the man has become like one of *us*."[72] These and other early passages from Scripture reveal a dialogue within the Godhead, and for a monotheistic religion, this is quite confusing. Why is God, who is absolutely One, speaking as if he were multiple, and who is God speaking to when he is speaking to himself? Is it possible that God can converse within himself? If so, to whom is he speaking?

The phenomenon of dialogue within the Godhead continues into the New Testament and is especially emphasized in the prologue of John's Gospel, whose opening lines state, "In the beginning was the Word (*logos*), and the Word was with God, and the Word was God." Here, the Godhead is seen as being both relational (the Word was *with* God), as well as united (the Word *was* God), and the Word can dialogue (*dia-logos*) with God because of a relationship within God himself. With these revelations, the internal dialogue found in Genesis is no longer explained as a mere semantic embellishing but instead is an expression of a reality about the nature of God himself: within the Godhead, there is true dialogue and authentic communication, and where there is communication, there is a relationship.

This communication within the Godhead was articulated in various ways through the words of Jesus Christ, but these words were often confusing. On the one hand, he spoke as if being merely related to God, as if he had only a relationship to the Father but was not actually the Father himself: "The Son can do nothing of his own accord, but only what he sees his Father doing," "Father, the hour has come; glorify your Son that the Son may glorify you" and "Father, not my will, but yours, be done."[73] In all of these passages, Jesus reveals himself as one who is in relationship with God, and so presumably distinct from God. Yet alongside these descriptions of relationship with God, Jesus also spoke of being *identical* with God, saying things like "he who hates me hates my Father also" and praying to the Father "that they may all be one; even as you, Father, are in me, and I in you."[74] Jesus also said that succinct but confusing line which enraged the Jews: "I and the Father are one."[75] The Jews knew how to interpret this statement, for they replied by saying, "you, being a man, make yourself God," but because they rejected the idea that a person could be equal to God, they chose to throw stones at him.[76] Though Jesus

72. Gen 1:26; 3:22.
73. John 5:19; 17:1; Luke 22:42.
74. John 15:23; 17:21.
75. John 10:39.
76. John 10:33.

proved his divine power by rising from the dead, he still left this question lingering within the Christian community: what, exactly, does Jesus mean when he says that "the Father and I are one"? What exactly does it mean to say that Jesus is "equal to God" and yet distinct from God?

In pondering these questions, the church discovered great riches about the role of the category of relationship, which alone was capable of explaining this seemingly-incoherent duality of distinction and equality. The church eventually came to articulate that Jesus was fully God, that he was "consubstantial (*homoousious*) with the Father" and thus truly One with the Father. But the church also maintained that there remained in the Godhead a real distinction between the Father and the Son. In order to explain this real distinction, the category of relation emerged as something that is inherent to being itself and not simply posterior to existence. Pope Benedict explains:

> With the insight that, seen as a substance, God is One but that there exists in him the phenomenon of dialogue, of differentiation, and of relationship through speech, the category *relatio* gained a completely new significance for Christian thought. To Aristotle, it was among the 'accidents's, the chance circumstances of being, which are separate from substance, the sole sustaining form of the real. The experience of the God who conducts a dialogue, of the God who is not only *logos* but also *dia-logos* . . . exploded the ancient division of reality into substance, the real thing, and accidents, the merely circumstantial. It now became clear that the dialogue, the *relatio*, stands beside the substance as an equally primordial form of being.[77]

Prior to Christian thought, the generally accepted conception of "being" consisted exclusively of the category of substance, "the sole sustaining form of the real." While the Western philosophers recognized the crucial importance of *relatio*, it was considered only an accident, one of the "chance circumstances of being," but with the emergence of the Christian creeds, relation came to be understood much more broadly and significantly. Zizioulas explains that now, "*to be* and *to be in relation* becomes identical. For someone or something to *be*, two things are simultaneously needed: being itself and *being-in-relation*."[78] Existence itself has an inherently relational dimension, and so the category of relation must henceforth be understood as "an equally primordial form of being." In the Trinity, being and relation have become forever inseparable.

---

77. Ratzinger, *Introduction to Christianity*, 182-183.
78. Zizioulas, *Being as Communion*, 88.

Though these insights on being and being-in-relation arose in the context of reflections about the Trinity, they also have a particular consequence for human beings, as Pope Francis explains: "Believing in one God who is Trinitarian communion suggests that the Trinity has left its mark on all creation."[79] What is true about the intrinsic nature of God must, in some sense, also be true about the intrinsic nature of the human person who is made in his image and likeness, and because God is not a monad but instead is a communion of persons, human existence itself must also bear an inherently relational dimension. Pope Benedict concludes,

> It is the nature of Christian existence *to receive and to live life as relatedness*, and thus to enter into that unity which is the ground of all reality and sustains it. This will perhaps make it clear how the doctrine of the Trinity, when properly understood, can become the nodal point of theology and of Christian thought in general.[80]

If God exists as fundamentally being-in-relationship, then man, too, exists as fundamentally being-in-relationship, and this doctrine is a nodal point for moral theology as much as any other branch of theology.

These revealed doctrines rooted in the Trinity influence our understanding of both human reason and human relationships, for instead of conceiving of the human person exclusively as a "thinking thing," as Descartes did, the Christian tradition conceives of the human person as both a thinking thing *and* a related thing. Through considerations of the Trinity, man is understood not primarily as a rational substance, but both a rational and a related substance, one whose dynamic of *relatio* stands alongside the substance as an "equally primordial form of being." Such a trinitarian understanding of the human person is of consequence for the human mind, for if being itself is inherently relational, then the rational faculty of human nature will also bear a relational dimension. Searching for and reflecting on these trinitarian consequences for the rational faculty is the motivating idea undergirding this thesis and is a theological prejudice which has influenced our own thinking on this topic. We acknowledge that we are violating Descartes's methodology by allowing such a prejudice to influence our decision to investigate these consequences, but if this thesis is true, then every rational decision is prejudiced in some way by one's relationships. Incapable of escaping such a hermeneutical contradiction within one's self, we must go outwards and consider these questions from other authorities besides the self.

79. Francis, *Laudato Si'*, 239.
80. Ratzinger, *Introduction to Christianity*, 188.

Chapter 2

The Democratic Mind

IN THE YEAR 1830, Alexis de Tocqueville was sent by the French government to the United States of America in order to conduct an investigation of the experience of democracy in this relatively new country. France herself had been experimenting with various expressions of democracy during the previous half-century, but instead of securing liberty, the people were left with only a series of intermittent revolutions which failed to firmly establish the democratic project.[1] As the democratic spirit of the people continued to revolt violently within its aristocratic social body, the French government was anxious for guidance on how to heal the social wounds brought on by these varied revolutions, and Tocqueville's mission to America was intended to be the source of this guidance.

He journeyed throughout the United States for nine months, and after returning to France, he worked for five years on his first volume of reflections from this journey, finally publishing it in the year 1835. Another five years of writing would be required for the completion of the second volume, but in the year 1840 it too was published, and together these two volumes make up a single, unified work titled *De la Démocratie en Amérique* (*Democracy in America*). It was met with great acclaim by the French intelligentsia, and not only did it accomplish the mission for which it was commissioned, it also is a work whose insights and conclusions have repercussions for the fields of political science, economics, sociology, history, and even moral

---

1. Tocqueville says, "The Revolution that reduced to dust the aristocratic society in which our fathers lived is the great event of our time. It has changed everything, modified everything, altered everything" (Tocqueville, *De la Démocratie en Amérique*, 691). All citations of de Tocqueville in this thesis come from this text.

theology. Originally written to guide the French government, it now serves as a canonical text for several academic disciplines, and we turn to it here in this thesis to expose what it has to reveal for our understanding of how the rational faculty of human nature develops in response to the relational dimension of the human person.

EQUALITY OF CONDITIONS

Tocqueville observed many intellectual, social, political, and religious tendencies among the citizens of the United States, but there was one social reality which united them all together: "equality of conditions." He states, "Among the new objects that attracted my attention during my stay in the United States, none struck me more vividly than the equality of conditions."[2] Equality of conditions had a pervasive influence on nearly every aspect of the culture, for "it gives a certain direction to the public mind, a certain turn to the laws; to those governing, new maxims, and particular habits to the governed."[3] Equality of conditions permeates the entirety of his work and will return numerous times throughout this exposition, so it is appropriate to now describe its essential characteristics.

Equality of conditions describes the social phenomenon in which nearly all of the citizens are more or less equivalent in terms of language, intellect, wealth, and status, and such a social state directly contrasts with an aristocratic society wherein one can find class stratifications based on the diverse concentrations of these same social factors. In fact, his work continually contrasts "democracy" and "aristocracy," making them indispensable reference points for each other, for what Tocqueville means by democracy can only be properly understood in light of what he means by aristocracy, and vice-versa. For Tocqueville, human nature is indivisible and unchanging, but when it is placed in either of these social environments, this same human nature will manifest itself in two very diverse and significant ways. Throughout his work, democracy and aristocracy are the two primary social lenses through which human nature will refract and break up into predictable customs, laws, and habits of mind.

Tocqueville's interest in equality extends beyond the American continent, for while equality of conditions was initially observed in American

---

2. "Parmi les objets nouveaux qui, pendant mon séjour aux États-Unis, ont attiré mon attention, aucun n'a plus vivement frappé mes regard que l'égalité des conditions" (*De la Démocratie en Amerique* [henceforth "DA"]), 4.

3. "il donne à l'esprit public une certaine direction, un certain tour aux lois; aux gouvernants des maximes nouvelles, et des habitudes particulières aux gouvernés" (DA, 4).

culture, he sees how it has already been established in some parts of the world and how it is emerging in others. For example, he says that China is a place where "equality of conditions is very great and very ancient," so America is not the first country to establish this social reality.[4] Regarding countries where it is currently emerging, he focuses on Europe, for he says, "I saw equality of conditions that, without having reached its extreme limits as in the United States, approached those limits more each day; and this same democracy that reigned in American societies, appeared to me to advance rapidly toward power in Europe."[5] Three important points emerge from this quote, and the first is that "democracy" and "equality of conditions" are used as nearly synonymous terms in this sentence, which is a recurring pattern in the writing of Tocqueville. The second important point is that Tocqueville considers equality of conditions to be a reality which is "advancing rapidly" within Europe; far from being a text primarily concerned with democracy only in America, Tocqueville's work actually serves as a guide to understanding the influence of democracy throughout the world, even in his own home. The third important point is that the United States serves as an "extreme limit" to equality of conditions. Tocqueville attributes this to its birth, for "The great advantage of the Americans is to have arrived at democracy without having to suffer democratic revolutions, and to have been born equal instead of becoming so."[6] Unlike France and other countries in Europe, the experience of equality of conditions in America did not grow from within an aristocratic culture; rather, Americans were "born" equal, thus allowing the country to serve as an extreme limit for what happens to human nature when it refracts under equality. America's purity of origin allows one to see more clearly the extent to which equality influences the development of the social fabric, but the consequences of this influence have repercussions in any society wherein equality of conditions begins to take root, even when that equality is not as well established as it is in America.

The primary causes of equality itself are not the focus of Tocqueville's work, for in reality, "democracy" is a social, religious, political, and historical phenomenon of dazzling complexity, so he concentrates his work

---

4. "l'égalité des conditions est très grande et très ancienne" (DA, 1123).

5. "Je vis l'égalité des conditions qui, sans y avoir atteint comme aux États-Unis ses limites extrêmes, s'en rapprochait chaque jour davantage; et cette même démocratie, qui régnait sur les sociétés américaines, me parut en Europe s'savancer rapidement vers le pouvoir" (DA, 5).

6. "le grand avantage des Américains est d'être arrivés à la démocratie sans avoir à souffrir de révolutions démocratiques, et d'être nés égaux au lieu de le devenir" (DA, 886).

on observing its consequences and illustrating the extent to which it has altered customs, opinions, sentiments, and human thought. Nonetheless, Tocqueville illustrates a few of the factors which contribute to equality of conditions before he embarks on the longer journey of showing how the social state of equality has altered the human experience, and so we will now examine one law and explore its role in bringing about a specific economic consequence and a specific intellectual consequence, and together, these various factors all contribute, in varied ways, towards the creation of equality of conditions.

The most important law in bringing about equality of conditions which Tocqueville considers at length is the law of inheritance, and its influence in America is best understood when contrasted with how the law of inheritance functions in an aristocratic society. Tocqueville defines an aristocratic society as a society wherein the laws of inheritance follow the law of primogeniture, which is the passing on of the entirety of one's property and a majority of one's wealth to the oldest son. In speaking about the law of primogeniture, Tocqueville observes that "it reunites, concentrates, gathers property and, soon after, power, around some head; in a way, it makes aristocracy spring from the soil."[7] Thus, the law of primogeniture has a great unifying and concentrating effect on land, wealth, and eventually some "power" which is often a family. This creates a certain bond between the family and the land, for the one who currently owns the land is a steward, and those who will one day own it are mentored and prepared for their reception of it and grow in their affection for it. Thus Tocqueville remarks, "The family represents the land; the land represents the family; the land perpetuates its name, origin, glory, power and virtues."[8] This bond between the family and the land is traced to the fact that, in each successive generation, the land and wealth passes on without being divided, culminating in the great landed estates of aristocratic cultures.

In aristocratic cultures, this law of primogeniture is often required, but in America, the laws of inheritance often allow for the equal division of the father's property among all the children, and in some states, this equal division is actually *required*. The consequences of this change are two-fold, both of which contribute to the creation of equality of conditions.

As to the most immediate effect, Tocqueville states that "the death of each owner leads to a revolution in property; not only do the holdings change masters, but so to speak, they change nature; they are constantly

    7. "elle réunit, elle concentre, elle groupe autour de quelque tête la propriété, et bientôt après le pouvoir; elle fait jaillir en quelque sorte l'aristocratie du sol" (DA, 79).

    8. "La famille représente la terre, la terre représente la famille; elle perpétue son nom, son origine, sa gloire, sa puissance, ses vertus" (DA, 81).

split into smaller portions."[9] As each generation sees the father's wealth equally split among the children, the concentration of wealth becomes fractured with each generational division, and thus wealth is found in smaller and smaller portions. This is simply the mathematical consequence of such a law, but there is also a second effect which, while indirect, is nonetheless the greatest contributor to the dissolution of great fortunes and great estates, and it is the fact that this law "destroys the intimate connection that existed between family spirit and keeping the land" and "from the moment you take away from landed proprietors any great interest—arising from sentiment, memory, pride, or ambition—in keeping the land, you can be sure that sooner or later, they will sell it."[10] This indirect effect, whereby those who inherit land are disposed to sell it, arises from the law's impact on their interest in the land, for if the land is fractured after each generation, the only hope for keeping the land united is for all those who will receive a piece of the estate to agree to keep it intact, and human history shows how unsuccessful brothers are at staying united when it comes to their parent's inheritance. But the presence of greed, ambition, and pleasure are also part of this desire to sell, for "Movable assets produce more income than other assets and lend themselves much more easily to satisfying the passions of the moment."[11] When the law is structured in such a way that the land itself can easily be divided after each generation, the bond between the land and the family erodes, and in the absence of such a bond, people are disposed towards literally "making the most" out of the situation and transferring their share of the inheritance towards movable assets, which involves selling the land.

Regarding the cumulative impact of both the direct and indirect effect arising from this change in the law of inheritance, Tocqueville remarks that "it succeeds in profoundly attacking landed property and in making families as well as fortunes rapidly disappear."[12] While the law of primogeniture unites land and wealth, the laws of inheritance in the United States cause the

9. "En vertu de la loi des successions, la mort de chaque propriétaire amène une révolution dans la propriété; non seulement les biens changent de maîtres, mais ils changent, pour ainsi dire, de nature; ils se fractionnent sans cesse en portions plus petites" (DA, 80).

10. "détruit la liaison intime qui existait entre l'esprit de famille et la conservation de la terre"; "du moment où vous enlevez aux propriétaires fonciers un grand intérêt de sentiment, de souvenirs, d'orgueil, d'ambition à conserver la terre, on peut être assuré que tôt ou tard ils la vendront" (DA, 82).

11. "les capitaux mobiliers produisant plus d'intérêts que les autres, et se prêtant bien plus facilement à satisfaire les passions du moment" (DA, 82).

12. "Des deux manières elle parvient à attaquer profondément la propriété foncière et à faire disparaître avec rapidité les familles ainsi que les fortunes" (DA, 83).

dissipation of land and wealth, and in this way, both land and fortunes are constantly being divided into smaller and smaller portions. The net result of these two effects is particularly striking because the indirect effect furthers what the law itself, in a purely mathematical way, is already destined to do. As great fortunes divide into smaller and smaller portions, we see the beginning of "equality," for the relative wealth of each member of society equalizes as large differences are diminished. It is in this way that a change in law can lead to equality of wealth, which is just one aspect of what Tocqueville means by equality of conditions.

We can be sure that we have not over-estimated the importance which Tocqueville places on the role of a single law in bringing about equality of conditions, for he says, "I am astonished that ancient and modern political writers have not attributed a greater influence on the course of human affairs to the laws of inheritance."[13] While he acknowledges that there are many other factors involved, this single law forms the nucleus around which many other factors revolve and depend. Having said this, the original cause which actually lead the American people to *change* the law of primogeniture is something more mysterious and remote, but identifying this cause is not Tocqueville's primary concern; instead, he is concerned with showing the effect that such a change has had on the concentration of wealth and how this change in wealth changes other dynamics of society. So while the factors which lead to changing the law of inheritance in America are complex, it nonetheless has a very simple economic consequence: a more equal distribution of wealth.

While wealth is more evenly distributed in America, this should not be confused with a diminished interest in money, for Tocqueville says, "I do not even know of a country where the love of money holds a greater place in the human heart and where a deeper contempt is professed for the theory of the permanent equality of property."[14] Because a love for money is deeply rooted in the American heart, we see that it is not "good" and "evil" which are driving conditions towards equality of wealth; rather, it is the way certain laws act on this human nature. For example, in aristocratic societies, Tocqueville says "What is called family spirit is often based on an illusion of individual egoism," which shows us how the vices of vainglory and egoism are alive and well in aristocratic cultures just as much as greed

13. "Je m'étonne que les publicistes anciens et modernes n'aient pas attribué aux lois sur les successions une plus grande influence dans la marche des affaires humaines" (DA, 79).

14. "je ne connais même pas de pays où l'amour de l'argent tienne une plus large place dans le cœur de l'homme, et où l'on professe un mépris plus profond pour la théorie de l'égalité permanente des biens" (DA, 85).

and materialism are present in democratic societies.[15] However, in a land where the love of money holds a special power over the human heart, and where this same land has laws of inheritance whereby each generation sees its family fortune divided, a situation comes about whereby "It is rare to see two generations reap the rewards of wealth."[16] So it is not the absence of vice or the presence of virtue which leads to equality; rather, it is the way certain virtues and vices of human nature interact with different laws which lead to equality.

It is also important to understand that fortunes are not smaller or rarer in America; they are only less continuous and rarely hereditary, causing wealth to fluctuate rapidly across the social landscape and arrive in new hands each generation. This constant fluctuation of money, and not the quantitative decrease of money, is the real factor which leads to equality, which causes Tocqueville to remark that "Wealth circulates there with incredible rapidity."[17] This is the first time we see Tocqueville highlight an aspect of "equality" which returns at various times throughout his writing, which is the constant movement, fluctuation, and "agitation" of things which, in aristocracy, are more stable and permanent. Here, he is only referring to the movement of wealth, but this great movement and general instability has an impact on many other areas of life, particularly education and "jobs," as we will see below.

The emergence of equality of wealth leads to other changes in society, such as a tendency towards equality of intelligence. Because people in democratic societies cannot depend on receiving their wealth through their parents, every generation is required to pursue a job or career wherein they can create their own fortune. Thus, "Americans can devote only the first years of life to general cultivation of mind; at age fifteen, they begin a career; most often, therefore, their education concludes when ours begins."[18] At the age when an aristocratic culture would begin to train someone for a "general cultivation of mind," the democratic culture sends its citizens off to work because no one is rich enough to afford a life without work. Thus in America, "Primary education is available to everyone; higher education is hardly available to anyone."[19] Pulled up from below by their primary education, but

---

15. "Ce qu'on appelle l'esprit de famille est souvent fondé sur une illusion de l'égoïsme individuel" (DA, 82).

16. "est rare de voir deux générations en recueillir les faveurs" (DA, 85).

17. "la fortune y circule avec une incroyable rapidité" (DA, 85).

18. "Les Américains ne peuvent donc donner à la culture générale de l'intelligence que les premières années de la vie: à quinze ans, ils entrent dans une carrière; ainsi leur éducation finit le plus souvent à l'époque où la nôtre commence" (DA, 87).

19. "l'instruction primaire y est à la portée de chacun; l'instruction supérieure n'y est presque à la portée de personne" (DA, 87).

not pulled up from above by a higher education due to the need to pursue a career, American citizens in 1830 exhibited a relatively equal intelligence.

We must comment on what Tocqueville means by *l'instruction supérieure* or "higher education," for reading that phrase today can evoke the idea of colleges and universities, which are institutions which did exist in the 1830's in America. Tocqueville acknowledges that some Americans pursue extended studies into adulthood, but these studies are different from what he considers "higher education," for "directed only toward a specialized and lucrative field, they study a field of knowledge in the way they prepare for a trade; and they take only the applications recognized to have immediate utility."[20] Colleges and universities in America often promote precisely this type of education: the study of specialized knowledge which prepares someone for a lucrative field and which limits the scope of inquiry almost exclusively to immediate utility, and such education is in no way what Tocqueville considers "higher education." Without ever explicitly referencing an entire theory of education, Tocqueville takes it for granted that the pursuit of *l'instruction supérieure* requires a general cultivation of mind which is greatly impeded by the accumulation of only trade-specific knowledge.

Of all the factors important for a superior education, Tocqueville thinks that generational wealth is an essential component, for he says, "In America no class exists that honors intellectual work and in which the penchant for intellectual pleasures is handed down with affluence and hereditary leisure."[21] For Tocqueville, a higher education cannot come without "hereditary leisure," and leisure cannot come without "affluence." Lacking a class which is able to safeguard either of these necessities in a continuous way for its descendants, the equality of wealth leads to a necessary consequence, which is equality of intelligence.

Tocqueville sees plenty of wealthy people in America who enjoy leisure and have riches, but this wealth does not produce aristocracy for the following reason: "In America, most of the rich began by being poor; nearly all the men of leisure were busy men in their youth. The result is that when they could have the taste for study, they do not have the time to devote themselves to it; and when they have gained the time, they no longer have the taste."[22] Despite the existence of "men of leisure" in America who also

20. "elle ne se dirige plus que vers une matière spéciale et lucrative; on étudie une science comme on prend un métier; et l'on n'en saisit que les applications dont l'utilité présente est reconnue" (DA, 87).

21. "Il n'existe donc point en Amérique de classe dans laquelle le penchant des plaisirs intellectuels se transmettre avec une aisance et des loisirs héréditaires, et qui tienne en honneur les travaux de l'intelligence" (DA, 87).

22. "En Amérique, la plupart des riches ont commencé par être pauvres; presque tous les oisifs ont été, dans leur jeunesse, des gens occupés; d'où il résulte que, quand

possess commanding wealth, there is not a class who protects this leisure for each succeeding generation, and this prevents the possibility of safeguarding a core of society which can pursue *l'instruction supérieure*. All those wealthy enough to afford leisure had to work in their intellectually formative years because few of them received their wealth from their parents, so there is only situational wealth and not generational wealth in America, and this has considerable consequences on the general level of intelligence among the citizens.

We again pause to note Tocqueville's understanding of human nature in both aristocratic and democratic societies, for a natural distribution of various levels of intelligence exists in both of these societies, and it is only what these societies do with this natural variety which results in two different expressions of intelligence among the people. In a democratic society, "Intelligences, while still remaining unequal as the Creator intended, find equal means at their disposal."[23] Because the educational formation is nearly identical for most Americans, these "equal means" of education will blunt the edges of any natural inequalities and produce a more continuous distribution of intelligence among the populace. So we must insist again that Tocqueville does not consider human nature in democracy any different from human nature in aristocracy; instead, he illustrates how this same human nature refracts under two different environments.

The practical result of the natural inequality of intelligence being compressed into equal means of formation is that America is filled with "a great multitude of individuals who have about the same number of notions in matters of religion, history, the sciences, political economy, legislation, and government."[24] In America, the equality of intelligence naturally leads to equality of thought, and Tocqueville insists that this equality of thought is traced to equality of wealth. In America, one sees fewer landed estates but also fewer slums; in America, one sees neither intellectual brilliance nor barbarism; and for Tocqueville, the connection between these two equalities is causal and not just correlative.

We can now see how the interaction between a single law and its diverse consequences all contribute to equality of conditions in America. The string of causality linking the law of inheritance to equality of intelligence

---

on pourrait avoir le goût de l'étude, on n'a pas le temps de s'sy livrer; et que, quand on a acquis le temps de s'sy livrer, on n'en a plus le goût" (DA, 87).

23. "les intelligences, tout en restant inégales, ainsi que l'a voulu le Créateur, trouvent à leur disposition des moyens égaux" (DA, 88).

24. "une multitude immense d'individus qui ont le même nombre de notions à peu près en matière de religion, d'histoire, de sciences, d'économie politique, de législation, de gouvernement" (DA, 88).

forms only one string among dozens which Tocqueville uses to weave the web of "democracy" and illustrate its distinction from "aristocracy," and part of the genius of Tocqueville's work is his ability to illustrate strings of causality within nearly every aspect of society, from opinions, to religious devotion, to dress, to language, and even to the constructing of monuments. The first pages of *Democracy in America* begin with reflections on the string of causality exposed above, and at the end of his extensive work, Tocqueville returns to this initial string and remarks: "I come to see that what is noticeable in fortunes reappears again in a thousand other forms. Nearly all the extremes become softer and are blunted . . . things are less high and less low, less brilliant and less obscure than what was seen in the world."[25] And he details specifically what he sees in "democratic" societies which allows him to make such sweeping claims about the universal presence of equality:

> Life is not very ornate, but very comfortable and very peaceful. There are few very delicate and very coarse pleasures, little courtesy in manners and little brutality in tastes. You scarcely find very learned men or very ignorant populations. Genius becomes rarer and enlightenment more common.[26]

This whole ensemble of equality in manners, equality of thought, equality of living conditions, equality of wealth, and many other such equalities is what Tocqueville means by equality of conditions, and having shown in brief outline what this phrase means, and illustrating some factors leading to its creation, we now turn our attention to the rational consequences of such a social state.

DEMOCRATIC LOGIC

As mentioned in the introduction, Tocqueville's work is split into two volumes, and the second volume was finished five years after the completion of the first volume. Although these two volumes form one complete work[27],

    25. "j'arrive à voir que ce qui se remarque dans les fortunes se représente sous mille autres formes. Presque tous les extrêmes s'sadoucissent et s'sémoussent . . . qui est tout à la fois moins haut et moins bas, moins brillant et moins obscur que ce qui se voyait dans le monde" (DA, 1281).
    26. "L'existence des hommes devient plus longue et leur propriété plus sûre. La vie n'est pas très ornée, mais très aisée et très paisible. Il y a peu de plaisirs très délicats et très grossiers, peu de politesses dans les manières et peu de brutalité dans les goûts. On ne rencontre guère d'hommes très savants ni de populations très ignorantes. Le génie devient plus rare et les lumières plus communes" (DA, 1281).
    27. Tocqueville states in the introduction to the second volume: "The two parts complement one another and form only a single work" (DA, 691).

the scope of thought within the second volume reveals new depths from these additional years of concentrated thought on the topic of equality of conditions, and Tocqueville takes advantage of this maturity to enter into more philosophical and theoretical dimensions of "democracy" which enrich the seeds of thought introduced in the first volume.

This second volume is composed of four parts, all of which seek to understand the role of "democracy" and equality of conditions on particular dimensions of social and political life, as can be seen in their titles: "*Part I: Influence of Democracy on the Intellectual Movement in the United States,*" "*Part II: Influence of Democracy on the Sentiments of Americans,*" "*Part III: Influence of Democracy on Mores Properly So Called,*" and "*Part IV: On the Influence that Democratic Ideas and Sentiments Exercise on Political Society.*" Thus, the role of "democracy" on the intellectual movement, sentiments, mores, and political society form the locus of this second volume, and given that this thesis is concerned primarily with the mind and logic, we will concentrate on the first part of this second volume (*Influence of Democracy on the Intellectual Movement in the United States*), though segments from the other parts will naturally make their way into our exposition. Tocqueville's thought is circular but not redundant, so each time he returns to an idea from the first part, he will illustrate its connection to some new thought or highlight an aspect which was not possible earlier. In this way, his comments on the mind and intelligence in the first part are enriched by comments in the other three parts, and so they will weave in and out of this exposition where appropriate.

While the first volume of *Democracy in America* is heavily concentrated on a specific study of America, the second volume is more concerned with "democracy" in general.[28] America continues to be the reference point of his reflections, but the conclusions are not relevant only for the American form of democracy. We also note that from this point forward, the terms "democracy," "equality of conditions" and "America" often mean the same thing. For example, when he says that "Protestantism itself already announced that society had become very democratic," we are to understand him to mean that the society from which Protestantism emerged had given birth to equality of conditions.[29] Because of this equivalence of terms, we alert the reader to understanding that "democracy" rarely refers to a system

---

28. Tocqueville says this himself in his notes for the introduction to the second volume when he writes, "The first book more American than democratic. This one more democratic than American" (DA, 691).

29. "le protestantisme lui-même annonçait déjà que la société était devenue trés démocratique" (DA, 699).

CHAPTER 2: THE DEMOCRATIC MIND   39

of voting and "America" does not always refer to the country; instead, they almost always refer to a social state pervaded by equality of conditions.

In the introduction to this second volume, Tocqueville writes that the democratic social state in America "has given birth to a multitude of sentiments and opinions that were unknown in the old aristocratic societies of Europe. It has destroyed or modified relationships that formerly existed and established new ones."[30] It is this destruction and modification of relationships (*rapports*) which has brought about these new sentiments and opinions, giving us our first indication as to how a modification of the relational dimension of the human person can bring about a change in their rational faculty. At this point, such a statement remains only an assertion by Tocqueville, and the extent to which this is true can only be seen by entering more deeply into the text; so, having stated our intention, we now turn to this first part of the second volume and listen to Tocqueville's understanding of how democracy has impacted the mind.

At the start of the first part of the second volume, Tocqueville states,

> It is easy to see, however, that nearly all the inhabitants of the United States direct their minds in the same way, and conduct them according to the same rules; that is to say, they possess, without ever having taken the trouble to define its rules, a certain philosophical method that is common to all of them.[31]

We first note that Tocqueville is no longer referring to a common intelligence (*l'intelligence*) among the inhabitants; here, he is referring to a common mind (*esprit*). It is not just the content of thought which is the same among the Americans, but the way of thinking and the *règles* or "rules" of thought itself which are the same.

Tocqueville provides several examples of the rules which American minds almost always follow, such as the tendency to "to escape from the spirit of system," "to take tradition only as information," "to seek by yourself and in yourself alone the reason for things" as well as "to strive toward the result without allowing yourself to be caught up in the means."[32] Each

---

30. "fait naître, parmi eux, une multitude de sentiments et d'opinions qui étaient inconnus dans les vieilles sociétés aristocratiques de l'Europe. Il a détruit ou modifié des rapports qui existaient jadis, et en a établi de nouveaux" (DA, 691).

31. "Il est facile de voir cependant que presque tous les habitants des États-Unis dirigent leur esprit de la même manière, et le conduisent d'après les mêmes règles; c'est-à-dire qu'ils possèdent, sans qu'ils se soient jamais donné la peine d'en définir les règles, une certaine méthode philosophique qui leur est commune à tous" (DA, 699).

32. "échapper à l'esprit de système," "prendre la tradition que comme un renseignement," "chercher par soi-même et en soi seul la raison des choses," "tendre au résultat sans se laisser enchaîner au moyen" (DA, 699).

of these tendencies of the American mind form a particular type of logic which is shared among the inhabitants, and Tocqueville summarizes them all when he says, "If I go still further and, among these various features, look for the principle one and the one that can sum up nearly all the others, I discover that, in most operations of the mind, each American appeals only to the individual effort of his reason."[33] He calls this the "American philosophical method," and whenever Tocqueville references *méthode* in the quotes below, he is referring to this pattern of thought wherein one appeals almost exclusively to one's individual reason in the operations of the mind.

Tocqueville notes that such a way of thinking is purely Descartian, but he does not think that Americans have acquired this philosophical method by reading Descartes; rather, it is the social state itself which brought it about: "Americans do not read the works of Descartes, because their social state diverts them from speculative studies, and they follow his maxims because the same social state naturally disposes their mind to adopt them."[34] Two seeds of thought, one subtle and the other apparent, are present here. The more subtle point is that the social state of equality *diverts* the minds of Americans from speculative study, and this is rooted in various currents of the social state, such as the lack of hereditary wealth and thus the need for all citizens to take up a career, but it is also due to other currents which Tocqueville explains elsewhere, such as materialism and a "restless agitation" which both arise as a consequence of equality of conditions.[35] But the more apparent point is that the social state of equality of conditions is what Tocqueville considers to be responsible for bringing about this *méthode* within the American mind. The corollary to such an affirmation is the following: when equality of conditions becomes prevalent within a culture, one can expect the emergence of this type of logic. This is precisely what Tocqueville goes on to affirm, and he goes about demonstrating this point by contrasting it with how the mind works in a social state of aristocracy.

---

33. "Que si je vais plus loin encore, et que parmi ces traits divers, je cherche le principal et celui qui peut résumer presque tous les autres, je découvre que, dans la plupart des opérations de l'esprit, chaque Américain n'en appelle qu'à l'effort individuel de sa raison" (DA, 699).

34. "Les Américains ne lisent point les ouvrages de Descartes, parce que leur état social les détourne des études spéculatives, et ils suivent ses maximes parce que ce même état social dispose naturellement leur esprit à les adopter" (DA, 700).

35. Tocqueville explains these dynamics at length in "Chapter 10: Of the Taste for Well-Being in America," "Chapter 11: Of the Particular Effects Produced by the Love of Material Enjoyments in Democratic Centuries," and "Chapter 13: Why the Americans Appear so Restless Amid Their Well-Being." All three of these chapters appear in the first part of the second volume; see DA 930–47.

When Tocqueville states "in most operations of the mind, each American appeals only to the individual effort of his reason," a key word is "appeal," for he thinks that human nature appeals to something in order to form the basis of its thought. In democratic times, it is the individual effort of one's own reason which forms the basis of a person's thought, but there are three other forms of authority which, in the social state of aristocracy, have served to form the basis of a person's thought. These authorities are family, class, and the intelligence of other people, and Tocqueville shows how and why each one of these forms of authority are no longer authoritative to minds which develop in a social state of equality.

Regarding the family, he says, "Amid the constant movement that reigns within a democratic society, the bond that links generations together weakens or breaks; each man easily loses track of the ideas of his ancestors, or is hardly concerned about them."[36] Again, we note the subtle assertion that the milieu of democracy is one of "continual movement," with each person finding his social and economic status in a constant state of development. The result is that bonds between generations within a family are more easily broken when compared to an aristocratic society, which means that men in democratic times will not be disposed to look for family or tradition to guide their thought. When the stability of family tradition is broken or made significantly less stable, its authority over the mind of its members is also broken or at least made less stable.

Regarding the influence of classes, he says,

> Nor can the men who live in such a society draw their beliefs from the opinions of the class to which they belong, for there are so to speak no longer any classes, and those that still exist are composed of elements so fluid, that the corps can never exercise a true power over its members.[37]

Classes do not exist in a democracy, and even when there is differentiation of wealth, Tocqueville considers the "fluid movement" of members in each class to be an insufficient basis of authority over thought. Again, it is the *instability* of these classes, and not necessarily the amount of money present in each class or the power of members within the class, which contributes to

---

36. "au milieu du mouvement continuel qui règne au sein d'une société démocratique, le lien qui unit les générations entre elles se relâche ou se brise; chacun y perd aisément la trace des idées de ses aïeux, ou ne s'sen inquiète guère" (DA, 700).

37. "Les hommes qui vivent dans une semblable société ne sauraient non plus puiser leurs croyances dans les opinons de la classe à laquelle ils appartiennent, car il n'y a, pour ainsi dire, plus de classes, et celles qui existent encore sont composées d'éléments si mouvants, que le corps ne saurait jamais y exercer un véritable pouvoir sur ses membres" (DA, 700).

its weakened status as an authority over the mind of those who live in times of equality.

Finally, regarding the intelligence of other people, he says,

> As for the action that the intelligence of one man can have on that of another, it is necessarily very limited in a country where citizens, having become more or less similar, all see each other at very close range; and, not noticing in any one of them the signs of incontestable greatness and superiority, they are constantly brought back to their own reason as the most visible and nearest source of truth.[38]

Intellectual authority over the mind requires that this authority possess a power greater than its own, but not seeing this power or grandeur in other human beings with equivalent intelligence, the individual will look elsewhere for something to which it can "appeal" as the basis of its thought.

Thus Tocqueville concludes that when equality of conditions reigns within the social state, when the bonds of family easily dissipate with each generation, when wealth is similar and hereditary classes are non-existent, and when all minds are afforded the same means to rise from ignorance but are not afforded the leisure necessary for rising to grandeur, there is no longer a reliable source of authority for thought itself, which then disposes those living in these conditions to turn within themselves to find "the reason for all things." It is not that man necessarily prefers to look within himself for the reason of all things when conditions are equal; rather, man has looked outside himself, and finding nothing to convince him of power or grandeur beyond himself, he retreats within his own mind, from which he judges the world. Regarding the thesis of this paper, we would say that it is a change in man's relations with family, class, and others which has caused this change in logic.

Tocqueville mentioned above how this *méthode* is thoroughly Descartian, but he is so convinced that equality of conditions is the source of this *méthode* that he argues that it was the presence of equality of conditions which was responsible for forming the thought of Descartes himself. To argue this point, he takes the reader on a brief historical journey:

---

38. "Quant à l'action que peut avoir l'intelligence d'un homme sur celle d'un autre, elle est nécessairement fort restreinte dans un pays où les citoyens, devenus à peu près pareils, se voient tous de fort prés, et, n'apercevant dans aucun d'entre eux les signes d'une grandeur et d'une supériorité incontestables, sont sans cesse ramenés vers leur propre raison comme vers la source la plus visible et la plus proche de la vérité" (DA, 700–1).

In the 16th century, the men of the Reformation subject some of the dogmas of the ancient faith to individual reason; but they continue to exclude all the others from discussion. In the 17th, Bacon, in the natural sciences, and Descartes, in philosophy strictly speaking, abolish accepted formulas, destroy the rule of traditions and overthrow the authority of the master. The philosophers of the 18th century, finally generalizing the same principle, undertake to submit to the individual examination of each man the object of all his beliefs.[39]

When Tocqueville considers what led to the development of this method so that it might reign over all thought, he does not point to Luther, Descartes, or Voltaire; instead, he points to equality of conditions, and he asks a series of rhetorical questions to emphasize his point:

> Why did the men of the Reformation enclose themselves so narrowly in the circle of religious ideas? Why did Descartes want to use it only in certain matters, although he made his method applicable to everything, and declare that only philosophical and not political things must be judged by oneself? How did it happen that in the 18th century general applications that Descartes and his predecessors had not noticed or had refused to see were all at once drawn from that same method? Finally, why in that period did the method we are speaking about suddenly emerge from the schools to penetrate society and become the common rule of intelligence, and why, after becoming popular among the French, was it openly adopted or secretly followed by all the peoples of Europe?[40]

---

39. "Au XVI siècle les réformateurs soumettent à la raison individuelle quelques-uns des dogmes de l'ancienne foi; mais ils continuent à lui soustraire la discussion de tous les autres. Au XVII, Bacon, dans les sciences naturelles, et Descartes, dans la philosophie proprement dite, abolissent les formules reçues, détruisent l'empire des traditions et renversent l'autorité du maître. Les philosophes du XVIII siècle, généralisant enfin le même principe, entreprennent de soumettre à l'examen individuel de chaque homme l'objet de toutes ses croyances" (DA, 702–3).

40. "D'où vient que les réformateurs se sont si étroitement renfermés dans le cercle des idées religieuses ? Pourquoi Descartes, ne voulant se servir de sa méthode qu'en certaines matières, bien qu'il l'eût mise en état de s'appliquer à toutes, a-t-il déclaré qu'il ne fallait juger par soi-même que les choses de philosophie et non de politique ? Comment est-il arrivé qu'au XVIIIe siècle, on ait tiré tout à coup de cette même méthode des applications générales que Descartes et ses prédécesseurs n'avaient point aperçues ou s's'étaient refusés à découvrir ? D'où vient enfin qu'à cette époque la méthode dont nous parlons est soudainement sortie des écoles pour pénétrer dans la société et devenir la règle commune de l'intelligence, et qu'après avoir été populaire chez les Français, elle a été ostensiblement adoptée ou secrètement suivie par tous les peuples de l'Europe?" DA, 704).

So, this *méthode* grew slowly over the course of the preceding three centuries, and when one investigates the initial *cause* of such a development, Tocqueville argues that it was the reality of equality of conditions, for he states "It was discovered in a period when men began to become equal and similar to each other."[41] At the moment in history when Tocqueville sees social conditions becoming more similar and equality among men becoming more thoroughly established, this method emerged in the world and began to penetrate various religious and intellectual domains in proportion to the growing establishment of equality of conditions, eventually reaching the point where it was applied to all thought.

Even as this method developed over time, there were many other currents within the social fabric which prevented it from diffusing as completely as it has in the United States, for in Europe, "Political laws, the social state, the habits of the mind that flow from first causes, were opposed to it."[42] Though Tocqueville thinks equality of conditions began to emerge as early as the twelfth century in Europe, he acknowledges that political laws, the social state, and habits of mind were opposed to the ready acceptance of such a method, and it could only pervade society as these same social realities began to bend under the growing weight of equality of conditions. This growing weight of equality eventually reached a critical mass and began to impose itself on the mind, which was why he says this method was only "discovered" (*découverte*) or "born" (*naître*) in the sixteenth century, and it would take time for it to grow to maturity within the minds and social state of his day. Thus he concludes: "The philosophical method of the 16th century is not only French, but democratic," and he notes elsewhere that, "It is not Luther, Bacon, Descartes, Voltaire that must be blamed. They only gave form or application; the substance emerged from the state of the world in their time."[43] So Tocqueville does not credit the reformers or the philosophers with creating the *méthode* which has dominated American thought, for these reformers merely gave "form" or "application" to a type of logic which arose naturally from within the social fabric in which these same reformers and philosophers were enmeshed. Because Tocqueville insists that

41. "Elle a été découverte à une époque où les hommes commençaient à s'ségaliser et à se ressembler" (DA, 704). In the introduction to the first volume, Tocqueville demonstrates the development of equality over the previous 700 years in Europe in greater detail; see DA, 6–12.

42. "Les lois politiques, l'état social, les habitudes d'esprit qui découlent de ces premières causes, s'sy opposaient" (DA, 704).

43. "La méthode philosophique du XVIIIe siècle n'est donc pas seulement française, mais démocratique"; "Ce n'est pas à Luther, à Bacon, à Descartes, à Voltaire qu'il faut s'sen prendre. Ils n'ont donné que la forme ou l'application, le fond ressortait de l'ètat du monde de leur temps" (DA, 705).

this *méthode* is "democratic" and not exclusively "American," we have called it "democratic logic" and not "American logic," recognizing nonetheless that Tocqueville sees its prevalence in the United States. From the earliest pages of his work, and continuing to the end, Tocqueville will argue that equality of social conditions, both in America and elsewhere, has bent the rational faculty of human persons in a particular direction, and that direction is inwards.

At this point, we must introduce a few nuances to Tocqueville's comments about the presence of this *méthode* in Europe and America. For example, he states that this philosophical method is actually more prevalent in France than in America[44], and he attributes this to two primary reasons: the experience of revolution in France and the role of religion in America.

Regarding the experience of revolution in France, he states,

> When conditions become equal following a prolonged struggle between the different classes that formed the old society, envy, hatred and contempt for neighbor, pride and exaggerated confidence in self, invade, so to speak, the human heart and for some time make it their domain. This, apart from equality, contributes powerfully to divide men, to make them mistrust each other's judgment and seek enlightenment only within themselves alone.[45]

In these comments on the consequences of revolution, we see how there can be other causes within the social fabric which lead men to not trust others and subsequently to trust in their own reason as the basis for all things. So equality of conditions is not the only factor which can drive men to search within themselves for enlightenment; revolutions are also capable of bending man towards this philosophical method, and in a country like France, which experienced both the growth of equality of conditions while also experiencing a significant revolution, these two forces compounded one another and led France to a social fabric which has seen a more prevalent diffusion of this *méthode* even though social conditions in France are not "more equal" than in the United States. These comments also help us to see why Tocqueville considers America a pure example of equality: democratic

---

44. "Today, this same method is followed more rigorously and applied more often among the French than among the Americans" (DA, 705).

45. "Lorsque les conditions deviennent égales à la suite d'une lutte prolongée entre les différentes classes dont la vieille société était formée, l'envie, la haine et le mépris du voisin, l'orgueil et la confiance exagérée en soi-même, envahissent, pour ainsi dire, le cœur humain et en font quelque temps leur domaine. Ceci, indépendamment de l'égalité, contribue puissamment à diviser les hommes, à faire qu'ils se défient du jugement les uns des autres et qu'ils ne cherchent la lumière qu'en eux seuls" (DA, 708).

thought is not necessarily more prevalent in America, but it is free of more complex social developments like a revolution, and this allows Tocqueville to see more easily the role of equality itself on various changes in behavior, intelligence, and the rational faculty.

The fact that this philosophical method is more prevalent in France than America is due to a second compounding factor, which is the presence of religion in America, which moves the mind in a direction different from the inward curvature which is natural to the democratic social state. Though France is also a Christian country, Tocqueville notes two important differences which impact the way religion influences thought in America versus thought in France: first, "the religious order there has remained entirely distinct from the political order, so that they were able to change ancient laws easily without shaking ancient beliefs."[46] Maintaining a strict separation between church and state from the time of its founding, it was easy for the ancient laws (such as the law of primogeniture) to change in America without also changing the way people think about God. The second way religion uniquely influenced the expression of this *méthode* was due to the way in which Christianity provides limits to the possible range of content which is subject to this philosophical method. Tocqueville explains, "Christianity retained a great dominion over the mind of the Americans, and, what I want to note above all, it reigns not only as a philosophy that you adopt after examination, but also as a religion that you believe without discussion."[47] Because Christianity is accepted without discussion, it has a dogmatic characteristic which is of great profit to those who must search in themselves for the reason of *all* things, for such dogmas actually limit the number of things which can be subject to this *méthode*. Tocqueville explains:

> The Americans, having admitted the principal dogmas of the Christian religion without examination, are obliged to receive in the same way a great number of moral truths that arise from it and are due to it. That confines the work of individual analysis within narrow limits, and excludes from it several of the most important human opinions.[48]

46. "l'ordre religieux y est resté entièrement distinct de l'ordre politique, de telle sorte qu'on a pu changer facilement les lois anciennes sans ébranler les anciennes croyances" (DA, 707).

47. "Le christianisme a donc conservé un grand empire sur l'esprit des Américains, et, ce que je veux surtout remarquer, il ne règne point seulement comme une philosophie qu'on adopte après examen, mais comme une religion, qu'on croit sans la discuter" (DA, 707).

48. "Les Américains, ayant admis sans examen les principaux dogmes de la religion chrétienne, sont obligés de recevoir de la même manière un grand nombre de

Because professing faith in Christianity obliges one to receive "a great number of moral truths" which arise from Christian doctrines, the scope of individual reason is confined to "narrow limits," and these limits are not found in a country like France, or at least not to the same degree. Though many people in France are born Christian and may celebrate their religion, Christianity in America is unique because of the way people allow it to dominate their mind and set limits to their thought. Tocqueville argues that such a narrowing of the confines of reason is actually of profound benefit to the American mind, and to see how this is so, we must look at a key idea contained within all that precedes, which is the role of authority in rational thought.

The tendency of the human mind to look for authority and thus to place trust in someone (or something) beyond the self is not just a social convention; rather, Tocqueville thinks that it is rooted in the deepest realities of human nature. He explains,

> If man was forced to prove to himself all the truths that he uses every day, he would never finish doing so; he would wear himself out with preliminary demonstrations without advancing; as he has neither the time, because of the short span of his life, nor the ability, because of the limitations of his mind, to act in this way, he is reduced to holding as certain a host of facts and opinions that he has had neither the leisure nor the power to examine and to verify by himself, but that those more clever have found or that the crowd adopts. On this foundation he builds himself the structure of his own thoughts. It is not his will that leads him to proceed in this manner; the inflexible law of his condition compels him to do so.[49]

Here we see the *premier fondement* or "first foundation" of our thought, which is to look for "a host of facts and opinions" which we can trust without actually examining for ourselves whether or not these facts and opinions are

---

vérités morales qui en découlent et qui y tiennent. Cela resserre dans des limites étroites l'action de l'analyse individuelle, et lui soustrait plusieurs des plus importantes opinions humaines" (DA, 707).

49. "Si l'homme était force de se prouver à lui-même toutes le vérités dont il se sert chaque jour, il n'en finirait point; il s'sépuiserait en démonstrations préliminaires *sans avancer*; comme il n'a pas le temps, à cause du court espace de la vie, ni la faculté, à cause des bornes de son esprit, d'en agir ainsi, il en est réduit à tenir pour assurés une foule de faits et d'opinions qu'il n'a eu ni le loisir ni le pouvoir d'examiner et de vérifier par lui-même, mais que de plus habiles ont trouvés ou que la foule adopte. C'est sure ce premier fondement qu'il élève lui-même l'édifice de ses propres pensées. Ce n'est pas sa volonté qui l'amène à procéder ce cette manière; la loi inflexible de sa condition l'y contraint" (DA, 714).

certain. Without trustful acceptance of these facts and opinions, the human mind would exhaust itself in "preliminary demonstrations" and could neither advance to the higher realms of thought nor make choices which depend on these higher thoughts. Human nature requires that a person act and choose, and the human mind is incapable of constructing for itself the basis of *all* its beliefs upon which it must found its acts, and because this is an "inflexible law" of the human condition, it is permanent and unchangeable. Thus he says, "You cannot make it so that there are no dogmatic beliefs, that is to say, opinions that men receive on trust and without discussion."[50] Where there is rational human thought, there must be a large body of opinions received on trust, and without these dogmas, human thought cannot advance.

We can now see how Christianity itself is of great benefit to minds formed in a democratic age, for Tocqueville says,

> Religion, by providing the mind with a clear and precise solution to a great number of metaphysical and moral questions as important as they are difficult to resolve, leaves the mind the strength and the leisure to proceed with calmness and with energy in the whole area that religion abandons to it; and it is not precisely because of religion, but with the help of the liberty and the peace that religion gained for it, that the human mind has often done such great things in the centuries of faith.[51]

Giving the mind a realm of dogmatic certainty in the domains of metaphysics and morals, the mind is given the leisure to investigate with "calmness" and "energy" all those realms of thought which are not answered by these dogmas. Spared from a task that Tocqueville considers both exhausting and impossible (namely, to build a coherent system of thought solely on the basis of one's own reason), the mind is given intellectual vitality, the fruit of which can be seen in those ages of faith in which these dogmatic beliefs permeate society more completely, a time during which "the human mind has often done such great things." This is why Tocqueville considers the influence of Christianity to be a positive development for rational thought in

---

50. "on ne saurait faire qu'il n'y ait pas de croyances dogmatiques, c'est-à-dire d'opinions que les hommes reçoivent de confiance et sans les discuter" (DA, 714).

51. "La religion en fournissant à l'esprit la solution nette et précise d'un grand nombre de questions métaphysiques et morales aussi importantes que difficiles à résoudre, lui laisse la force et le loisir de se porter avec calme et avec énergie dans tout l'espace qu'elle lui abandonne, et ce n'est pas précisément par la religion mais à l'aide de la liberté et du repos que la religion lui avait procuré, que l'esprit humain a souvent fait de si grandes choses dans les siècles de foi" (DA, 716). This text is found in the original manuscript, but it did not appear in the first published edition.

America, and it would be right to say that he values it primarily because of the degree of certainty with which it influences the American mind and not necessarily because of the content of these beliefs.[52] Thus "certainty" in the critical domains of metaphysics and morals (and we note that "certainty" here has nothing to do with *proving* something as certain; rather, it is the result of *receiving* something as certain) allows a person to apply their mind freely to those areas which do not pertain directly to these metaphysical and moral certainties. For Tocqueville, it is this type of certainty which is the only possible foundation of free thought and true intellectual liberty.

In summary, we have seen the way by which equality of conditions influences the development of the human mind, and within this discussion, we saw the essential role of authority in forming a person's thought. Unable to find commanding authority in class, family, or other people, those who live in "democratic" cultures tend to turn within themselves and search by themselves for the reason of all things. There are other social realities, like revolutions and religions, which can either accentuate or moderate this inward curvature of the mind, but they cannot eliminate it. Furthermore, in the section which follows, we will examine a great paradox, for Tocqueville observed how these same people, who are disposed to search within themselves for all truth, simultaneously exhibit a nearly irresistible tendency to consult the majority as the exclusive authority over their own thought, something which he calls the "tyranny of the majority." Such a tyranny forms the great paradox of thought in times of equality, and by examining its intricacies, we can see more definitively the way in which the rational faculty of human nature is dependent on the relational dimension of the human person.

THE TYRANNY OF THE MAJORITY

There are two main sections in Tocqueville's work where he draws attention to this "tyranny of the majority." In the first volume, he dedicates a section to exploring the role which the majority exercises over political thought specifically, and then he returns to this same topic in the second volume, looking at how the majority exercises a commanding influence over nearly all dimensions of thought. Therefore, we will first expose what is written in the

---

52. The strength of his belief in this point leads him to state, "Assuredly, metempsychosis is not more reasonable than materialism; but if it were absolutely necessary for a democracy to make a choice between the two, I would not hesitate, and I would judge that its citizens risk becoming brutalized less by thinking that their soul is going to pass into the body of a pig than by believing that it is nothing" (DA, 958).

first volume on political thought in America specifically, and then we will integrate the key ideas from the second volume, which together reveal the extent to which the human mind is dependent on the relational dimension.

Tyranny of the Majority in America

Tocqueville begins his reflections on the tyranny of the majority by stating, "The very essence of democratic governments is that the dominion of the majority be absolute; for, in democracies, nothing outside of the majority can offer resistance."[53] Tocqueville thinks that the majority has an essential role in all democracies and that it will always have a natural strength over the citizens, but in America, he sees that this natural strength has been augmented by various laws and customs which give the majority a nearly indomitable strength. The primary source of this strength lies in the way in which the legislature is elected, as Tocqueville explains,

> Of all political powers, the legislature is the one that most willingly obeys the majority. The Americans have wanted the members of the legislature to be named directly by the people, and for a very short term, in order to force them to submit not only to the general views, but also to the daily passions of their constituents.[54]

Because the people nominate this power directly, and because their terms are very short, the legislature becomes subservient to the immediate will of the majority, for they will depose them in little time if their will is not obeyed. The consequences of such a system impacts other branches of government, such as the judiciary power, for Tocqueville says, "In several states, the law delivered the judicial power to election by the majority; and in all, it made the existence of the judicial power dependent, in a way, on the legislative power, by leaving to the representatives the right to fix the salaries of judges annually."[55] Some states actually make the election of the judiciary

53. "Il est de l'essence même des gouvernements démocratiques que l'empire de la majorité y soit absolu; car en dehors de la majorité, dans les démocraties, il n'y a rien qui résiste" (DA, 403).

54. "La législature est, de tous les pouvoirs politiques, celui qui obéit le plus volontiers à la majorité. Les Américains ont voulu que les membres de la législature fussent nommés directement par le peuple, et pour un terme très court, afin de les obliger à se soumettre non seulement aux vues générales, mais encore aux passions journalières de leurs constituants" (DA, 403).

55. "Dans plusieurs États, elle livrait le pouvoir judiciaire à l'élection de la majorité, et dans tous elle faisait, en quelque sorte, dépendre son existence de la puissance législative, en laissant aux représentants le droit de fixer chaque année le salaire des juges" (DA, 404).

directly dependent on the will of the majority, and even in states which do not have such a system, the judicial power is partially dependent on the majority because all states give the legislature the right to fix the annual salaries of the judges. Furthermore, the executive power is also elected by the majority in the states, for both the governor of the state and the president of the nation are elected by the majority. Thus all three of branches of government, at the state level and partially at the federal level, are subject to the immediate will of the majority.

One way in which the absolute political dominion of the majority can be seen is in the speed with which laws change in America, for Tocqueville states that "America today is, therefore, the country in the world where laws have the shortest duration."[56] The reason why the laws change so rapidly in America is because of the omnipotence of the majority, and this power extends even to the execution of these laws and their impact on public administration:

> Since the majority is the only power important to please, the works that it undertakes are ardently supported; but from the moment when its attention goes elsewhere, all efforts cease; whereas in the free States of Europe, in which administrative power has an independent existence and an assured position, the will of the legislator continues to be executed, even when he is occupied by other objects.[57]

Because the majority is "the only power important to please," a law is effective and a work is carried out only for as long as it appeals to the desire of the majority. Once the majority changes its mind or simply neglects the urgency it once attached to a law or public work, both this law and its works are rendered ineffective, which leads to either neglecting the law or revising it, and this results in a situation where laws have the shortest duration of any country.

Tocqueville's concern over the absolute power of the majority lies not in the short duration of laws or in the fickle nature of the execution of various public works; rather, he is concerned that this majority can dominate

---

56. "l'Amérique est-elle de nos jours le pays du monde où les lois ont le moins de durée" (DA, 408).

57. "La majorité étant la seule puissance à laquelle il soit important de plaire, on concourt avec ardeur aux œuvres qu'elle entreprend; mais du moment où son attention se porte ailleurs, tous les efforts cessent; tandis que dans les États libres de l'Europe, où le pouvoir administratif a une existence indépendante et une position assurée, les volontés du législateur continuent à s'exécuter, alors même qu'il s'soccupe d'autres objets" (DA, 408).

citizens and perpetuate injustice, creating a situation which he calls the "tyranny of the majority." He explains:

> When a man or a party suffers from an injustice in the United States, to whom do you want them to appeal? To public opinion? That is what forms the majority. To the legislative body? It represents the majority and blindly obeys it. To the executive power? It is named by the majority and serves it as a passive instrument. To the police? The police are nothing other than the majority under arms. To the jury? The jury is the majority vested with the right to deliver judgments. The judges themselves, in certain states, are elected by the majority. However iniquitous or unreasonable the measure that strikes you may be, you must therefore submit to it or flee. What is that if not the very soul of tyranny under the forms of liberty?[58]

In these comments, Tocqueville shows how in America, nearly all the political instruments which can secure justice in society are rooted in the power of the majority, and the problem arises when a person is treated unjustly by something which the majority approves. In such a situation, a person is not afforded any assurance of attaining justice, for all the usual instruments of justice, whether it is the executive power or the judicial power, whether jury or public opinion, whether the police or legislators, all serve and reflect the will of the majority.

Tocqueville thinks that the transformation of the omnipotence of the majority into an experience of tyranny is not currently widespread in America, for he states, "I am not saying that at the present time in America tyranny is frequently practiced; I am saying that no guarantee against tyranny is found there, and that the causes for the mildness of government must be sought in circumstances and in mores, rather than in laws."[59] The omnipotence of the majority in America has the potential to exercise unlimited and

---

58. "Lorsqu'un homme ou un parti souffre d'une injustice aux États-Unis, à qui voulez-vous qu'il s'adresse ? À l'opinion publique ? c'est elle qui forme la majorité; au corps législatif ? il représente la majorité et lui obéit aveuglément; au pouvoir exécutif ? il est nommé par la majorité et lui sert d'instrument passif; à la force publique ? la force publique n'est autre chose que la majorité sous les armes; au jury ? le jury, c'est la majorité revêtue du droit de prononcer des arrêts: les juges eux-mêmes, dans certains États, sont élus par la majorité. Quelque inique ou déraisonnable que soit la mesure qui vous frappe, il faut donc vous y soumettre ou fuir. Qu'est-ce que cela sinon l'âme même de la tyrannie sous les formes de la liberté ?" (DA, 414).

59. "Je ne dis pas que dans le temps actuel on fasse en Amérique un fréquent usage de la tyrannie, je dis qu'on n'y découvre point de garantie contre elle, et qu'il faut y chercher les causes de la douceur du gouvernement dans les circonstances et dans les mœurs plutôt que dans les lois" (DA, 415).

unrestrained dominion over others, and the fact that it has yet to do so must be found in something other than the laws which this democratic people have made for themselves.

But when Tocqueville says that the tyranny of the majority is not currently widespread, he nonetheless sees disturbing instances of such a tyranny, especially in the treatment of Negroes, who are often denied justice even when the law demands that justice be given to them. Tocqueville provides only one story to illustrate how the omnipotence of the majority already exercises a tyranny over some citizens, so despite its length, we quote it here because of its importance to his thought:

> I said one day to an inhabitant of Pennsylvania: "Please explain to me why, in a state founded by Quakers and renowned for its tolerance, emancipated Negroes are not allowed to exercise the rights of citizens. They pay taxes; isn't it just that they vote?"—"Don't insult us, he answered, by thinking that our legislators have committed such a gross act of injustice and intolerance."—"So, among you, Blacks have the right to vote?"—"Undoubtedly."—"Then, how come at the polling place this morning, I did not see a single one in the crowd?"—"This is not the fault of the law," the American said to me; "Negroes, it is true, have the right to present themselves at elections, but they abstain voluntarily it seems."—"That is very modest of them."—"Oh! it isn't that they refuse to go, but they are afraid that they will be mistreated there. Among us, it sometimes happens that the law lacks force when the majority does not support it. Now, the majority is imbued with the greatest prejudices against Negroes, and magistrates do not feel they have the strength to guarantee to the latter the rights that the legislator has conferred."—"What! the majority which has the privilege of making the law, also wants to have that of disobeying the law?"[60]

Tocqueville reveals here the heart of his critique of the omnipotence of the majority in America, which is not that Americans use the majority to *make* the law, but that this same majority can instantaneously *break* the law, which is to say that the law is no law at all, and when the law is broken in order to deny justice to others, there one has encountered a tyrannical moment. So, the "tyranny of the majority" is not just a seed lying dormant in American society; rather, it is a sapling whose poisonous fruit can already be tasted by some of the citizens living within the country.

---

60. (DA, 414). Because this is a story whose relevance does not depend on semantic precision, and because of its length, we have provided only the English translation.

Tocqueville explains that the original source of this limitless power given to the majority comes from two Enlightenment realities. First, he says, "The moral dominion of the majority is based in part on the idea that there is more enlightenment and Wisdom in many men combined than in one man alone, more in the number than in the choice of legislators. It is the theory of equality applied to minds."[61] When this equality of minds is applied to political questions, one has confidence that the majority cannot err as often as the individual, and thus power comes from the number of people who are making the decision as opposed to the individual characteristics of these decision-makers. The second source of the power of the majority comes from the fact that an equivalence of minds coexists with equality of ideas. Tocqueville explains,

> The moral dominion of the majority is based as well on the principle that the interests of the greatest number must be preferred to those of the few. Now, it is easily understood that the respect professed for this right of the greatest number naturally increases or decreases depending on the state of the parties. When a nation is divided among several great irreconcilable interests, the privilege of the majority is often unrecognized, because it becomes too painful to submit to it.[62]

The disposition to trust the majority will not manifest itself so extensively if there exists any natural and permanent dissidence between factions, and the majority will have a difficult time establishing itself as a basis of power when there is significant intellectual or factional differentiation among the members, but because Americans possesses not only equivalent intelligence but also nearly equivalent ideas, they are greatly disposed to trust the majority. We can say that they trust the majority because, in most instances, they are in agreement with the majority.

Tocqueville notes that these Enlightenment principles lead some people to suggest that "in objects that concern only itself, a people could not go entirely beyond the limits of justice and reason, and that we should not be

---

61. "L'empire moral de la majorité se fonde en partie sur cette idée, qu'il y a plus de lumières et de sagesse dans beaucoup d'hommes réunis que dans un seul, dans le nombre des législateurs que dans le choix. C'est la théorie de l'égalité appliquée aux intelligences" (DA, 404).

62. "L'empire moral de la majorité se fonde encore sur ce principe, que les intérêts du plus grand nombre doivent être préférés à ceux du petit. Or, on comprend sans peine que le respect qu'on professe pour ce droit du plus grand nombre augmente naturellement ou diminue suivant l'état des partis. Quand une nation est partagée entre plusieurs grands intérêts inconciliables, le privilège de la majorité est souvent méconnu, parce qu'il devient trop pénible de s'sy soumettre" (DA, 405).

CHAPTER 2: THE DEMOCRATIC MIND   55

afraid, therefore, to give all power to the majority that represents a people."[63] The majority, it is argued, will always keep itself within the bounds of justice, but Tocqueville opposes this faith placed in the majority when he states,

> Now, if you admit that an individual vested with omnipotence can abuse it against his adversaries, why would you not admit the same thing for the majority? Have men, by gathering together, changed character? By becoming stronger, have they become more patient in the face of obstacles? As for me, I cannot believe it; and the power to do everything that I refuse to any one of my fellows, I will never grant to several.[64]

According to Tocqueville, the majority is just as capable as any individual of transgressing the rights of others, of destroying justice, and of behaving tyrannically. Having gathered together with others, this potency for tyranny does not dissolve; instead, it remains dormant within the law so constructed. He elaborates this point conclusively when he states,

> No one would want to maintain that a people is not able to abuse strength vis-à-vis another people. Now, parties are like small nations within a large one; in relation to each other, they are like foreigners. If you agree that a nation can be tyrannical toward another nation, how can you deny that a party can be so toward another party?[65]

The history of the world shows that it is quite possible for large bodies of people in one nation to behave tyrannically towards another body of people, and because parties function "like small nations within a large one," this historical phenomenon causes Tocqueville to place little hope in the majority's ability to safeguard against tyranny. Instead, he noted an instance above in which this tyranny of the majority is currently practiced, and

---

63. "qu'un peuple, dans les objets qui n'intéressaient que lui-même, ne pouvait sortir entièrement des limites de la justice et de la raison, et qu'ainsi on ne devait pas craindre de donner tout pouvoir à la majorité qui le représente" (DA, 411).

64. "Or, si vous admettez qu'un homme revêtu de la toute-puissance peut en abuser contre ses adversaires, pourquoi n'admettez-vous pas la même chose pour une majorité ? Les hommes, en se réunissant, ont-ils changé de caractère ? Sont-ils devenus plus patients dans les obstacles en devenant plus forts ? Pour moi, je ne saurais le croire ; et le pouvoir de tout faire, que je refuse à un seul de mes semblables, je ne l'accorderai jamais à plusieurs" (DA, 411).

65. "Personne ne voudrait soutenir qu'un peuple ne peut abuser de la force vis-à-vis d'un autre peuple. Or, les partis forment comme autant de petites nations dans une grande ; ils sont entre eux dans des rapports d'étrangers. Si on convient qu'une nation peut erre tyrannique envers une autre nation, comment nier qu'un parti puisse l'être envers un autre parti ?" (DA, 411).

combined with his knowledge of world history, he seems to have little hope that the majority will not abuse its power in various ways in the future. Men in democratic ages are disposed to be of equivalent intelligence, but whether or not this equivalent intelligence is directed towards justice or injustice will depend on something other than the majority and instead must be directed by some other thread within the social fabric.

There is another reason why Tocqueville fears the extent to which the majority exercises power over Americans, and that is because he sees how it influences not only laws but also the expression and articulation of political thought. He begins his remarks on this topic by stating, "When you come to examine how thought is exercised in the United States, you notice very clearly to what extent the power of the majority surpasses all the powers that we know in Europe."[66] The reason the majority in America surpasses the power of the majority in Europe is that in America, the majority "is vested with a strength simultaneously physical and moral, which acts on the will as well as on actions and which at the same time prevents the deed and the desire to do so."[67] It is this ability of the majority to control both the execution of laws, and the desire to think or write something contrary to these laws, which gives it a supreme power that surpasses anything seen in Europe. This causes Tocqueville to remark, "I know of no country where, in general, there reigns less independence of mind and true freedom of discussion than in America."[68] Because the majority has taken it upon itself to decide irrevocably what must be thought, there is minimal independence of mind or freedom of discussion about political matters in America, and Tocqueville distinguishes such a practice from what happens in Europe to demonstrate his point:

> Today, the most absolute sovereigns of Europe cannot prevent certain ideas hostile to their authority from circulating silently within their States and even within their courts. It is not the same in America; as long as the majority is uncertain, people speak; but as soon as the majority has irrevocably decided,

---

66. "Lorsqu'on vient à examiner quel est aux États-Unis l'exercice de la pensée, c'est alors qu'on aperçoit bien clairement à quel point la puissance de la majorité surpasse toutes les puissances que nous connaissons en Europe" (DA, 416).

67. "est revêtue d'une force tout à la fois matérielle et morale, qui agit sur la volonté autant que sur les actions, et qui empêche en même temps le fait et le désir de faire" (DA, 417).

68. "Je ne connais pas de pays où il règne, en général, moins d'indépendance d'esprit et de véritable liberté de discussion qu'en Amérique" (DA, 417).

everyone is silent, and friends as well as enemies then seem to climb on board together.[69]

So it is not that there is no independence of political thought in America; rather, there is no independence of thought on those subjects wherein the majority has already decided, and this contrasts with the reality of Europe wherein even the most powerful monarchs must tolerate the circulation of ideas which are hostile to their rule.[70] Citizens feel free to discuss and debate those topics in which the majority is still undecided, but beyond these undecided issues, debate will cease and the majority alone is the voice which speaks for all.

The process by which the majority exercises such influence over the entire populace is described in the following remarks:

> In America, the majority draws a formidable circle around thought. Within these limits, the writer is free; but woe to him if he dares to go beyond them. It isn't that he has to fear an auto-da-fé, but he is exposed to all types of distasteful things and to everyday persecutions. A political career is closed to him; he has offended the only power that has the ability to open it to him. Everything is denied him, even glory. Before publishing his opinions, he believed he had some partisans; it seems to him that he has them no longer, now that he has revealed himself to all; for those who censure him speak openly, and those who think as he does, without having his courage, keep quiet and distance themselves. He gives in; finally, under the daily effort, he yields and returns to silence, as though he felt remorse for having told the truth.[71]

---

69. "De nos jours, les souverains les plus absolus de l'Europe ne sauraient empêcher certaines pensées hostiles à leur autorité de circuler sourdement dans leurs États et jusqu'au sein de leurs Cours. Il n'en est pas de même en Amérique : tant que la majorité est douteuse, on parle ; mais dès qu'elle s'est irrévocablement prononcée, chacun se tait, et amis comme ennemis semblent alors s'attacher de concert à son char" (DA, 417).

70. To this point, Tocqueville cites the example of monarchs having plays performed for them in their own courts wherein this very play criticizes the monarch. See DA, 419.

71. "En Amérique, la majorité trace un cercle formidable autour de la pensée. Au-dedans de ces limites, l'écrivain est libre ; mais malheur à lui s'il ose en sortir. Ce n'est pas qu'il ait à craindre un autodafé, mais il est en butte à des dégoûts de tous genres et à des persécutions de tous les jours. La carrière politique lui est fermée : il a offensé la seule puissance qui ait la faculté de l'ouvrir. On lui refuse tout, jusqu'à la gloire. Avant de publier ses opinions, il croyait avoir des partisans ; il lui semble qu'il n'en a plus, maintenant qu'il s'est découvert à tous ; car ceux qui le blâment s'expriment hautement, et ceux qui pensent comme lui, sans avoir son courage, se taisent et s'éloignent. Il cède, il plie enfin sous l'effort de chaque jour, et rentre dans le silence, comme s'il éprouvait des remords d'avoir dit vrai" (DA, 418).

By asserting opinions contrary to those adopted by the majority, a writer is immersed in a cycle of rejection which results in becoming publicly ostracized, and even those who supported him will keep silent when they are in the public square, for they know that speaking up will only cast them into this same cycle of rejection. Tocqueville goes on to consider how such a tyranny over thought is a sort of "intellectual violence," a violence which attacks not the body but the soul. He explains:

> Under the absolute government of one man, despotism, to reach the soul, crudely struck the body; and the soul, escaping from these blows, rose gloriously above it; but in democratic republics, tyranny does not proceed in this way; it leaves the body alone and goes right to the soul. The master no longer says: You will think like me or die; he says: You are free not to think as I do; your life, your goods, everything remains with you; but from this day on you are a stranger among us. You will keep your privileges as a citizen, but they will become useless to you. If you aspire to be the choice of your fellow citizens, they will not choose you, and if you ask only for their esteem, they will still pretend to refuse it to you. You will remain among men, but you will lose your rights to humanity. When you approach your fellows, they will flee from you like an impure being. And those who believe in your innocence, even they will abandon you, for people would flee from them in turn. Go in peace; I spare your life, but I leave you a life worse than death.[72]

Thus, the majority does not tyrannize by way of physical violence; instead, it leaves the body intact but attacks the deeper and more glorious aspects of the human person. Those who speak against the majority are not exiled from their land, but they are exiled from fellowship; they retain their right to speak, but they lose their right to be heard; they can still host dinner parties, but no one will show up. Such are the consequences of speaking

---

72. "Sous le gouvernement absolu d'un seul, le despotisme, pour arriver à l'âme, frappait grossièrement le corps ; et l'âme, échappant à ces coups, s'élevait glorieuse au-dessus de lui ; mais dans les républiques démocratiques, ce n'est point ainsi que procède la tyrannie ; elle laisse le corps et va droit à l'âme. Le maître n'y dit plus : Vous penserez comme moi, ou vous mourrez ; il dit : Vous êtes libre de ne point penser ainsi que moi ; votre vie, vos biens, tout vous reste ; mais de ce jour vous êtes un étranger parmi nous. Vous garderez vos privilèges à la cité, mais ils vous deviendront inutiles ; car si vous briguez le choix de vos concitoyens, ils ne vous l'accorderont point, et si vous ne demandez que leur estime, ils feindront encore de vous la refuser. Vous resterez parmi les hommes, mais vous perdrez vos droits à l'humanité. Quand vous vous approcherez de vos semblables, ils vous fuiront comme un être impur ; et ceux qui croient à votre innocence, ceux-là mêmes vous abandonneront, car on les fuirait à leur tour. Allez en paix, je vous laisse la vie, mais je vous la laisse pire que la mort" (DA, 418–19).

against the majority, but because hardly anyone dares to doom themselves to such relational suicide, there remains only passive submission to the majority and very little "freedom of mind" in America.

Tocqueville compares such a restriction of thought to the Inquisition, though the majority in America is even more effective: "The Inquisition was never able to prevent the circulation in Spain of books opposed to the religion of the greatest number. The dominion of the majority does better in the United States: it has removed even the thought of publishing such books."[73] The inquisitorial nature of the majority in America impacts all writing and leads Tocqueville to conclude that it is the reason why America lacks any great writers, for he states, "If America has not yet had great writers, we do not have to look elsewhere for the reasons: literary genius does not exist without freedom of the mind, and there is no freedom of the mind in America."[74] Fearful of the consequences of contradicting the majority, one sells their freedom of thought in order to purchase freedom of fellowship with the community.

We would be mistaken to think that such a bartering of freedom of thought is commonly practiced in America; on the contrary, Tocqueville says that such dominating power "is still felt only weakly in political society."[75] This power is, at the time of his writing, only discreetly present in the political society of America, and the only example he provides to show how it is already present is in some of his comments on the role of the majority in denying justice to Negroes. However, while it is only discreetly present in the political world, it is nonetheless penetrating the national character of the people. For example, he contrasts the types of minds present in the early days of the republic to its current state, and regarding these early days, he states,

> When the American Revolution broke out, outstanding men appeared in large number; then public opinion led and did not tyrannize over wills. The famous men of this period, freely joining the movement of minds, had a grandeur of their own; they shed their brilliance on the nation and did not derive it from the nation.[76]

73. "L'Inquisition n'a jamais pu empêcher qu'il ne circulât en Espagne des livres contraires à la religion du plus grand nombre. L'empire de la majorité fait mieux aux États-Unis: elle a ôté jusqu'à la pensée d'en publier" (DA, 419).

74. "Si l'Amérique n'a pas encore eu de grands écrivains, nous ne devons pas en chercher ailleurs les raisons: il n'existe pas de génie littéraire sans liberté d'esprit, et il n'y a pas de liberté d'esprit en Amérique" (DA, 419).

75. "se fait encore sentir que faiblement dans la société politique" (DA, 420).

76. "Lorsque la révolution d'Amérique éclata, (hommes remarquables) parurent

This grandeur and brilliance of the founding fathers contrasts with the political men observed in Tocqueville's day:

> Among the immense crowd, in the United States, that pushes into a political career, I saw very few men who showed this virile candor, this manly independence of thought, that often distinguished Americans in former times and that, wherever it is found, forms the salient feature of great characters.[77]

The lack of "virile candor" and "manly independence of thought" among those in politics is a grave weakness for the political fabric of the United States, and Tocqueville attributes the lack of these men to the despotic nature of the majority: "I think that the small number of outstanding men who appear today on the political stage must be attributed, above all, to the always increasing action of the despotism of the majority in the United States."[78] America does not lack minds which could rise above the majority and direct it more effectively, but those who do possess these minds know that to contradict the majority would be equivalent to social rejection and political exile.[79] They are capable of leading well, but the majority will never afford them the opportunity to lead them anywhere other than where the majority has already decided; and knowing that the majority will not tolerate any violation of their pre-determined opinions, any potential leaders will turn their skills and interests elsewhere.

So while the ill effects of a tyranny of the majority are not often expressed in America, Tocqueville already sees how it is depriving the government of quality leadership, and over time, he fears that this power will grow to such an extent that it becomes a tyrant who executes its will at the expense of inflicting injustice. This leads him to conclude:

---

en foule ; l'opinion publique dirigeait alors les volontés et ne les tyrannisait pas. Les hommes célèbres de cette époque, s'associant librement au mouvement des esprits, eurent une grandeur qui leur fut propre : ils répandirent leur éclat sur la nation et ne l'empruntèrent pas d'elle" (DA, 421).

77. "Parmi la foule immense qui, aux États-Unis, se presse dans la carrière politique, j'ai vu bien peu d'hommes qui montrassent cette virile candeur, cette mâle indépendance de la pensée, qui a souvent distingué les Américains dans les temps antérieurs, et qui, partout où on la trouve, forme comme le trait saillant des grands caractères" (DA, 422).

78. "Je pense que c'est à l'action toujours croissante du despotisme de la majorité, aux États-Unis, qu'il faut surtout attribuer le petit nombre d'hommes remarquables qui s'sy montrent aujourd'hui sur la scène politique" (DA, 420).

79. He has met people who have the ideas which are capable of leading well, but he observes that these men, instead of fighting the majority, quietly walk away and choose some other field of activity. See DA, 422.

So in the United States the majority has an immense power in fact and a power of opinion almost as great; and once the majority has formed on a question, there is, so to speak, no obstacle that can, I will not say stop, but even slow its course and leave time for the majority to hear the cries of those whom it crushes as it goes. The consequences of this state of affairs are harmful and dangerous for the future.[80]

This ability of the majority to act quickly and speedily on so much of the social fabric, moderating its laws absolutely and moderating political opinions with nearly equivalent power, moving along hastily and "crushing" all those who oppose it, is a considerable danger to the American people, so much so that Tocqueville summarizes a whole section of his writing with the following title: "*That the Greatest Danger to the American Republics Comes from the Omnipotence of the Majority.*"[81] The reason why it presents the "greatest danger" to the republic is evident from the comments above.

Tyranny of the Majority in Equality

In the previous section, we demonstrated the way in which the majority influences both political thought and laws in American society, and we noted the way in which this is distinct from the experience of the majority in Europe. This sweeping influence of the majority in America over political thought was not rooted in equality of conditions; rather, we saw how it arises from a complex mix of laws, sentiments, and methods of electing members of the various branches of government, and these all interact and enhance one another in such a way that they give a unique and dominating power to the majority. However, Tocqueville believes there are other factors, independent of these laws and sentiments, which lead to a tyranny of the majority, and one of these factors is the equality of conditions. We have already seen how equality of conditions played a role in leading to the tendency of Americans to place so much trust and power in the hands of the majority, and in the following comments, Tocqueville isolates this variable of equality and considers how it can, of itself, lead to the tyranny of the majority. To see how this is so, we must return to his second volume and

---

80. "La majorité a donc aux États-Unis une immense puissance de fait et une puissance d'opinion presque aussi grande ; et lorsqu'elle est une fois formée sur une question, il n'y a pour ainsi dire point d'obstacles qui puissent, je ne dirai pas arrêter, mais même retarder sa marche, et lui laisser le temps d'écouter les plaintes de ceux qu'elle écrase en passant. Les conséquences de cet état de choses sont funestes et dangereuses pour l'avenir" (DA, 407).

81. DA, 424.

explore the role which equality of conditions plays in leading the intellect of isolated individuals towards faith in the majority.

We saw previously how Tocqueville considers authority to have an essential role in the formation of coherent thought, even in democratic societies where the citizens "appeal only to the individual effort of their reason," and this role of authority is so pervasive and so necessary for rational thought that Tocqueville concludes,

> So, no matter what happens, authority must always be found somewhere in the intellectual and moral world. Its place is variable, but it necessarily has a place. Individual independence can be greater or lesser; it cannot be limitless. Thus, the question is not to know if an intellectual authority exists in democratic centuries, but only to know where its repository is and what its extent will be.[82]

Thus, authority will always have a place in forming one's intellect and morals, and having demonstrated above how this must be so, Tocqueville proceeds to show how and why the majority is this authority within those democratic societies where equality of conditions is pervasive.

The first step in his reasoning is the affirmation that, when conditions are equal, citizens are disposed to take their own reason as the lone guide for reasoning, and this *méthode* leads their minds to other habits, such as depending on themselves: "Since they see that they manage without help to solve all the small difficulties that their practical life presents, they easily conclude that everything in the world is explicable, and that nothing goes beyond the limits of intelligence."[83] Having a habitual disposition to turn to one's self in daily situations, and seeing that they are able to manage these small but real situations successfully, a habit is formed whereby the intellect is presumed to have an unlimited power and is able to explain all things. Thus Tocqueville states, "men who live during these times of equality are not easily led to place the intellectual authority to which they submit outside and above humanity. It is in themselves or their fellows that they ordinarily

---

82. "Il faut donc toujours, quoi qu'il arrive, que l'autorité se rencontre quelque part dans le monde intellectuel et moral. Sa place est variable, mais elle a nécessairement une place. L'indépendance individuelle peut être plus ou moins grande; elle ne saurait être sans bornes. Ainsi, la question n'est pas de savoir s'il existe une autorité intellectuelle dans les siècles démocratiques, mais seulement où en est le dépôt et quelle en sera la mesure" (DA, 716–17).

83. "Comme ils voient qu'ils parviennent à résoudre sans aide toutes les petites difficultés que présente leur vie pratique, ils en concluent aisément que tout dans le monde est explicable, et que rien n'y dépasse les bornes de l'intelligence" (DA, 701).

look for the sources of truth."[84] Thus the "sources of truth" in a democratic society will always be within the people themselves, and even when there are supernatural truths which permeate a democratic society, the authority with which they seek to influence minds must be comprehensible to their individual reason.

Given such a disposition to look for an authority within humanity, Tocqueville first explains how an aristocracy provides sources of authority from within humanity:

> When conditions are unequal and men dissimilar, there are some individuals very enlightened, very learned, very powerful because of their intelligence, and a multitude very ignorant and very limited. So men who live in times of aristocracy are naturally led to take as guide for their opinions the superior reason of one man or of one class, while they are little disposed to recognize the infallibility of the mass.[85]

Because the multitude is composed of "very ignorant" (*très ignorante*) and "very limited" (*fort bornée*) men in an aristocratic society, and also because of the presence of very learned and intelligent men in the leading class, they easily recognize authority in these men of brilliance and thus the citizens are not disposed to find authority in the majority.

Yet when conditions become equal, the opposite happens: "As citizens become more equal and more similar, the tendency of each blindly to believe a certain man or a certain class decreases. The disposition to believe the mass increases, and more and more it is opinion that leads the world."[86] When conditions are equal, neither the shining brilliance of great men, nor the debasing ignorance of many men, are present to a degree in which class stratification can be established. Thus, the majority is now no longer a multitude of *très ignorante* and *fort bornée* men; instead, it is full of similar

---

84. "Les hommes qui vivent dans ces temps d'égalité sont donc difficilement conduits à placer l'autorité intellectuelle à laquelle ils se soumettent en dehors et au-dessus de l'humanité. C'est en eux-mêmes ou dans leurs semblables qu'ils cherchent d'ordinaire les sources de la vérité" (DA, 717).

85. "Lorsque les conditions sont inégales et les hommes dissemblables, il y a quelques individus très éclairés, très savants, très puissants par leur intelligence, et une multitude très ignorante et fort bornée. Les gens qui vivent dans les temps d'aristocratie sont donc naturellement portés à prendre pour guide de leurs opinions la raison supérieure d'un homme ou d'une classe, tandis qu'ils sont peu disposés à reconnaître l'infaillibilité de la masse" (DA, 717).

86. "À mesure que les citoyens deviennent plus égaux et plus semblables, le penchant de chacun à croire aveuglément un certain homme ou une certaine classe diminue. La disposition à en croire la masse augmente, et c'est de plus en plus l'opinion qui mène le monde" (DA, 718).

men with modest intelligence. The consequences of such a situation are as follows:

> In times of equality, men, because of their similarity, have no faith in each other; but this very similarity gives them an almost unlimited confidence in the judgement of the public; for it does not seem likely to them that, since all have similar enlightenment, truth is not found on the side of the greatest number.[87]

In searching for the truth, democratic minds are disposed to look to the greatest number as its source of authority to guide its thought. In such a situation, "common opinion is the sole guide that remains for individual reason," and we note that it is not just a "helpful" guide but rather the "sole" guide to individual reason, giving the majority "an infinitely greater power" than is observed in the social state of aristocracy.[88] Tocqueville elaborates on this point:

> When the man who lives in democratic countries compares himself individually to all those who surround him, he feels with pride that he is equal to each of them; but, when he comes to envisage the ensemble of his fellows and to place himself alongside this great body, he is immediately overwhelmed by his own insignificance and weakness. This same equality that makes him independent of each one of his fellow citizens in particular, delivers him isolated and defenseless to the action of the greatest number.[89]

In an aristocracy, it was the grandeur of *specific* men which imposed authority on those in the society, but in times of democracy, it is the intimidating spectacle of the great *number* of men which forms the basis of authority. Overwhelmed by one's own individual weakness when compared to a great multitude of similar minds, the isolated mind conforms itself to the

---

87. "Dans les temps d'égalité, les hommes n'ont aucune foi les uns dans les autres, à cause de leur similitude ; mais cette même similitude leur donne une confiance presque illimitée dans le jugement du public ; car il ne leur paraît pas vraisemblable qu'ayant tous des lumières pareilles, la vérité ne se rencontre pas du côté du plus grand nombre" (DA, 718-19).

88. "l'opinion commune est le seul guide qui reste à la raison individuelle" (DA, 718).

89. "Quand l'homme qui vit dans les pays démocratiques se compare individuellement à tous ceux qui l'environnent, il sent avec orgueil qu'il est égal à chacun d'eux ; mais, lorsqu'il vient à envisager l'ensemble de ses semblables et à se placer lui-même à côté de ce grand corps, il est aussitôt accablé de sa propre insignifiance et de sa faiblesse. Cette même égalité qui le rend indépendant de chacun de ses concitoyens en particulier, le livre isolé et sans défense à l'action du plus grand nombre" (DA, 719).

majority, trusting that so many similar minds cannot be lead astray. Thus Tocqueville states, "So the public among democratic peoples has a singular power the idea of which aristocratic nations would not even be able to imagine. It does not persuade, it imposes its beliefs and makes them penetrate souls by a kind of immense pressure of the mind of all on the intelligence of each."[90] In democratic ages, the majority exerts "an immense pressure of the mind," imposing its power over the mediocre minds who view it in the isolation of their own selves, and in this way it imposes its beliefs and penetrates souls.

From these considerations, we can see how authority has not disappeared from rational thought within democratic peoples; instead, it is the majority which is the real authority over the democratic mind. It is the very tendency of democratic citizens to "appeal only to the individual effort of their reason," combined with the equality of minds of those who make up the majority, which makes the majority the real authority in "democracy."

We saw in the previous section how the majority in America possesses an immense power over *political* thought, and in what precedes, we have seen how the majority among democratic people's exercises immense power over *all* thought. By now, we should see that there is a strong degree of similarity between the way the majority rules political thought in America compared to the way the majority rules over all thought when conditions are equal. Tocqueville also sees the points of resonance, and because America is also a democratic people, he considers the degree to which the political institutions of America versus the experience of equality of conditions is responsible for the pervasive influence of the majority in America. Is the majority so powerful in the United States primarily because of its institutions of government, or because of the presence of equality of conditions? To this question Tocqueville remarks,

> This political omnipotence of the majority in the United States increases, in fact, the influence that the opinions of the public would have without it on the mind of each citizen there; but it does not establish it. The sources of this influence must be sought in equality itself, and not in the more or less popular institutions that equal men can give themselves.[91]

---

90. "Le public a donc chez les peuples démocratiques une puissance singulière dont les nations aristocratiques ne pouvaient pas même concevoir l'idée. Il ne persuade pas ses croyances, il les impose et les fait pénétrer dans les âmes par une sorte de pression immense de l'esprit de tous sur l'intelligence de chacun" (DA, 719).

91. "Cette omnipotence politique de la majorité aux États-Unis augmente, en effet, l'influence que les opinions du public y obtiendraient sans elle sur l'esprit de chaque citoyen; mais elle ne la fonde point. C'est dans l'égalité même qu'il faut chercher les

So for Tocqueville, the political institutions in America augment the tendency to give the majority such vast authority over intelligence, but these institutions do not establish this authority; rather, it is the presence of equality of conditions which is the true "source" of this authority. Tocqueville explains his point further:

> It is to be believed that the intellectual dominion of the greatest number would be less absolute among a democratic people subject to a king, than within a pure democracy; but it will always be very absolute, and, whatever the political laws may be that govern men in centuries of equality, you can predict that faith in common opinion will become a sort of religion whose prophet will be the majority.[92]

Tocqueville says that equality leads to "faith" in common opinion which has become a sort of "religion" wherein the majority acts like a "prophet," and we note that these words (faith, religion, prophecy) are not words which are associated exclusively with reason; rather, they are associated with trust and authority. This leads Tocqueville back to his previous comments about the inevitable presence of authority in forming rational thought:

> Thus intellectual authority will be different, but it will not be less; and, far from believing that it must disappear, I foresee that it would easily become too great and that it might well be that it would finally enclose the action of individual reason within more narrow limits than are suitable for the grandeur and happiness of the human species.[93]

This is the essential criticism of Tocqueville: it is not that the majority should never be an authority over thought, for authority must exist within the intellectual world; rather, it is the fact that this majority is able to rule so extensively and so pervasively that it risks containing human reason "within more narrow limits than are suitable for the grandeur and happiness of the

---

sources de cette influence, et non dans les institutions plus ou moins populaires que des hommes égaux peuvent se donner" (DA, 723).

92. "Il est à croire que l'empire intellectuel du plus grand nombre serait moins absolu chez un peuple démocratique soumis à un roi, qu'au sein d'une pure démocratie ; mais il sera toujours très absolu, et, quelles que soient les lois politiques qui régissent les hommes dans les siècles d'égalité, l'on peut prévoir que la foi dans l'opinion commune y deviendra une sorte de religion dont la majorité sera le prophète" (DA, 724).

93. "Ainsi l'autorité intellectuelle sera différente, mais elle ne sera pas moindre ; et, loin de croire qu'elle doive disparaître, j'augure qu'elle deviendrait aisément trop grande et qu'il pourrait se faire qu'elle renfermât enfin l'action de la raison individuelle dans des limites plus étroites qu'il ne convient à la grandeur et au bonheur de l'espèce humaine" (DA, 724).

human species." There is a certain "grandeur" and "happiness" which is appropriate to the human person, but these traits cannot manifest themselves in an environment whereby the mind is constricted to blindly obeying the mandates of a great number of moderately-intelligent men who may or may not have justice in view. If such a people were to emerge from an aristocratic culture which wants to revolt against the role of aristocratic authority, they would find themselves in an ironic position, for "after breaking all the obstacles that were formerly imposed on it by classes or men, the human mind would bind itself narrowly to the general wills of the greatest number."[94] After breaking bonds imposed on the mind by class or individual men, human reason risks still being enslaved to something even more arbitrary: a numerical majority. So Tocqueville concludes,

> If, in place of all the diverse powers that hindered or slowed beyond measure the rapid development of individual reason, democratic peoples substituted the absolute power of a majority, the evil would only have changed character. Men would not have found the means to live independently; they would only have discovered, a difficult thing, a new face of servitude.[95]

This "face of servitude" is not unique to America; rather, it risks manifesting itself, in varying degrees, whenever men begin to become equal. Thus, it is equality of conditions which naturally leads to entrusting the majority with a potentially despotic dominion over the minds of men, but just as despotism can be resisted in aristocracies, so too can this form of despotism be resisted. How democratic societies can achieve true "freedom of mind" in the presence of such a natural tendency towards cognitive despotism is the subject of our next section.

FREE ASSOCIATIONS

In order to ensure both political and intellectual freedom among democratic peoples, nothing is more necessary than securing the right to establish free associations and learning how to create and maintain them, which is why

---

94. "de telle sorte qu'après avoir brisé toutes les entraves que lui imposaient jadis des classes ou des hommes, l'esprit humain s'enchaînerait étroitement aux volontés générales du grand nombre" (DA, 724).

95. "Si, à la place de toutes les puissances diverses qui gênaient ou retardaient outre mesure l'essor de la raison individuelle, les peuples démocratiques substituaient le pouvoir absolu d'une majorité, le mal n'aurait fait que changer de caractère. Les hommes n'auraient point trouvé le moyen de vivre indépendants ; ils auraient seulement découvert, chose difficile, une nouvelle physionomie de la servitude" (DA, 724).

Tocqueville remarks, "There are no countries where associations are more necessary, to prevent the despotism of parties or the arbitrariness of the prince, than those where the social state is democratic."[96] Whether subject to the despotism of an erratic prince or the despotism of a fickle majority, the ability to form associations among a democratic people is a political necessity if this same people wants to maintain their independence. This need to form and maintain free associations is quite foreign to those who live in aristocratic societies, and the reasoning is as follows:

> In aristocratic societies, men do not need to unite in order to act, because they are held tightly together. There, each citizen, rich and powerful, is like the head of a permanent and compulsory association that is composed of all those who are dependent on him and who are made to cooperate in the execution of his plans.[97]

Because real wealth and substantial power reside in a diversity of aristocratic heads, men can act together without the need of the political and material support of the government, and a type of natural association exists around this head because of the dependence which many lesser citizens have on this aristocrat. But this natural form of unity no longer exists when conditions are equal: "Among democratic peoples, on the contrary, all citizens are independent and weak; they can hardly do anything by themselves, and no one among them can compel his fellows to lend him their help. So they all fall into impotence if they do not learn to help each other freely."[98] In a democratic society where conditions are equal, the powerful individuals of an aristocracy can no longer be found; instead, all the citizens are "independent and weak" and must unite together in order to achieve any collective goal.

Tocqueville distinguishes between political associations and civil associations, where political associations are concerned with the policies

---

96. "il n'y a pas de pays où les associations soient plus nécessaires, pour empêcher le despotisme des partis ou l'arbitraire du prince, que ceux où l'état social est démocratique" (DA, 307).

97. "Dans les sociétés aristocratiques, les hommes n'ont pas besoin de s'unir pour agir, parce qu'ils sont retenus fortement ensemble. Chaque citoyen, riche et puissant, y forme comme la tête d'une association permanente et forcée qui est composée de tous ceux qu'il tient dans sa dépendance et qu'il fait concourir à l'exécution de ses desseins" (DA, 898).

98. "Chez les peuples démocratiques, au contraire, tous les citoyens sont indépendants et faibles; ils ne peuvent presque rien par eux-mêmes, et aucun d'entre eux ne saurait obliger ses semblables à lui prêter leur concours. Ils tombent donc tous dans l'impuissance s'sils n'apprennent à s'saider librement" (DA, 898).

of government and the affairs of the state, and civil associations are those concerned with *la vie ordinaire* and often have a commercial, intellectual, or moral focus. Both of these associations are prevalent in America, and both are necessary for sustaining liberty, but to different degrees and for different reasons.

Political associations are necessary for a democratic people like America because these associations help people to defend themselves "against the despotic action of a majority or against the encroachments of royal power," and "if each citizen, as he becomes individually weaker and therefore more incapable of preserving his liberty by himself alone, did not learn the art of uniting with his fellows to defend his liberty, tyranny would necessarily grow with equality."[99] Thus, political association is a necessary way to mitigate the despotic potential of the majority.

Given Tocqueville's statement that the tyranny of the majority is "the greatest danger" among democratic peoples, one is initially surprised to hear him claim that, between political associations and civil associations, civil associations are actually more essential to the preservation of liberty among the people. He states,

> If men who live in democratic countries had neither the right nor the taste to unite for political ends, their independence would run great risks, but they could for a long time retain their wealth and their enlightenment; while, if they did not acquire the custom of associating in ordinary life, civilization itself would be in danger. A people among whom individuals lost the power to do great things separately without acquiring the ability to achieve them together would soon return to barbarism.[100]

For Tocqueville, there is something more vital to existence than political liberty, and that is "civilization itself." Without political associations, a people will lose political liberty, but their wealth and intelligence could endure for a long time and existence would carry on; but without civil associations,

---

99. "contre l'action despotique d'une majorité ou contre les empiétements du pouvoir royal"; "si chaque citoyen, a mesure qu'il devient individuellement plus faible, et par conséquent plus incapable de préserver isolément sa liberté, n'apprenait pas l'art de s'sunir à ses semblables pour la défendre, la tyrannie croîtrait nécessairement avec l'égalité" (DA, 895–96).

100. "Si les hommes qui vivent dans les pays démocratiques n'avaient ni le droit ni le goût de s'sunir dans des buts politiques, leur indépendance courrait de grands hasards, mais ils pourraient conserver longtemps leurs richesses et leurs lumières ; tandis que s'sils n'acquéraient point l'usage de s'sassocier dans la vie ordinaire, la civilisation elle-même serait en péril. Un peu le chez lequel les particuliers perdraient le pouvoir de faire isolément de grandes choses sans acquérir la faculté de les produire en commun retournerait bientôt vers la barbarie" (DA, 898).

civilization itself is threatened, for the very fabric of a democratic society would deteriorate to a state of barbarism. Tocqueville said above that democratic citizens "all fall into impotence if they do not learn to help each other freely," and this is not just a helplessness in their ability to control political life but is also a helplessness which descends to the very depths of civil life.

Americans seem to have spontaneously understood this need to associate for civil purposes, for civil associations exist in great numbers and form the great majority of associations present, as Tocqueville remarks, "The political associations that exist in the United States form only a detail amid the immense tableau that associations as a whole present there."[101] This "immense tableau" of associations in America is made up of many associations which enrich and sustain civil life while not directly serving a political purpose, and we quote Tocqueville at length in order to appreciate the myriad ways these associations impact civil life:

> Americans of all ages, of all conditions, of all minds, constantly unite. Not only do they have commercial and industrial associations in which they all take part, but also they have a thousand other kinds: religious, moral, intellectual, serious ones, useless ones, very general and very particular ones, immense and very small ones; Americans associate to celebrate holidays, establish seminaries, build inns, erect churches, distribute books, send missionaries to the Antipodes; in this way they create hospitals, prisons, schools. If, finally, it is a matter of bringing a truth to light or of developing a sentiment with the support of a good example, they associate. Wherever, at the head of a new undertaking, you see in France the government, and in England, a great lord, count on seeing in the United States, an association.[102]

From the paragraph above, we can now understand more clearly what Tocqueville means when he says that civilization itself would be threatened

---

101. "les associations politiques qui existent aux États-Unis ne forment qu'un détail au milieu de l'immense tableau que l'ensemble des associations y présente" (DA, 896).

102. "Les Américains de tous les âges, de toutes les conditions, de tous les esprits, s'sunissent sans cesse. Non seulement ils ont des associations commerciales et industrielles auxquelles tous prennent part, mais ils en ont encore de mille autres espèces: de religieuses, de morales, de graves, de futiles, de fort générales et de très particulières, d'immenses et de fort petites; les Américains s'sassocient pour donner des fêtes, fonder des séminaires, bâtir des auberges, élever des églises, répandre des livres, envoyer des missionnaires aux antipodes; ils créent de cette manière des hôpitaux, des prisons, des écoles. S'agit-il enfin de mettre en lumière une vérité ou de développer un sentiment par l'appui d'un grand exemple, ils s'sassocient. Partout où, à la tête d'une entreprise nouvelle, vous voyez en France le gouvernement et en Angleterre un grand seigneur, comptez que vous apercevrez aux États-Unis une association" (DA, 896).

if men in democratic nations did not learn the art of uniting for a common purpose, for it is by way of association that schools are built, seminaries established, books are distributed, and holidays are celebrated. Due to their vital role in sustaining not only independence of thought but also culture itself, Tocqueville concludes, "The liberty to associate is, therefore, more precious and the science of associating more necessary among those people than among all others, and it becomes more precious and more necessary as equality is greater."[103] The "science" of association is therefore the primary way which American's ensure both intellectual liberty and cultural vitality, and the necessity of this science extends to any social state in which equality is pervasive.

Tocqueville acknowledges that some thinkers disagree with his assessment, for they hold that a centralized government could just as easily fill the role of associations. Granted, this government must be made "more skillful and more active" so that it can fill this role, but it is argued that, if the government grew in power and activity, it could replace associations with its own form of civil maintenance.[104] On this point, Tocqueville is in clear disagreement.

He acknowledges that the government could replace some associations, but he asks the rhetorical question, "But what political power would ever be able to be sufficient for the innumerable multitude of small enterprises that the American citizens carry out every day with the aid of the association?"[105] It is the great immensity of civil associations, and their wide diversity of purposes, which Tocqueville cannot foresee any government ever replacing successfully. There is another factor which leads to Tocqueville's distaste for this theory: "The more government puts itself in the place of associations, the more individuals, losing the idea of associating, will need it to come to their aid."[106] As the government replaces associations, men will need this same government more frequently, and Tocqueville considers this a problem, not necessarily because he is opposed to "big government," but because encouraging the art of association in local matters is

---

103. "La liberté de s'sassocier est donc plus précieuse et la science de l'association plus nécessaire chez ces peuples-là que chez tous les autres et elle devient plus précieuse et plus nécessaire à mesure que l'égalité est plus grande" (DA, 899). Text in original manuscript but not in the first printed version of the book.

104. DA, 899.

105. "Mais quel pouvoir politique serait jamais en état de suffire à la multitude innombrable de petites entreprises que les citoyens américains exécutent tous les jours à l'aide de l'association?" (DA, 900).

106. "Plus (l'pouvoir social) se mettra à la place des associations, et plus les particuliers, perdant l'idée de s'sassocier, auront besoin qu'il vienne à leur aide" (DA, 900).

essential for preparing people to learn the art of associating in more critical matters: "So the government, even when it lends its support to individuals, must never discharge them entirely from the trouble of helping themselves by uniting; often it must deny them its help in order to let them find the secret of being self-sufficient, and it must withdraw its hand as they better understand the art of doing so."[107] As this art of associating becomes less frequently practiced, the people find themselves incapable of associating for larger and more critical matters, and we have seen above that such associating is the only consistent protection against the tyranny of the majority among democratic peoples.

Up to this point, Tocqueville has only demonstrated the principal political and social reasons for rejecting the idea that a government could replace associations, but there are other reasons which touch more directly on the thesis of this paper and which ultimately are the root of his strongest objection, which is that the morals and intelligence of the people are threatened when associations are replaced by government. Tocqueville explains,

> The morals and intelligence of a democratic people would run no lesser dangers than their trade and industry, if the government came to take the place of associations everywhere. Sentiments and ideas are renewed, the heart grows larger and the human mind develops only by the reciprocal action of men on each other. I have demonstrated that this action is almost nil in democratic countries. So it must be created there artificially. And this is what associations *alone* are able to do.[108]

If associations were replaced by government, men might have their schools built, their seminaries constructed, and their books printed just as well as if they had been done by an association, but something essential would still be missing, and that is the reciprocal influence of men on each other. Tocqueville seems to think that the human mind does not develop as broadly and extensively when speaking to a government clerk as it does

107. "Il faut donc que le gouvernement, alors même qu'il prête son appui à des particuliers, ne les décharge jamais entièrement du soin de s'aider eux-mêmes en s'unissant, que souvent il leur refuse son concours afin de leur laisser trouver le secret de se suffire, et qu'il retire sa main à mesure qu'ils comprennent mieux l'art de la faire" (DA, 904).

108. "La morale et l'intelligence d'un peuple démocratique ne courraient pas de moindres dangers que son négoce et son industrie, si le gouvernement venait y prendre partout la place des associations. Les sentiments et les idées ne se renouvellent, le cœur ne s'agrandit et l'esprit humain ne se développe que par l'action réciproque des hommes les uns sur les autres. J'ai fait voir que cette action est presque nulle dans les pays démocratiques. Il faut donc l'y créer artificiellement. Et c'est ce que les associations *seules* peuvent faire" (DA, 900; emphasis added).

when it is forced to unite with equal minds to achieve a common goal, and given the fact that democratic citizens are already disposed to look only within themselves for the reason of all things, Tocqueville considers it essential that this reciprocal influence of minds must be created intentionally, something which associations can provide in abundance. A strong central government might accomplish similar tasks as those which associations set out to accomplish, but Tocqueville thinks there is something being accomplished which is more important than the task itself, and this "something more" is the development of the human mind. To diminish or remove associations in civil society would thus impede the mind's growth, which is why he says that such a democratic society would risk receding into barbarism.

In perhaps the most succinct summary of his thought on this topic, Tocqueville states, "I believe firmly that you cannot establish an aristocracy again in the world; but I think that simple citizens by associating together can constitute very wealthy, very influential, very strong beings, in a word aristocratic persons."[109] This idea of associations forming a sort of "aristocratic person" compliments an idea he states elsewhere: "Associations, among democratic peoples, must take the place of the powerful individuals that equality of conditions has made disappear."[110] There is a contribution to the civil and political world which only persons can accomplish, and if these persons do not exist naturally (as they do in an aristocratic state), they must be created. To replace these persons with a governmental power is insufficient for the reasons mentioned above. If all a people want from their government is wealth, comfort, or property, then associations are unnecessary; but the moment a people ask for something beyond these material benefits and instead seek to secure things such as grandeur of mind and a developed intelligence, the enrichment of sentiments and a strengthening of morals, then a democratic people is forced to develop the "science" of associations, which is why Tocqueville calls this the "mother science" among democratic peoples.[111]

We recall that Tocqueville was writing for French readers, and to them he addresses the following words,

> There is nothing, in my opinion, that merits our attention more than the intellectual and moral associations of America. The

109. "Je crois fermement qu'on ne saurait fonder de nouveau, dans le monde, une aristocratie; mais je pense que les simples citoyens en s'assosciant, peuvent y constituer des êtres très opulents, très influents, très forts, en un mot des personnes aristocratiques" (DA, 1268).

110. "Ce sont les associations qui, chez les peuples démocratiques, doivent tenir lieu des particuliers puissants que l'égalité des conditions a fait disparaître" (DA, 901).

111. DA, 902.

political and industrial associations of the Americans easily fall within our grasp, but the others escape us; and, if we discover them, we understand them badly, because we have hardly ever seen anything analogous. You must recognize, however, that the intellectual and moral associations are as necessary as the political and industrial ones to the American people, and perhaps more.[112]

We thus see that both the *art* of association and the *types* of associations are essential for providing the kind of intellectual and moral vigor which Tocqueville desires to see in society and which he knows must be present in order to avoid barbarism. By maintaining an "immense tableau" of associations in which the moral and intellectual associations are as robust as the political and industrial, human reason need not fear being constrained "within more narrow limits than are suitable for the grandeur and happiness of the human species," and such grandeur of mind is important not only for the individual, but also for civilization itself.

RATIO IN RELATIONE WITHIN THE DEMOCRATIC MIND

It is the claim of this thesis that the rational faculty of human nature develops according to the relational dimension of the human person, and Tocqueville's *Democracy in America* provides strong evidence to support such a thesis, for even among those democratic minds which claim to think "by themselves," there exists an observable pattern for human reason to be formed by the type of relations within a culture. In aristocratic times, men allowed their mind to be formed by class, family, or brilliant men, giving evidence of how, even in aristocratic minds, the rational faculty is developed through one's relationships. Though democratic minds do not acknowledge this same source of authority, these same democratic minds invest the majority with an authority greater and more vast than the authority formerly given to class, family, and brilliant men. This is the great paradox which emerges from this exposition, for even when a people profess faith in a *méthode* which embraces a self-constructed rationality, these same people

---

112. "Il n'y a rien, suivant moi, qui mérite plus d'attirer nos regards que les associations intellectuelles et morales de l'Amérique. Les associations politiques et industrielles des Américains tombent aisément sous nos sens; mais les autres nous échappent; et, si nous les découvrons, nous les comprenons mal, parce que nous n'avons presque jamais rien vu d'analogue. On doit reconnaître cependant qu'elles sont aussi nécessaires que les premières au peuple américain, et peut-être plus" (DA, 902).

are nonetheless overwhelmed by relationally-dependent factors which bend their mind and mold their thought in a particular direction. The rational faculty of democratic persons is just as relationally-dependent as the rational faculty of aristocratic persons, for in both "aristocracy" and "democracy," how a person thinks is very much dependent on what a person is related to.

Yet another paradox emerges which supports our thesis when we see that the remedy to curing the tyrannical influence of the majority over the human mind is the formation of free associations. This is paradoxical for a democratic people, for though they may claim to appeal to their own thought as the basis of all things, they nonetheless seem to intuit a need to associate in order to remain free. They may have a philosophical method which is relationally-independent, but put them in society without a strong central government, and quickly they begin to associate to build schools, establish seminaries, print books, celebrate holidays, and even to eradicate liquor.[113] It is as if the isolated minds of these citizens naturally drift towards one another, intuiting that an isolated self is not a very effective way to build society, and left alone, very little can be accomplished. We reiterate that this is true not just for building "things" but also for developing minds and enhancing intelligence, for the "vital effect" of free associations is not rooted exclusively in their ability to bring about a certain result, but also in their ability to help expand the human mind by way of relationship. If it is true that "sentiments and ideas are renewed, the heart grows larger and the human mind develops only by the reciprocal action of men on each other," then the surest hope for authentic growth of one's rational faculty is growth in one's relationships. This is something which American citizens have naturally discovered on their own, just as they discovered their philosophical method. They had no need to read Descartes in order to learn how to "search by oneself alone" for the reason of all things; but neither did they need anyone to tell them that such a philosophy is a short-cut to social and intellectual barbarism. A relationally-independent rationality may exist in

---

113. The use of associations to eradicate liquor both confused and enlightened Tocqueville. He explains: "The first time I heard in the United States that one hundred thousand men had publicly pledged not to use strong liquor, the thing seemed to me more amusing than serious, and I did not at first see clearly why these citizens, who were so temperate, would not be content to drink water within their families. I ended by understanding that these hundred thousand Americans, frightened by the progress that drunkenness was making around them, had wanted to give their patronage to temperance. They had acted precisely like a great lord who dressed very plainly in order to inspire disdain for luxury among simple citizens. It may be believed that if these hundred thousand men lived in France, each one of them would have individually addressed the government in order to beg it to oversee the taverns throughout the entire kingdom" (DA, 901).

theory, but it does not exist for long among people who seek to be politically and intellectually free.

So we see in several important ways how the rational faculty of human nature develops in response to the relational dimension of the human person, and perhaps the best reason to believe this is to observe what happens when a society embraces a philosophical method to the contrary, for even then, forces begin to emerge which reveal how much the rational faculty is permeated by relations and, in the process, molded and developed. We repeat: the influence of these relations is not only on the content of thought but also on the type of thinking involved; these relations not only develop *what* a person thinks but also *how* a person thinks. Despite philosophical claims to the contrary, how a person thinks is not solely dependent on "self-evident" rational principles but is also very much dependent on what a person is related to.

CHAPTER 3

The Technocratic Mind

IN THE PREVIOUS CHAPTER, we conducted an examination of the role of equality of conditions in creating a democratic logic, and this chapter aims to conduct a similar examination by identifying the role of technology in creating a technocratic logic. The motivation for examining this logic comes from the church's most recent social encyclical, *Laudato Si'*, which focuses on care for the earth but also contains conceptual landmarks that are continuous with, but also a development of, ideas nascent within the Catholic Social Tradition. One such conceptual landmark is found in Pope Francis's teaching about the "technocratic paradigm," and while teachings about technology are present in other social encyclicals, *Laudato Si'* expands upon this topic in new and important ways. Most important for this thesis is the fact that Pope Francis speaks about the "logic" inherent in technology and warns humanity about the way that this logic can dominate the mind of modern man, and given that this thesis is focused on the way the rational faculty develops in response to one's relational dimension, our specific focus on the technocratic paradigm will further illustrate this dynamic interplay between the *ratio* and *relatio* of the human person.

THE TECHNOCRATIC PARADIGM

Although *Laudato Si'* is rightly considered an encyclical about "care for our common home," it is important not to reduce it to a commentary on merely environmental concerns. Pope Francis states, "We are not faced with two separate crises, one environmental and the other social, but rather with *one complex crisis* which is both social and environmental."[1] Thus, the deterioration of the biological environment is intimately connected to the deterioration of the social environment, and the breakdown of both is attributable to "one complex crisis." In seeking to articulate a unifying cause of this complex crisis, Pope Francis points to the "assault of the technocratic paradigm."[2] The "technocratic paradigm" is a phrase which is new to the social doctrine of the church, and it has various social and environmental consequences, so only after considerable hermeneutic recuperation can we then establish its connections to this thesis.

Part of the hermeneutical challenge to understanding the technocratic paradigm is rooted in the fact that Pope Francis does something that is unprecedented in the other social encyclicals: he extensively cites a single author who is outside the Magisterial and ecclesial documents traditionally cited in other social encyclicals. This author is Romano Guardini, who is cited six times in chapter three, which is the chapter which deals with the technocratic paradigm. Given that Pope Benedict XVI is cited seven times in this chapter and Pope John Paul II nine times, Guardini's thought is given an almost-pontifical status in the document, and just as one cannot understand the social encyclicals in isolation, neither can one understand the technocratic paradigm without understanding Romano Guardini. To that end, we must conduct a preliminary investigation of the works of Guardini which are cited by Pope Francis or which explicitly speak about this topic, and then we can analyze and better understand the phrase "technocratic paradigm" as it is used in *Laudato Si'*.

The Rise of the Machines

In both *Letters from Lake Como* and *The End of the Modern World*, Romano Guardini provides a detailed description of the role of machines and technology in forcing social conformity and reducing the human experience of reality. Fundamental to his thought on this topic is an essential distinction between "tools" and "machines," for in the use of natural tools, one can experience "a vital and sympathetic power, an ability to follow the inner courses of reality and to shape it accordingly"; but in the use of machines, "materials and forces are harnessed, unleashed, burst open, altered, and directed at will. There is no feeling for what is organically possible or tolerable in any living sense. A rationally constructed and arbitrarily set goal reigns

---

1. Francis, *Laudato Si'*, 139 (emphasis added).
2. Francis, *Laudato Si'*, 111.

supreme."[3] Machines, as a medium of interaction, are unsympathetic to the inner realities of material goods; instead, they are attuned only to what is possible, a situation in which a "rationally constructed and arbitrarily set goal reigns supreme," and Guardini sees this as a true loss of proportionality, beauty, and humanity. Guardini employs the analogy of a plow to illustrate his point:

> Think of the plow. It, too, is a primitive cultural artifact. How did this implement with the animal in front and the farmer behind turn up the soil? In a purely secondary way, I as a city dweller have seen the mystery of humanity as plowmen worked across the field and tore up the earth to make it receptive to the seed . . . But what happens when the plow is mechanized? Certainly this is a wonderful work of technology, and it gives us more bread and raises the standard of living. But riding on the tractor is different from following the plow.[4]

Why is riding on a tractor different from following the plow? Because with a tractor, a crucial separation has now been introduced between the user and reality. A man following a plow must, in a very real sense, *follow* the plow, which in turn has a subtle responsiveness to the inner contours of the earth, whereas a man riding a tractor optimizes the use of the land according to preconditioned, mathematically determined functions of the machine that are not in tune with these inner realities. Thus, Guardini's criticism of machines is that they are inherently reductionist, that they reduce natural contours and force a superficial conformity to rigidly controlled optimization. This is what could be termed "reduction-by-mechanization," a situation in which the mechanical process reduces reality to a pre-conditioned, logically derived standard and forces a synthetic unity of form.

This reduction-by-mechanization has permeated nearly all aspects of the human experience, and this is not for the betterment of humanity according to Guardini. Because "a system of machines is engulfing life," and because machines reduce or compress all of reality, he laments that "the world of natural humanity, of nature in which humanity dwells, is perishing."[5] As the use of machines continues to increase in daily life, the experience of natural humanity is subsequently lost, to the detriment of humanity itself: "As the machine is perfected, the intimate relation of man to his work, in which his eye, will, sense of material, imagination, and general

---

3. Guardini, *Letters from Lake Como*, 46.
4. Guardini, *Letters from Lake Como*, 15.
5. Guardini, *Letters from Lake Como*, 49.

creativeness cooperate, disappears."⁶ As man's intimate relation to his work disappears, the human person becomes more and more distant from reality itself, and the erosion of man's relatedness results in an erosion of his very being. Thus Guardini concludes

> As a result, in some respects, man himself grows poorer. He loses the rich satisfaction of personal creativity, consenting instead to invent, utilize, and service mechanical contraptions. But even as he puts them to ever more varied tasks, gaining through them ever greater power, his own will and creativeness must conform ever more to the mechanism in question, for one-sided effects do not exist. This means that the producer renounces individuality in his product and learns to content himself with producing only what the machine allows. The more perfect the apparatus, the fewer the possibilities for personal creativeness.⁷

As technical apparatuses are perfected, man is able to *produce* more but *create* less, and insofar as man actually needs to create something with his life and through his work, this inhibition of creativity by way of the machine is experienced as a loss for the human person. In reality, it is the machine which actually "works" and "creates," whereas man is reduced to a "servicer of machines."⁸ The net effect of all these machines, contraptions, and apparatuses which have replaced the creative work of man is the emergence of a new humanity which Guardini calls the "non-human humanity." In order to fully understand what Guardini means by this term, a brief journey into the past is required.

Guardini asserts that, in the past, the works of man were permeated with the "organic," which

> suggests that in ancient man's manner of interpreting nature, of reacting to it, utilizing and developing it, his rational, instinctive, and creative aspects held each other in check. He took possession of the given conditions, strengthened their forms, increased their effectiveness; but on the whole, he respected their structure and did not break it up.⁹

---

6. Guardini, *End of the Modern World*, 155.
7. Guardini, *End of the Modern World*, 156.
8. Guardini says, "In place of the artisan, we have the worker, servicer of machines" (*End of the Modern World*, 156).
9. Guardini, *End of the Modern World*, 154.

CHAPTER 3: THE TECHNOCRATIC MIND

Thus, the "organic" works of pre-modern man are those in which the rational, instinctive, and creative aspects are all held in balance, and all are mutually integrated in each creative work. But then

> something new happened: man began to explore nature with methodical thoroughness and precision. It was no longer enough to comprehend it with his senses or to grasp it symbolically or practically. (We really ought to say that he gradually unlearned these approaches to nature.) Now he begins to disintegrate nature both experimentally and theoretically.[10]

According to Guardini, man "unlearned" the organic approach to nature and began to disintegrate the natural world by way of experiment and rational abstraction, and "through increasingly precise mathematical-experimental methods, man bends nature to his will."[11] Whereas the rational, instinctive, and creative were once in an organic balance, this new humanity is characterized by a nearly exclusive dependence on rational abstraction to bend nature according to the will of man.

As the organic was overwhelmed by technics, as technology invaded nearly every aspect of human life, a new "structural order" came about. Guardini explains:

> From all this a *structural order* evolves which has been invented and created by man, but which in its construction as well as in its effects is ever farther removed from direct human manipulation. It complies to human will and achieves human goals, but in the process it seems to develop a peculiar autonomy of function and growth.[12]

What is unique about this structural order is that it is invented by man and yet it has obtained a "peculiar autonomy" of its own, independent of the intention of those who invented it. In so far as this structural order has attained "autonomous growth," we could say that this technocratic world of machines and gadgets has come "alive," so much so that Guardini says that this technocratic world has created a "shift in the human condition."[13] The term he applies to this shift in the human condition is "non-human humanity," which refers to "man in whom the earlier relative agreement between the fields of knowledge and works on the one hand, and of experience on the other, is no longer found. He exists in a world of knowledge-works

---

10. Guardini, *End of the Modern World*, 154.
11. Guardini, *End of the Modern World*, 154.
12. Guardini, *End of the Modern World*, 155 (emphasis added).
13. Guardini, *End of the Modern World*, 158.

possibilities that have outstripped the earlier norms."[14] This non-human humanity has seen the harmonious balance of the organic replaced by a technocratic rationality which has radically altered man's relationships. Guardini makes this point more explicit when he states that this non-human humanity creates

> a man shaped by a certain cultural pattern, an historic pattern which the passage of time increasingly sharpens. He is a man of increasing alienations between his experience and his understanding, between his experience and his field of work. Under the impact of this historic change, we must repeat, *man's relations with nature have changed radically*. Man himself is less capable of attaining nature, of representing it and of experiencing it.[15]

First, we note that Guardini thinks that this non-human humanity has "radically changed" man's relations with nature, which is why such a man is one of "increasing alienations." Second, this is a "cultural pattern" and not merely a tendency within a few members of society, which is why Guardini calls it a "structural order" above. Because this first point coincides so intimately with the thesis of this paper, we will comment on it more extensively in the conclusion to this chapter, but for the moment, we must further examine the details of this structural order and cultural pattern.

This systematic cultural pattern is far reaching, extending beyond the individual and encroaching both the order of the family and the state. With regard to the family, Guardini says,

> The dissolution of organic creativity finds a counterpart in the dissolution of the basic unit of mature human life. The family is losing its significance as an integrating, order-preserving factor. Congregation, city, country are being influenced less and less by the family, clan, work-group, class. Humanity itself appears ever more as a formless mass to be purposefully "organized."[16]

Just as the works produced by man have been dissolved of their integral "organic creativity," so too has the family lost its status as the organic backbone of the social environment, leading humanity away from a stratified diversity composed of hierarchical differentiation and moving it closer to a "formless mass" which is strikingly undifferentiated. What is seen in the family is seen also among cities: "modern cities everywhere are alike, whether in Western

---

14. Guardini, *End of the Modern World*, 158.
15. Guardini, *End of the Modern World*, 70 (emphasis added).
16. Guardini, *End of the Modern World*, 161–62.

Europe, China, North or South America, or Russia."[17] And a similar phenomenon manifests itself within the modern state:

> The modern state shares the characteristic just described. It too is losing its organic structure, becoming more and more a complex of all-controlling functions. In it the human being steps back, the apparatus forward. Constantly improving techniques of stock-taking, man-power survey, and bureaucratic management—to put it brutally, increasingly effective social engineering—tend to treat people much as the machine treats the raw materials fed into it.[18]

From the individual, to the family, to the city, to the nation-state, Guardini sees a systematic erosion of the "organic structure" of these institutions and finds instead that they have been replaced by a radical homogeneity. Within all this leveling, uniformity, and social conformity, Guardini sees correlations to the machine, noting that the state "tends to treat people much as the machine treats the raw material fed into it." Once again, Guardini advances his thesis that the methodology of the machine is manifesting itself among those who so frequently use machines; it is as if those who use machines so naturally within their daily lives are simultaneously being formed into the image and likeness of the machine itself.

Guardini's concern about such a loss of "natural humanity" does not stem from a nostalgic longing for a return to the past but rather from a concern about the loss of the constituent elements of human existence. His critique is perhaps best revealed in the following words:

> Things, forces, processes have become "worldly"—the word stripped of its former religious richness and given a new sense which implies "rationally understandable and technically controllable." This means that both man as a whole as well as important individual aspects of human life—the defenselessness of childhood, the special nature of woman, the simultaneous physical weakness and rich experience of the aged—all lose their metaphysical worth. Birth is now considered the appearance of a new unit of the species homo sapiens; marriage but an alliance of a man and a woman with certain personal and legal consequences; death the end of a total process known as life.[19]

---

17. Guardini, *End of the Modern World*, 162.
18. Guardini, *End of the Modern World*, 162.
19. Guardini, *End of the Modern World*, 167.

The loss of the "metaphysical worth" of things is Guardini's fundamental critique of this technocratic culture, a culture wherein the inherent transcendence and meaning of reality is increasingly lost and thus gives rise to a "non-human humanity." As man has learned to control his surroundings, these same surroundings have become devoid of meaning and stripped of their inner worth. Guardini presupposes, of course, that there is more to birth than increasing the species, that there is more to marriage than personal and legal consequences, that there is indeed a "metaphysical worth" to the relationships and events of human existence that extends beyond their utilitarian or pragmatic effects, and lamenting man's increasing metaphysical blindness, Guardini compares such a "structural order" to a tyranny:

> When we examine the development as a whole, we cannot escape the impression that nature as well as man himself is becoming ever more vulnerable to the domination—economic, technical, political, organizational—of power. Ever more distinctly our condition reveals itself as one in which man progressively controls nature, yes, but also men; the state controls the citizens; and an autonomous technical-economic-political system holds all life in thrall.[20]

Man is increasingly dominated by the very structural order which his machines have helped to create and on which man has grown increasingly dependent, and the result is a technical-economic-political system which has an ironclad grip on humanity and made it a "thrall." This is the tyranny of modern man according to Guardini: man has learned to control nature with technical machines, and yet he has also come to be controlled in a similar machine-like fashion, and a blindness to the "metaphysical worth" of reality is the net result. The humanity which arises from such a tyrannical structural order is what Guardini refers to when he speaks of a "non-human humanity."

These considerations cause Guardini to conclude that technology "moves forward in the final analysis neither for profit nor for the well-being of the human race," a conclusion that is cited by Pope Francis in *Laudato Si'*.[21] Guardini does not deny the advances that technology has provided to human life, for he stated above that the tractor brings about "more bread" and a higher standard of living; but he is alerting a technological world that something deeply human is being lost in all of its technological sophistication. Guardini is insistent that there is a real cost for acquiring more bread and a higher standard of material living by way of machines, and this cost

---

20. Guardini, *End of the Modern World*, 163–64.
21. Guardini, cited in Francis, *Laudato Si'*, 108.

is a decrease in natural humanity. Furthermore, he views this exchange as something to be lamented, and we will soon see the extent to which such a view is shared by Catholic Social Teaching.

The Technocratic Paradigm in *Laudato Si'*

From this preliminary introduction of Guardini's thought, we are now prepared to properly interpret the teachings of Pope Francis about the technocratic paradigm. Like Guardini, Pope Francis sees a great amount of good coming from technological advances, stating, "How can we not feel gratitude and appreciation for this (technological and scientific) progress, especially in the fields of medicine, engineering and communications?"[22] He says that it is "right to rejoice in these advances," for he sees true growth and real development coming about as a consequence, just as Guardini recognizes tractors are responsible for more bread.[23] Yet all this technical advancement has come at a cost: it contributes to the emergence of a new mind and a new way of thinking which is deficient. Citing Guardini, Pope Francis explains that "The technological *mind* sees nature as an insensate order, as a cold body of facts, as a mere 'given', as an object of utility, as raw material to be hammered into useful shape; it views the cosmos similarly as a mere 'space' into which objects can be thrown with complete indifference."[24] Pope Francis goes on to explain that this technological mind operates according to a "technocratic paradigm," whose essential features are the following:

> This paradigm exalts the concept of a subject who, using logical and rational procedures, progressively approaches and gains control over an external object. This subject makes every effort to establish the scientific and experimental method, which in itself is already a technique of possession, mastery and transformation. It is as if the subject were to find itself in the presence of something formless, completely open to manipulation.[25]

The parallels between these words of Pope Francis and the words of Romano Guardini are abundant, for like Guardini, Pope Francis understands the technocratic paradigm to be radically out of tune with the natural proportions and the inherent qualities of nature and reality. Like the tractor, the technocratic paradigm is insensitive to any intrinsic qualities of the

---

22. Francis, *Laudato Si'*, 103.
23. Francis, *Laudato Si'*, 102.
24. Guardini, cited in Francis, *Laudato Si'*, 115.
25. Francis, *Laudato Si'*, 106.

surrounding environment and instead uses only "logical and rational procedures" which allow one to "gain control over an external object." Nothing is received as it is; rather, it is shaped into what it can be, and the sole criterion for what something can be is determined exclusively by logical and rational analysis, something which Guardini called "a rationally constructed and arbitrarily set goal."

We recall again that this is not to criticize rational or logical analysis *per se*, which have done so much good in developing and sustaining modern existence; rather, it is to criticize the elevation of rationality as the supreme and exclusive criterion for how to interact with and relate to an exterior object. Pope Francis explains,

> Men and women have constantly intervened in nature, but for a long time this meant being in tune with and respecting the possibilities offered by the things themselves. It was a matter of receiving what nature itself allowed, as if from its own hand. Now, by contrast, we are the ones to lay our hands on things, attempting to extract everything possible from them while frequently ignoring or forgetting the reality in front of us.[26]

Francis is affirming that reality is not just formless matter to be manipulated at will but rather is something to be received; reality has something to give us and something to tell us. Guardini celebrated the plow because it has a "vital and sympathetic power, an ability to follow the inner courses of reality and to shape it accordingly," but the technocratic paradigm is a mindset which rushes past these "inner courses of reality" and arrives at a simple abstraction of reality. This is what distinguishes more acceptable and "organic" ways of manipulating reality from the modern, technocratic ways of manipulating reality: according to the technocratic paradigm, there is nothing to be received in reality but only matter to be controlled. The consequence of this skewed vision is to flatten reality, to force a sort of reduction-by-mechanization on all of reality, resulting in a machine-like rationality that is no longer able to see the inner nature of things. Thus Guardini could say that such a paradigm "evinces a growing *inability to see*, a progressive cooling of the heart, an indifference to the people and things of existence."[27] This is a blindness which touches all of reality because it impacts all of the "people and things of existence," and thus it is a systematic blindness and not just a temporary blindness.

So what, exactly, is the technocratic paradigm? It is a mindset which values "technical thought over reality itself," thus causing the intrinsic

---

26. Francis, *Laudato Si'*, 106.
27. Guardini, *End of the Modern World*, 158 (emphasis added).

dignity of reality to be compromised.[28] It is a systematic disregard for, and ignorance of, "the message contained in the structures of nature itself."[29] It is, fundamentally, *a blindness to the metaphysical worth and inner reality of exterior objects*. It is, above all, an assault on the category of relation.

The consequences of this mentality are extensive, for it touches on every object external to the observer. Pope Francis explains, "The effects of imposing this model on reality as a whole, human and social, are seen in the deterioration of the environment, but this is just one sign of a reductionism which affects every aspect of human and social life."[30] All of reality is now filtered through a mind habituated to reductionism-by-mechanization, and therefore all of reality is incapable of being seen for what it truly is and remains only formless matter to be manipulated at will. This complete deformation of all of reality by way of a technocratic mind gives rise to a great array of consequences.

In the environmental crisis, the technocratic paradigm expresses itself in a mindset which neglects any interior limitations of the external environment and treats it as an object for unlimited exploitation. Taken to an extreme, as it has been in recent decades, this application of the technocratic paradigm to the environment has led to extensive decay, such that "the earth, our home, is beginning to look more and more like an immense pile of filth."[31] Treating the earth like an object to be limitlessly exploited is to risk exposing it to the same fate of over-used material objects: an item worthy of the trash bin.

In the economic sector, the technocratic paradigm gives rise to an exclusive focus on the priority of financial profit without concern for how the methods to acquire this profit may have an impact on others or on the environment. This is exhibited in many businesses where the "bottom line" refers, quite literally, only to profit, but making profit the sole criterion for economic success blinds one to the other realities within a certain market, and it can even lead to blindness about the reality of the people engaged in the market. Unfortunately, this devaluation of human beings in preference for unrestrained access to profit can be seen in many ways, most especially in the tendency to replace workers with machines, and "to stop investing in people, in order to gain greater short-term financial gain, is bad business for society."[32] Yet the social costs of economic decisions are negligible to a

---

28. Francis, *Laudato Si'*, 115.
29. Francis, *Laudato Si'*, 117.
30. Francis, *Laudato Si'*, 107 (emphasis added).
31. Francis, *Laudato Si'*, 21.
32. Francis, *Laudato Si'*, 128.

technocratic mind, because social costs are not part of a bottom line and are not a significant variable in "technocratic" economic analysis. Guardini shares Pope Francis's concern about the relationship between the technocratic paradigm and economic models accepted today, for he says that "By means of all those inventions and procedures which we call technics man came to dominate nature. Finally, technics were joined *indissolubly* to an economy of greed. Thus was begotten the many-faceted system of modern capitalism."[33] According to Guardini, the technocratic paradigm and an economy of greed are the ideological parents of the prevailing economic model of western society, and this union which he says is indissoluble is a union which Pope Francis hopes to annul.

The indissoluble union of greed and technics has deleterious consequences for the private sector, for unlimited profit is dependent on establishing and promoting mechanisms of unlimited consumption, requiring the creation of a "culture of consumerism" in which people are lead to believe that "they are free as long as they have the supposed freedom to consume."[34] If humanity can now create unlimited goods, then men must be taught how to consume unlimited goods, and so "the market tends to promote extreme consumerism in an effort to sell its products."[35] Pope Francis once again quotes Guardini to explain his position:

> The gadgets and technics forced upon him by the patterns of machine production and of abstract planning, mass man accepts quite simply; they are the forms of life itself. To either a greater or lesser degree mass man is convinced that his conformity is both reasonable and just.[36]

To "mass man," the gadgets and technics "are the forms of life itself," meaning that mass man learns to consider it reasonable to do anything to attain this life-by-material-possession. Unfortunately, this can only be an empty experience, for material goods can never actually be the form of "life itself" and are instead only a shallow imitation of that vitality and force of life which Guardini sees coursing through animate beings.

In these and other ways, it can be seen that the technocratic paradigm is a pervasive mentality, an entire logical structure which influences all that passes through one's rational faculty. It is a hermeneutical lens for interpreting all that is brought to the rational faculty, and thus Pope Francis calls it

---

33. Guardini, *End of the Modern World*, 75 (emphasis added).
34. Francis, *Laudato Si'*, 184, 203.
35. Francis, *Laudato Si'*, 203.
36. Guardini, quoted in Francis, *Laudato Si'*, 203.

"an *epistemological paradigm* which shapes the lives of individuals and the workings of society."[37] As Guardini already foresaw, this paradigm permeates an entirely new "structural order"; it has given rise to a new "cultural pattern" which has brought about "a new sociological type"; and from all this restructuring of relationship, it gives birth to a unique type of rationality which Guardini calls the "technocratic mind." Such a mind has its own logic, and in the following section, we seek to better illustrate the origins of this logic and the way in which it arises from one's relationship with technology.

TECHNOCRATIC LOGIC

In seeking to understand the technocratic paradigm, there is a particular hermeneutical challenge that has not been addressed, and it concerns the relationship between the use of technology and the presence of the technocratic paradigm. A precise articulation of this interaction between technology and the technocratic paradigm is not so simple, as the technocratic paradigm is used in no other social encyclical, appears in few other extraneous sources, and is, at times, interchangeable with just the word "technology." The precise theological language of someone like Pope Benedict is notably absent from the text of *Laudato Si'*, and although this does not mean it contains any less significance, it does mean that a sensitivity to stylistic differences between the two Popes is helpful for proper interpretation.[38] To properly understand Pope Francis, it is often more helpful to zoom out than to zoom in, and so we will zoom out and look at how the technocratic paradigm interacts with technology throughout the encyclical as a whole.[39]

When one looks at the whole framework of Pope Francis's encyclical, it becomes clear that his understanding of technology in human life stands in opposition to a more laissez-faire attitude to technology, for he makes numerous references to the idea that technology itself has a deleterious impact on human thinking and relationship. He states, "We have to accept that

37. Francis, *Laudato Si'*, 107.

38. It is helpful to recall that Jorge Bergoglio spent many years as a literature professor, whereas Joseph Ratzinger spent most of his life as a theology professor and academic theologian. Bergoglio's mind is a literary mind, one in which analogy and imagery takes precedence over technical linguistic precision, and this should inform how we read his works as Pope Francis.

39. In speaking about how to interpret Pope Francis, Pope-Emeritus Benedict XVI affirmed the need to "zoom out" and see the whole when he stated, "If one isolates things, takes them out of context, one can construct opposites, but not if one looks at the whole" (Benedict XVI, *Last Testament*, 34).

technological products are not neutral, for they create a framework which ends up conditioning lifestyles and shaping social possibilities along lines dictated by the interests of certain powerful groups."[40] The word choice is important here: "technological products," and not just the technocratic paradigm, are capable of conditioning lifestyles and shaping social possibilities, which means that they limit the human experience in a distinct and powerful way, and they do so by way of creating a "framework" which is structurally nested within the culture.

In perhaps some of the most evocative language in the encyclical, Pope Francis, quoting Guardini, states that technology "moves forward in the final analysis neither for profit nor for well-being of the human race" and that "in the most radical sense of the term, power is its motive—a lordship over all."[41] The claim is that technology itself, and not just the technocratic paradigm, is something that does not move forward for the profit or well-being of the human race. These are strong words which seem to be in opposition to previous statements by the church in which technological advances are seen as a "gift from God" and to be used for the spreading of the gospel.[42] But a more sober reading of the encyclical, and not a literal emphasis of single phrases, is needed, for elsewhere the Pope states that he is not advocating "a return to the Stone Age."[43] In reading these provocative words of Pope Francis, it is helpful to continually recall that he himself has a Twitter account and rides in a car and uses a cell phone. He is conducting a critique of technology, which is not to be confused as a contempt for technology. But having said this, there clearly is some relationship between the proliferation of technology and the proliferation of the technocratic paradigm, and although the dynamics of this interaction are not made explicit in the encyclical, we venture in the following section to propose one possible explanation.

The Logic of Reduction

In considering the relationship between the technocratic paradigm and technology itself, we must clarify what is meant by "technology" in the encyclical and in this paper. Guardini is helpful for such a task, for he provides several ideas which all contribute to greater clarity about this term.

---

40. Francis, *Laudato Si'*, 107.
41. Guardini, cited in Francis, *Laudato Si'*, 108.
42. Pontifical Council for Social Communications, *Communio et Progressio*, 2; see also Pius XII, *Miranda Prorsus*; Pontifical Council for Social Communications, *Ethics in Internet*.
43. Francis, *Laudato Si'*, 114.

In Guardini's comments above, we saw how technology was almost synonymous with machines, a term used to describe how rational abstraction has come to dominate the things produced by man. Elsewhere, Guardini defines technology as "the striking complex of knowledge, theory, skill, and mode of production summed up in the term 'technics's."[44] Here, he understands technology as a composite of various elements which all contribute to a specific task, and because such tasks are increasingly self-defined, he also defines technology as "a concentration of processes allowing man to posit ends in conformity with his own desires."[45] For Guardini, technology is a "complex" or a "concentration of processes" which all interact and allow man to achieve rationally determined ends with machine-like means.

In this thesis and in *Laudato Si'*, such a definition of technology is often employed, but there is another more specific definition used occasionally, and that is the definition of technology as a "technological product": things like cell phones, computers, email, and the internet all fall under this more specific definition, and we will refer to these things as "digital technology" whenever we intend to mean this more specific definition. Many of these technological products were not invented at the time of Guardini's writings, and yet they have become the most visible form of technology in modern culture and thus form an important subset within these comments on technology. Guardini himself would recognize such digital technology as just one more expression of that "concentration of processes" which allow man to attain certain ends with machine-like means, and such digital technology will be our main focus in this discussion on understanding how a technocratic paradigm can arise from one's use of technology.

We saw above that Guardini's problem with machines was that they habituate the user to a reductionism-by-mechanization, and when reflecting on the use of digital technology specifically, one can see how it, too, follows a certain reductionism-by-mechanization. The primary way that digital technology brings about this reductionism is due to its "inner logic" in which qualitative reality is transformed into quantitative information, a transformation which happens through binary code. This code is the inner language of digital technology, and it is a programming language that consists of a lengthy series of ones and zeroes which represent either the absence or the presence of an electron. As an example, one can consider the creation of a sound file: a digital recorder must reduce all of the qualitative features of that sound and store it as a quantifiable number that can then be transferred digitally to other instruments which then reinterpret these

---

44. Guardini, *End of the Modern World*, 55.
45. Guardini, *End of the Modern World*, 42.

numbers to recreate the original sound. The end result of such a process is a file that is purely digital, a file that has transferred complex qualitative reality into a simplified numerical reality. This simplification is comprehensive, for the original sound itself has become lost in the reduction and can never be replicated perfectly, although it can be imitated (and imitated with increasing accuracy as technology advances). What happens in an audio file happens in nearly every use of digital technology, and so this "logic of reduction" permeates every digital product. The digital landscape is one in which sound waves are reduced to digital files, where the human face is reduced into a digital image that is then transferred on a screen, where nuances of hand-writing are reduced to a strict and consistent form of digital letters, and where education by a human person is reduced into a digital video that can repeat the same way every time.

The problem with this logic of reduction is that our experience of reality is not quantitative but qualitative. Feser explains,

> Our ordinary experience of nature is of course *qualitative* through and through. We perceive colors, sounds, flavors, odors, warmth and coolness, pains and itches, thoughts and choices, purposes and meanings. Physics abstracts from these rich concrete details, ignoring whatever cannot be expressed in terms of equations and the like and thereby radically simplifying the natural order.[46]

What physics has always done, digital technology continues to do, for both physics and its technological derivatives in the modern world are possessed of a logic which "radically simplifies the natural order" by way of abstracting out "rich concrete details" that are impossible to include in equations. For example, in calculating the velocity of an airplane, an equation only considers the mass, wind speed, and other such factors, and so the "airplane" is actually reduced to only numerical abstractions. There are many details that do not directly impact the equation (such as what the people on the plane want to eat, their names and occupation, etc.) and because these concrete details cannot correspond to an exact numerical equivalent, they are removed from the equation. Of course, such simplification by way of abstraction is essential for certain purposes in physics, for calculating the velocity of a plane is not greatly impacted by the color of the plane.[47] But

---

46. Feser, *Scholastic Metaphysics*, 13 (emphasis original).

47. However, even this statement is an abstraction because certain colors absorb more light, causing miniscule changes in surface temperature, which would also then impact its velocity moving through the air. It should always be remembered that the fundamental theorems of modern physics are not equations but *probabilities*. The

there is a danger in forgetting that an abstraction has been done, and just such an abstraction is inherent within the logic of all technological derivatives spawned from exclusively quantitative analysis.

When compressing a single audio file, not much is lost in the world, but as more and more reality passes through the digital medium, more and more reality suffers from this logic of reduction. If the consumption of digital content were to grow to significant levels, it is conceivable that virtual reality would eventually become confused with actual reality, embedding the digital users in a virtual world that has reduced many layers of nuance that are now long forgotten and imperceptible to the technocratic mind. Only hearing Beethoven's *Ode to Joy* at an orchestra is sufficient evidence to demonstrate what is lacking in a high-fidelity digital recording, and as digital fidelity increasingly matches reality, the distinction between the two becomes more and more difficult to detect. As quantitative reality increasingly approximates qualitative reality, there is a diminished sense that something has been lost in the transfer. Swimming in a world of technological gadgets that are all inherently reductionist, the human mind can soon forget that qualitative features *do* exist, and by reducing qualities to quantities, technology can obscure one's encounter with reality itself. Thus, in our saturated use of digital technology, there will naturally arise the symptoms of the technocratic paradigm, which has been defined above as a blindness to the inner realities of reality itself.

What has been explained above is the hypothesis of the author of this paper, and so it needs to be understood as such. However, there is implicit agreement with the conclusions of this argument in recent social encyclicals. For example, Pope Francis thinks that this modern gluttony of digital consumption is causing a transformation that is problematic for the human person and for human development. He thinks humanity has passed some threshold of technological conditioning, regretting that "it has become countercultural to choose a lifestyle whose goals are even partly independent of technology" and that for many, "life becomes a surrender to situations conditioned by technology."[48] In man's surrender to the conditioning effect of technology, Pope Francis is calling attention to the deleterious impact of an over-exposure to technology in human existence and human relationship. Pope Benedict XVI shares this same concern in other sources outside the Magisterial documents, noting in a homily in 2011 that "virtuality risks predominating over reality. Unbeknownst to them, people are increasingly becoming immersed in a virtual dimension because of the

---

fundamental basis of modern physics is not certainty; it is estimation.

48. Francis, *Laudato Si'*, 110.

audiovisual messages that accompany their life from morning to night."[49] He, too, shows a deep concern about the virtual dimension dominating reality itself, and in this same homily, he goes on to wonder if today we are seeing an "anthropological mutation" in humanity because of this excessive saturation of the virtual medium.[50]

These concerns of both Pope Benedict and Pope Francis regarding the negative impacts of the digital medium stand in direct contrast to the supposed "neutrality" of technology that is found in earlier church documents on technology and social communication. For example, the Pontifical Council for Social Communications states "the media do nothing by themselves; they are instruments, tools, used as people choose to use them."[51] Furthermore, they also state that whether or not the internet leads to good or harm is "largely a matter of choice" and that the main question is only "Are the media being used for good or evil?"[52] All these comments neglect consideration of whether or not the medium itself is harmful, and as we grow in our understanding of the negative impact of a technocratic paradigm, it becomes more and more difficult to argue that technology as a medium is always morally neutral; instead, it is becoming more common for the Magisterium to suggest that use of the medium itself, consumed at elevated levels, is not a neutral experience but rather diminishes our humanity into something that Guardini calls a "non-human humanity."

Part of the genius of Guardini is that he long ago identified this logic of reduction inherent within machines and lamented so much loss that is now only accelerated in the modern digital world. He foresaw how the world of natural humanity is crippled under the compressive load of so many invisible recalibrations of the human experience, and this compressive load has had an impact on every facet of the human experience, for what facet of human life is not permeated by machines and technology? The central thesis of Guardini is that every use of modern machines and technology only furthers the destruction of natural humanity, as the logic of reduction becomes inescapable in each use and confines the human experience to an inherent

---

49. Benedict XVI, "Homily of His Holiness Benedict XVI," para. 6.

50. "The youngest . . . seem to want to fill every empty moment with music and images, out of fear of feeling this very emptiness. This is a trend that has always existed, especially among the young and in the more developed urban contexts but today it has reached a level such as to give rise to talk about *anthropological mutation*. Some people are no longer able to remain for long periods in silence and solitude" (Benedict XVI, "Homily of His Holiness Benedict XVI," para. 7).

51. Pontifical Council for Social Communications, *Ethics in Communications*, para. 4.

52. Pontifical Council for Social Communications, *Ethics in Internet*, 2.

divorce from natural reality and replaces it instead with a mechanized or technocratic reality.[53] Because this logic is inherent within technology and can never be separated from our use of it, attention to its formative capacity on the human mind is essential for properly understanding the ethical dimensions of technology itself and will be a subject to which we return several more times in this chapter.

Technology as an Ideology

Pope Benedict once expressed a concern that "the process of globalization could replace ideologies with technology," and we are now in a position to better understand the extent to which that may be taking place in Western culture.[54] To analyze this comment properly, we must first articulate what is meant by an "ideology," and we take our definition from Luigi Giussani:

> Ideology is a theoretical-practical construction developed from a preconception. More precisely, it is a theoretical-practical construction based upon an aspect of reality—even a true aspect—which is formulated for the aims of a philosophy or political project, is taken unilaterally and made, in principle, into an absolute.[55]

According to Giussani, an ideology takes an aspect of reality and exalts it as the whole of reality. For example, the ideology of mechanism accurately recognizes that physical objects are mechanistically determined by outside forces, such as gravity exerting a specific force on the human body, and this true observation becomes an ideology as soon as someone exalts it as the absolute truth of all reality. In doing so, the ideology of mechanism would then rigorously uphold a preconceived idea that *every* physical object, in *all* of its interactions, is *completely* determined by *only* physical forces and would reject, *a priori*, any idea that contradicts this preconceived idea, as does indeed happen in the ideologies of some strict mechanists.

This rigid restructuring of all of reality, based only on a partial aspect of reality, allows Giussani to compare ideology with a sort of nearsightedness: it creates a situation in which the ideologue

> acts as if he were nearsighted, and within a centimeter of a painting, he fixes his gaze upon a certain point, exclaiming: 'What a

---

53. Besides the citations above in *Letters from Lake Como*, see also Guardini, *End of the Modern World*, 69–70.
54. Benedict XVI, *Caritas in Veritate*, 72 (emphasis added).
55. Giussani, *Religious Sense*, 95.

spot here!" And because the painting is rather large, this person could go over the whole thing, centimeter by centimeter, exclaiming at every point, 'What a spot here!' The painting would appear as a senseless collection of spots.[56]

This analogy of myopia illustrates how ideology is not so much about inherent lies as it is about proposing incomplete truths. Ideology is not a failure to see; it is a failure to see fully. Where it should see a whole painting in all its complexity, an ideology sees only the fragmented parts that make up the whole. As Giussani's analogy makes clear, seeing only fragments of the whole is to miss the whole completely.

With this definition of ideology, Pope Benedict's comparison of technology to ideology is fitting, for technology manifests an inner logic of reductionism, a compression of complex qualitative features into simplistic quantitative numbers. This reduction happens in the use of all digital technological products and is inherent within the virtual medium itself, and as human existence has grown increasingly nested within this virtual, technological domain, Pope Francis sees a simultaneous proliferation of the technocratic paradigm which functions as an *a priori* limitation on the mind and "conditions lifestyles" and "shapes social possibilities."[57] Thus, Pope Francis is arguing that the use of digital technology does contribute in a real way to the proliferation of the technocratic paradigm, and that technology in all its forms is increasingly functioning like a restrictive ideology.

Although Pope Francis's comments notably contrast with more laissez-faire approaches to technology found in other documents of church teaching, it is not a line of thought that is new to the church, for as early as 1971, Pope Paul VI spoke about the danger of "universalized technology as the dominant form of activity, as the overwhelming pattern of existence, even as a language, without the question of its meaning being really asked."[58] Here, universalized technology is not seen as a neutral good but instead a pattern that "overwhelms" human existence and prevents it from being able to encounter reality itself. Pope Paul VI is warning that technology could one day become a new ideology, and as such, a new tyranny.

It was Pope Benedict XVI who picked up this comment from Paul VI and developed it further when he explained that technology could replace ideologies. In order to better understand what Pope Benedict meant, it will be helpful to return to the full context of his comment:

---

56. Giussani, *Religious Sense*, 124.
57. Francis, *Laudato Si'*, 107.
58. Paul VI, *Octogesima Adveniens*, 29.

the process of globalization could replace ideologies with technology, allowing the latter to become an ideological power that threatens to confine us within an *a priori* that holds us back from encountering being and truth. Were that to happen, we would all know, evaluate and make decisions about our life situations from within *a technocratic cultural perspective* to which we would belong *structurally*, without ever being able to discover a meaning that is not of our own making.[59]

Pope Benedict is essentially coalescing the thought of Guardini and Pope Paul VI, exhibiting caution about the potential for technology to become an ideological power that "holds us back from encountering being and truth." He shares the same concern of Guardini and Pope Paul VI that people would be nested in this "technocratic cultural perspective" structurally, and because it limits and "confines" our experience of reality, it would rightly be considered a new form of ideology.

Though we can see many parallels between Pope Francis, Pope Benedict XVI, and Pope Paul VI, there does remain a striking difference between the language of the three popes, and it is a difference that goes much deeper than stylistic emphasis. Whereas Pope Benedict XVI and Pope Paul VI *wondered* if this technocratic mindset could become an ideological power, Pope Francis emphatically *insists* that it has permeated the social fabric to an alarming degree. Not only do we belong to this power structurally, but it also is becoming increasingly difficult to escape, for it "dominates" and "overwhelms" nearly every aspect of life.[60] Furthermore, there is a marked difference in length of argumentation, for Pope Paul VI wrote one sentence about this possibility of technology becoming a new tyrannical ideology, and Pope Benedict XVI writes a few paragraphs in *Caritas in Veritate* on this topic, but in *Laudato Si'*, nearly an entire chapter (chapter 3) is dedicated to explaining how this tyrannical ideology has taken root within society. This elaboration should not be considered simply an extraneous commentary of an already exhausted topic but instead should be understood as a significant and consequential development in Catholic Social Teaching, for it is an argument about the moral dynamics involved in the use of the digital medium itself, independent of how a person chooses to use it. This development stands in contradistinction to more laissez-faire statements about the use of technology, such as "the media do nothing by themselves; they are instruments, tools, used as people choose to use them," and this

---

59. Benedict XVI, *Caritas in Veritate*, 72 (emphasis added).

60. The words "dominate" and "overwhelm" often appear alongside references to the technocratic paradigm, especially in paragraphs 108–9.

development makes such statements increasingly disharmonious with the developed Magisterium.[61] Even Pope Benedict said "it seems quite absurd to maintain that (the means of social communication) are neutral—and hence unaffected by any moral considerations concerning people," illustrating how Pope Francis is not the only Pope to challenge the language of a supposed moral neutrality. No development of doctrine should ever be taken lightly, and so it is fitting to ask if there is any empirical evidence to support the argument sustained by Pope Francis, implicit within Guardini, and familiar to Pope Benedict which argues against the moral neutrality of technology. As it turns out, one does not need to look far to find significant evidence.

In the domain of scientific and empirical research, there is a growing body of knowledge demonstrating how a hyper-saturation of the digital medium is having a negative impact on users, particularly in their experience of relationship. Some of the most convincing evidence comes from Sherry Turkle, a distinguished professor of psychology at the Massachussets Institute for Technology (MIT) and one of the leading researchers on the role of technology and its impact on relationship with others. Her research indicates that our use of technology is not just changing what we can do; it is changing *who we are*, noting that "We make our technologies, and they, in turn, shape us."[62] Crucial to her research, however, is not just the fact that technology shapes us; what her research shows most clearly is that technology (most specifically, digital technology) shapes us in a *negative* way. She observes the compressive and reductionist nature of the digital medium in a way similar to what is found in Pope Francis and Guardini, for on social networks, "people are *flattened* into personae . . . and *reduced* to their profiles." She calls all of this "flattening" and "reducing" the "new language of abbreviation"[63], and her years of research point to the varied ways that an over-saturation in this medium reshapes the person into a more isolated self which sees all of reality, including other people, in a limited and reduced way.[64] All of her key points demonstrate how life in the digital world impacts our experience of the real world, and the net impact of a compressive virtual environment is to experience a compressed natural environment.[65] Furthermore, her work continues to be corroborated by the work of other

---

61. Pontifical Council for Social Communications, *Ethics in Communications*, para. 4.

62. Turkle, *Alone Together*, 19.

63. This "language of abbreviation" at least mimics the dominant language which Pope Paul VI foresaw.

64. Turkle, *Alone Together*, 18 (emphasis added).

65. Turkle, *Alone Together*, 223.

researchers in several other domains.⁶⁶ Thus, there is substantial evidence in the fields of psychology, biology, and neuro-cognitive science that supports the idea that using technology is not a morally-neutral experience because of its reductionist impact on our experience of reality which can lead to isolation, alienation, and a reconditioning of human relationships.

It should be noted, however, that Turkle's research does not show that technology "causes" social fragmentation. She says, "It is people who are disappointing each other. Technology merely enables us to create a mythology in which this does not matter."⁶⁷ Her point is that social fragmentation by way of diffused technology still contains a very real human element, and so the social fabric is not rigidly determined merely by the technology itself; however, it is true that over-saturation in this medium does have real social costs. As humanity grows increasingly immersed in virtual reality, we become "accustomed to the reductions and betrayals" that occur in the environment and eventually grow attracted to these simpler, more controlled relationships that a digital medium can provide.⁶⁸ While there still remains a very human element behind the use of technology, excessive immersion in the digital medium does bring about negative consequences for relationship with others and contributes to the growth of shallow connections and an erosion in authentic human relationship.

There is one other domain in which evidence supports the assertion that the use of technology is not a morally-neutral phenomenon, and we find this in the domain of praxis. For example, in 2009, Pope Benedict and some Italian bishops encouraged people to consider giving up texting and other forms of digital technology for Lent. Pope Benedict later explained why: "If the desire for virtual connectedness becomes obsessive, it may in fact function to isolate individuals from real social interaction while also disrupting the patterns of rest, silence and reflection that are necessary for healthy human development."⁶⁹ This praxis of giving up digital technology makes an important statement: over-saturation of this medium is bad for the human person, for it leads to patterns of "isolation" and diminished human development which can prevent one from discovering the metaphysical depths of their surroundings.

Something unique is happening here, for while some documents of the church speak of technology as a morally-neutral tool, the church is also

---

66. See the research compiled by Nicholas Carr in *The Shallows: What the Internet is Doing to Our Brains* (2011) and *The Glass Cage: How Our Computers are Changing Us* (2015).

67. Turkle, *Alone Together*, 237.

68. Turkle, *Alone Together*, 285.

69. Benedict XVI, "New Technologies, New Relationships," para. 7.

inviting her members to refrain from using these digital tools precisely because of their inner-logic of reduction which can be isolating and unhealthy, which is to say that their excessive use is immoral. The church has never asked people to give up writing letters for Lent, but she has asked people to give up texting for Lent, and this praxis is informative to our consideration of how the medium of digital texting differs from the more organic medium of hand-writing.

Many others in the secular world have initiated a similar praxis and reduced their use of technology. For example, CEOs and other tech-savvy users sometimes participate in a "media fast" in which they give up their phones for several days.[70] The reason people say they are doing this is because these devices and the constant presence of the internet are a "hindrance to life," which resonates with Pope Francis's assertion that so much information and media acts as a sort of "mental pollution."[71] Even for those with no direct connection to Catholic Social Teaching, it is becoming important to establish some separation from their use of digital technology, and they are doing so because they are experiencing the negative impact of the medium itself. The hyper-saturation of digital technology is changing people, and many people do not like the person it is making them become, and some people are seeking a way to escape. It is almost as if they are trying to flee from a tyrant who is literally inhibiting their life; it is almost as if technology itself has become a global tyrant.[72]

From all that has been said above, it is now evident that Pope Francis's assertion that technology is "conditioning lifestyles" and "shaping social possibilities" is not grounded in pontifical naïveté but instead is an insightful description of contemporary culture. Various cultural markers converge with Pope Francis's assertion that it is becoming increasingly difficult to escape the "dominating" and "overwhelming" influence of technology in our lives, and thus it is cogent to assert that technology is already, in some sense, replacing the tyrannies of previous centuries with a tyranny of its own. Where traditional tyrannies restrict reality to their own ideology, digital technology reinterprets reality with its own logic of reduction and "language of abbreviation." Where traditional tyrannies impose large financial burdens on the people and create disastrous social fracturing, digital technology comes at an exorbitant financial cost and is contributing to deterioration of the social environment. Where traditional tyrannies make it

---

70. Richtel, "Your Brain on Computers."

71. Turkle, *Reclaiming Conversation*, 116; Francis, *Laudato Si'*, 47.

72. Turkle seems to agree, for she calls global technology a "regime" (*Alone Together*, 155).

nearly impossible for anyone under their domain to escape their grip, digital technology is so nested within the culture that escaping it is nearly impossible. The escalating presence of digital technology and its translation of so much actual reality into virtual reality is an emerging presence of tyranny in Western culture, and it remains to be seen how much this tyrant will spread and what can be done to resist it.

BEYOND TECHNOLOGY

It was articulated above that the fundamental characteristic of the technocratic paradigm is a blindness to the inner reality of things, and we turn now to three authors (Guardini, Francis, and Turkle) who all converge on a similar way to reform a mind which is under the dominion of such a paradigm.

In explaining how to overcome the technocratic cult and the rise of machines, Guardini's solution is the following:

> We must try to rediscover something of what is called the contemplative attitude, actually experience it ourselves, not just talk about it interestingly. All around, we see activity, organization, operations of every possible type; but what directs them? An inwardness no longer really at home within itself; which thinks, judges, acts from the surface, guided by mere intellect, utility, and the impulses of power, property, and pleasure . . . Before all else, then, man's depths must be reawakened.[73]

Guardini's vision here is one in which the inner qualities of reality would be more deeply encountered, enjoyed, appreciated, and developed, a vision which will come about only by recovering a "contemplative attitude" which has a deeper engagement with the intrinsic value of all external objects. Though the technocratic paradigm systematically reduces all of reality, this contemplative attitude would cause a reexpansion of the fullness of reality, giving one the adequate time, space, and perspective to see things as they are in their essence and not merely as dictated by the logic of the machine. It would allow one to see the same things but in a fuller and truer way, which would be akin to seeing them for the first time. It would be, as Guardini calls it, a "reawakening."

There are two primary ways one would bring about this reawakening of unseen and forgotten depths. First, it requires man to return to meditation and prayer, though Guardini states that this prayer need not acquire the patterns or words of Judeo-Christian prayer to resist effectively the assault

---

73. Guardini, *End of the Modern World*, 214 (emphasis added).

of the technocratic paradigm. The central feature of this meditation and prayer is that it must allow one to "step aside from the general hustle and bustle," that it must allow one to become tranquil and really present, "opening (wide) his mind and heart to some word of piety or Wisdom or ethical humor, whether he takes it from Scripture or Plato, from Goethe or Jeremias Gotthelf."[74] There are many creeds that offer this type of contemplative assistance for the internally-blind citizens of the modern world, and Guardini does not articulate a particular preference of one over another. There really seems to be only one requirement: that the subject open up his mind to some truth that lies beyond his technocratically-enclosed self.

The second way to bring about this reawakening is to foster a renewed asceticism, "for how can men control the growing monstrousness of power when they cannot even control their own appetites?"[75] Self-control (the defining feature of all true asceticism) is thus a pre-requisite for external control, and integrating this asceticism into modern living will help foster within contemporary man an adequate response-ability that is needed to successfully control the vast power now in his hands. This asceticism would have many dimensions beyond just controlling an appetite for food, for the truly modern ascetic envisioned by Guardini is someone who "must fight for inner health and freedom—against the machinations of advertising, the flood of loud sensationalism, against noise in all its forms. He must acquire a certain distance from things; must train himself to think independently, to resist what 'they' say."[76] This is the profile of a modern ascetic: one who is removed from the pulsating flood of digital messages, who possesses a reflex-aversion to the pomp and garish novelty of a world of professional marketing that is "indissolubly" united to greed, and who fosters a deep love for the stillness and peace that will always be incompatible with restless "noise in all its forms." These are the inner appetites that the modern man must learn to govern, and in so doing, he will then be able to govern the more remote and external powers that have been placed in his hands by way of modern technology.

As should be expected at this point, there is a strong correlation between these insights of Romano Guardini and Pope Francis's own proposals in *Laudato Si'*. When articulating what might be done, Pope Francis states that we need to "slow down and look at reality in a different way," to "recover the values and the great goals swept away by our unrestrained delusions

---

74. Guardini, *End of the Modern World*, 215.
75. Guardini, *End of the Modern World*, 216.
76. Guardini, *End of the Modern World*, 217.

of grandeur."[77] This is simply more pastoral language to express Guardini's desire for the recovery of a contemplative attitude in man, one which would allow man to "pause" and "recover depth" amidst so much reductionism.[78] The goal of this contemplation is the same for Francis as for Guardini, which is a renewed vision of the fullness of reality, noting that "the time has come to pay renewed attention to reality and the limits it imposes."[79] It is the reductionism of reality which is the problem, so only a fuller penetration of reality is a proper solution. By building "the human capacity for contemplation and reverence," man is given the space he needs to see things as they truly are and not just as formless matter that can be used for any purpose.[80]

But Pope Francis also recognizes that a renewed attention to reality is often impaired by the modern fury of "constant noise, interminable and nerve-wracking distractions, (and) the cult of appearances."[81] So we should not be surprised to find that, just like Guardini, he too proposes the ascetic life as a path moving forward: "We need to take up an ancient lesson, found in different religious traditions and also in the Bible. It is the conviction that 'less is more.'"[82] There are two important features about this quote. First, Pope Francis follows Guardini in emphasizing the ecumenical possibility of recovering from the tyranny of technology, noting that this basic ascetic principle is found in many sources outside the Christian tradition, and so it can be a key point of contact with other religions. Second, he reveals the conviction that this ascetic lifestyle does not diminish the good a person experiences but is about giving them "more," noting that "it is not a lesser life or one lived with less intensity. On the contrary, it is a way of living life to the full."[83] The ascetic can enjoy a better and fuller life because

> those who enjoy more and live better each moment are those who have given up dipping here and there, always on the lookout for what they do not have. They experience what it means to appreciate each person and each thing, learning familiarity with the simplest things and how to enjoy them . . . Even living on little, they can live a lot.[84]

77. Francis, *Laudato Si'*, 114.
78. Francis, *Laudato Si'*, 113.
79. Francis, *Laudato Si'*, 116.
80. Francis, *Laudato Si'*, 127.
81. Francis, *Laudato Si'*, 225.
82. Francis, *Laudato Si'*, 222.
83. Francis, *Laudato Si'*, 223.
84. Francis, *Laudato Si'*, 223.

The argument presented here, and in various other religious traditions, is that less attention to superficial goods is vital to gaining renewed appreciation for the intrinsic fullness of each material good already possessed. The problem with modern man is not a lack of possessions; his problem is an inability to appreciate and enjoy his possessions rightly, and regaining an ascetic discipline towards superfluity is a powerful corrective to this distorted logic.

However, the goal of all this contemplation and asceticism is not only about seeing our material possessions rightly but, perhaps most importantly, it is also about more properly understanding our relationships with one another. Pope Francis laments modern man's inability to see the fullness of reality, and he thinks that the reality that we neglect most often is that of the human person. Through growth in the contemplative life and regaining an ascetic control of basic appetites, one is allowed to approach life with "serene attentiveness," which then allows one to be "fully present to someone without thinking of what comes next."[85] Pope Francis cites the example of Jesus himself who "was completely present to everyone and to everything, and in this way he showed us the way to overcome that unhealthy anxiety which makes us superficial, aggressive, and compulsive consumers."[86] Rewiring minds in such a way that they resist the assault of the technocratic paradigm is ultimately about so much more than renewing one's appreciation of material things; it is also concerned with renewing one's appreciation of human relationships. This is why Pope Francis says that "we cannot presume to heal our relationship with nature and the environment without healing all fundamental human relationships."[87] The technocratic paradigm is ultimately an assault on the category of relation, so it is fitting that resistance to this assault would help bring about a restoration of human relationship.

The third and final contribution to a solution for rewiring technocratic minds comes from Sherry Turkle, who recognizes that many people today are living "moments of more but lives of less," that we see time "as a resource to exploit," that we have become accustomed to "a life of constant interruption" that has created people who are "rushed, impatient, not interested in process, unable to be alone with their thoughts."[88] Though she may have never read *Laudato Si'*, she is observing all of the traditional symptoms of a culture swimming in the technocratic paradigm, and though she does not

---

85. Francis, *Laudato Si'*, 226.
86. Francis, *Laudato Si'*, 226.
87. Francis, *Laudato Si'*, 119.
88. Turkle, *Reclaiming Conversation*, 35, 66, 76.

give it the same name, she does suggest the same solution: fostering a contemplative attitude towards reality, and also a bit of asceticism.

In the midst of all this manic desire for more, she proposes a return to what she calls "solitude," which is quite distinct from "being alone." According to Turkle, solitude is a time for internal dialogue with one's self, a time to "be contentedly and constructively alone," a time to "construct a stable sense of self" and "understand ourselves better."[89] She asserts that it is only by way of this sort of internal dialogue with the self that a convincing encounter with the inner courses of reality can first begin to blossom. In solitude, the self is revealed to be something which is much more complex and more expansive than what the reductive load of a technocratic culture is capable of describing, and this expanded reality has far-reaching consequences, most especially for our relations with others.[90] Turkle thinks that failure to develop this internal dialogue will erode all other relationships, for "you end up isolated if you don't cultivate the capacity for solitude, the ability to be separate, to gather yourself . . . If we're not able to be alone, we're going to be more lonely."[91] Turkle's conception of solitude, therefore, does not consist in "being alone," but is rather a development of an inner sensitivity to the deeper realities of life, starting with one's self. It is about developing what Guardini and Pope Francis called "the contemplative attitude" towards all reality. It is about restoring an inner vision of the complexities and fullness of things that have too long been misunderstood as thin, flat, and uniform.

For Turkle, the revival of the technocratic mind is also predicated on cultivating a sense of digital asceticism. She thinks that the deprecating over-exposure to technology is inhibiting healthy emotional, physical, and psychological development, and only a reduced exposure to such a medium can bring about a healthy balance in one's ability to reflect and stay recollected. Her reason for proposing such digital asceticism is similar to Pope Francis: because it makes people happier. She cites the many people who are already embracing a digital asceticism by way of various media fasts, but going on a media fast is not about giving something up; it is about restoring life. This modern asceticism, as Pope Francis said, is about a desire to "live life to the full," and somehow, without conducting any research or theological studies on the topic, many people are sensing that their over-consumption of digital technology is inhibiting this quest to "live life to the full" and are already seeking a way out. They are doing so by way of some digital asceticism.

---

89. Turkle, *Reclaiming Conversation*, 61, 65, 79.
90. Turkle, *Reclaiming Conversation*, 61.
91. Turkle, "Connected, but Alone?" 14:21–15:18.

We shall make one final comment about the parallels between all three of these thinkers, and it is that all of them uphold the great value of technology and argue that it has an indispensable role in the development of modern culture. Guardini says that

> We need not less technology but more. Or more accurately, we need stronger, more considered, more human technology. We need more science, but it must be more intellectual and designed; we need more economic and political energy, but it must be more mature and responsible, able to see the details in the whole contexts to which it belongs.[92]

He is arguing here not for an elimination of technology; rather, he wants those who use it to be capable of wielding its vast power, for only truly human users can ensure that technology gets used in a truly human way.[93] Pope Francis, per usual, takes up a similar line of argumentation, explaining that "We can put technology at the service of another type of progress, one which is healthier, more human, more social, more integral."[94] He, too, envisions a more human user as the key element in the development of the emerging technocratic reality. Similarly, Turkle is clear that her argument "is not anti-technology" but rather "pro-conversation."[95] She recognizes that there is a benefit to technology, but she also asserts what digital ideologues often fail to see, which is that that these benefits also come at a cost, for "technology helps us manage life stresses but generates anxieties of its own."[96] The use of technology for the sake of managing life stresses creates, ironically, its very own set of stresses which somehow need to be managed.

This leads us to the following point: technology itself cannot be a remedy for problems caused by the use of technology, and so a solution to these problems must be found in something beyond technology. If the way forward is through a "more human" technology, and if the standard product of the current technocratic culture is a "non-human humanity,"

---

92. Guardini, *Letters from Lake Como*, 83.

93. This should not be considered a contradiction of Guardini's previous arguments that technology itself is destructive of natural humanity. He explains his reasoning as follows: "We must not oppose what is new and try to preserve a beautiful world that is inevitably perishing. Nor should we try to build a new world of the creative imagination that will show none of the damage of what is actually evolving. Rather, we must transform what is coming to be. But we can do this only if we honestly say yes to it and yet with incorruptible hearts remain aware of all that is destructive and nonhuman in it" (Guardini, *Letters from Lake Como*, 80–81).

94. Francis, *Laudato Si'*, 102.

95. Turkle, *Reclaiming Conversation*, 25.

96. Turkle, *Alone Together*, 243.

CHAPTER 3: THE TECHNOCRATIC MIND 107

then something from beyond this non-human culture must reintroduce this human element. So implicit within the development of these "more human" users is the need for some degree of separation from technology itself, for the fullness of humanity is diminished when immersed in excessive technology. In so far as authentic human development is predicated on being immersed in reality, there will never be "more human" users of technology without some degree of technological asceticism. Technology will always be limited in its ability to form humans, for technology will always be limited in communicating Reality.[97] This is the deeper reason why all three of these thinkers are arguing, not for a reduction of technology, but rather an increase in humanity; what is required is a human user who is more deeply in tune with the metaphysical worth of reality and who exhibits an ascetic disposition towards the impulses that are triggered by so much digital interaction and "noise." Only such an integrated and developed humanity can successfully wield the modern tools of technology and solve problems created by their use.

So it is seen that the observations of a twentieth-century German theologian, a modern Pope, and an American psychologist all converge on similar conclusions about the technocratic paradigm. In exchange for a frantic hurriedness, they propose a slowed down pace of contemplation and reflection. In exchange for the ceaseless pursuit of more material and technological goods, they propose an asceticism of tempered renunciation. In exchange for a reduction of reality to some rational calculation, they propose a contemplative beholding which seeks to regain a vision of the deeper truths of external objects and to receive their deeper meaning. Their response to the technocratic paradigm is not concerned with what we should actively do; it is concerned with allowing the world to do something new to us, which is to communicate to us about the true essence of things.

It is quite fitting, then, that their solution is thoroughly non-technocratic, for even by asking the question, "What can one *do* about the technocratic paradigm?," one is already betraying deference to a technocratic solution. The technocratic paradigm is so entrenched in the culture that it is already conditioning one's response by way of conditioning the question.[98]

---

97. This is actually a dogmatic point, for there can be no Sacraments on the internet because the digital medium cannot transmit the fullness of Reality: "Virtual reality is no substitute for the Real Presence of Christ in the Eucharist, the sacramental reality of the other sacraments, and shared worship in a flesh-and-blood human community. There are no sacraments on the Internet; and even the religious experiences possible there by the grace of God are insufficient apart from real-world interaction with other persons of faith" (Pontifical Council for Social Communications, *Church and Internet*, 9).

98. If one is not careful, the technocratic paradigm will itself dominate our response to the paradigm, which is why Pope Francis warns "the best ecological initiatives can find themselves caught up in the same globalized logic" (Francis, *Laudato Si'*, 111).

In reversing the question, what these thinkers actually propose is a real lack of formal activity and instead encourage a return to solitude and contemplation. Perhaps a better question would be: what can anyone *not* do about it?

We close this section with the following words of Dietrich von Hildebrand, someone of whom Pope Benedict wrote, "I am personally convinced that (when) the intellectual history of the Catholic Church in the twentieth century is written, the name of Dietrich von Hildebrand will be most prominent among the figures of our time."[99] His piercing insights into many moral, political, and theological debates of the twentieth century give good reason to expect he may have something valuable to contribute to the discussion of the technocratic paradigm, and given his own experience in resisting National Socialism, he has also proven to be a reliable source for fighting tyranny in all its forms. Thus, we turn to his words which provide an excellent recapitulation of much that was written above:

> The predominance of the artificial in the epoch which was influenced by the liberalism of the Enlightenment; the triumphal march of technology during much of the nineteenth century and the beginning of the twentieth; the overgrowth of action when compared to contemplation; the primacy of a person's achievements over his being as person; the relegating of all of modern life to the periphery of existence—modern life, with its haste and its hurry, its inner impatience which no longer leaves any time for an event to develop from within; in a word, its so called "Americanism"—all this has devalued the person, who is viewed as the origin of everything that is non-organic and artificial. But the real path out of the dead-end street of the artificial back to the organic does not pass via the cult of the vital. It passes via the rediscovery of the real essence of the spiritual person and what constitutes his true center of gravity.[100]

In one short paragraph, he has interwoven the technocratic paradigm with the modern project, with the need to go "back to the organic," with the closed self, and with the diffusion of technology. But not only has he identified the problem; he also identifies the solution. Only a recovery of our inner vision by means of a "rediscovery of the real essence of the spiritual person" is sufficient to overcome the technocratic illness within Western culture. By fostering a contemplative attitude, which is continually opening oneself to a habitual receptivity to the inner courses of reality, can one escape the "dead-end street of the artificial" and arrive at a proper view

---

99. Ratzinger, "Foreword," 9.
100. Hildebrand, *My Battle against Hitler*, 312.

of things. If we look for solutions to the technocratic paradigm by way of activity, we pay homage to the "cult of the vital" and undermine the entire quest for inner freedom. In the end, there really is not much to *do*; there is only a need to *see*.

RATIO IN RELATIONE WITHIN THE TECHNOCRATIC MIND

Having surveyed a few illuminating thinkers on the subject of technology, we can now articulate how this chapter supports and strengthens this thesis. It is Pope Francis himself who, in several places in *Laudato Si'*, speaks about the logic inherent within technology which is then absorbed by the users of technology. For example, he says that "technology tends to absorb everything into its ironclad *logic*" and that "the technological paradigm has become so dominant that it would be difficult to do without its resources and even more difficult to utilize them without being dominated by their internal *logic*."[101] Similarly, he says that we need to work to "generate resistance to the assault of the technocratic paradigm. Otherwise, even the best ecological initiatives can find themselves caught up in the same globalized *logic*."[102] For Pope Francis, the "technocratic paradigm" is interchangeable with "technocratic logic," and this is fitting because a paradigm itself is a logical structure which conditions all that is interpreted by this paradigm.[103]

The previous sections of this chapter describe the ways in which such a techno-logical structure functions, how it conditions the human experience, and only indirectly have we illustrated its origins. Now, we must articulate more fully what lies within these references and show the way in which this specific paradigm or logic is developed according to the relational dimension of the human person.

First and foremost, this technocratic logic is not derived exclusively from the autonomous mind of a thinking person; rather, it is received by being in relationship to specific techno-logical realities which then impose their logic on the user. Guardini insists on this point, stating that

> The rise of technology is creating a radically different sociological type and attitude. The new man finds the ideal of the self-made and creative personality inimical; he refuses to grant that the autonomous subject is the measure of human perfection.

101. Francis, *Laudato Si'*, 108 (emphasis added).
102. Francis, *Laudato Si'*, 111 (emphasis added).
103. The word "paradigm" will be defined more explicitly in the fourth chapter of this thesis.

> Sharpest evidence for the denial of the older idea of personality comes with that human type—who stands at the extreme pole from the autonomous—the Mass Man. When used in this connection the term does not connote a man who is worthless; it simply designates the man who is absorbed by technology and rational abstraction. This new human type strikes us unfavorably at first because it has entered history with no tradition of its own; in fact, it must assert itself against those traditions which until now have carried the day.[104]

In comments preceding this paragraph, Guardini shows how the "autonomous subject" is the ideal of man formed by that intellectual tradition called "modernity." This autonomous subject must strive to become a "self-made" and "creative" personality which, as all these words imply, is a purely autonomous and self-driven initiative which derives from man himself. Guardini insists, however, that the technocratic man stands in direct opposition to this sort of logic; to the man "absorbed by technology and rational abstraction," this autonomous logic is a foreign tradition which he opposes with his own technocratic logic. This is the fullest meaning of the title *The End of the Modern World*, for Guardini's central thesis is that the world created by Enlightenment ideals is "perishing" and a new world order is emerging.[105] A new type of man with a new type of prevailing logic is now ruling the cultural framework, and it is Guardini's task to illustrate the development of this logic to the best of his ability.

The second point naturally follows on this first point, for if man did not inherit this technocratic logic from previous traditions, from whence did it come? If "Mass Man" did not learn this logic in school or from his parents, if he did not read about it in his books and did not hear it proclaimed in lecture halls, what is the actual source of this tradition? The answer to this question reveals the critical convergence of thought between Tocqueville

---

104. Guardini, *End of the Modern World*, 58.

105. In affirming this idea, Guardini is not suggesting modernity will no longer have an impact on mankind; he is only affirming the essence of something new. Thus he can say, "Today the modern age is essentially over. The chains of cause and effect that it established will of course continue to hold. Historical epochs are not neatly severed like the steps of a laboratory experiment. While one era prevails, its successor is already forming, and its predecessor continues to exert influence for a long time. To this day, we find elements of a still-vital antiquity in southern Europe, and we run across strong medieval currents in many places. Thus in the yet nameless epoch which we feel breaking in on us from all sides, the last consequences of the modern age are still being drawn, although that which determined the essence of that age no longer determines the character of the historical epoch now beginning" (Guardini, *End of the Modern World*, 118).

CHAPTER 3: THE TECHNOCRATIC MIND   111

and Guardini, for both thinkers showed how a specific logic was derived from an altering of man's relations.

Earlier in this chapter, Guardini commented that technocratic man

> is a man of increasing alienations between his experience and his understanding, between his experience and his field of work. Under the impact of this historic change, we must repeat, *man's relations with nature have changed radically*. Man himself is less capable of attaining nature, of representing it and of experiencing it.[106]

As the proliferation of technics alter relationships, Guardini argues that they have also altered the mind; as man becomes increasingly alienated from qualitative reality, he becomes increasingly nested within a technocratic logic which trains the mind to view the natural order in the same way in which the machine interacts with the natural order. He continually comes back to this point, stating elsewhere that

> Man's *relations* with nature have been altered radically, have become indirect. The old immediateness has been lost, for now his *relations* are transmitted by mathematics or by instruments. Abstract and formalized, nature has lost all concreteness; having become inorganic and technical, it has lost the quality of real experience.[107]

According to Guardini, the use of technology alters our relations, leading us to acquire a new logic. Guardini suggests that what is actually happening is that man has "unlearned" his former relationship with nature, that the "metaphysical worth" of things slowly disappeared from the vision of modern man as this same man came to rely more and more on a mechanical and technical apparatus to work and create within the natural world. The old way of relating to the world has been lost, and it was replaced instead by mathematical and instrumental relations. Given that these mechanical contraptions and mathematical instruments are "blind" to the metaphysical worth of things and can only comprehend their abstraction of them, it is not surprising to discover that those who use them slowly lose their vision of these metaphysical realities which were once more apparent to the man who had more "natural" and "organic" relationships.

What is suggested by all of the above is an intriguing paradox, for although man himself is the one who creates technology, who constructs scientific equations and builds technical gadgetry and perfects mechanical

---

106. Guardini, *End of the Modern World*, 70.
107. Guardini, *End of the Modern World*, 69.

contraptions, man finds his own mind altered by his use of these technics. Man can choose to use technology, but he cannot choose to be uninfluenced by this technology; man can "bend nature according to his will," but he cannot control the rational consequences of such a relationship. We could say that the abstract relationship with nature is chosen, but the derivative logic of such a relationship is a necessary consequence of such a choice.

Guardini is not surprised by this paradox, for he says that "It is a dangerous illusion to think that a deed can remain 'outside' the doer. In reality, it permeates him, is in him even before it reaches the object of his act. The doer is constantly becoming what he does."[108] If this is true, then it is no surprise that one who uses rationally abstract technics will become a rationally abstract thinker who misses the metaphysical worth of things; it is no surprise that the one who uses machines that transform qualitative reality into quantitative numerology will see within himself a similar transformation in his own way of thinking. Elsewhere, Guardini speaks of "the act of knowing, in which the object cannot be considered apart from the subject, in which the observer and the observed coinhere; or again, in regard to causality, in which there exist no one-sided effects among beings, but every effect is bipolar."[109] Guardini shows how the logic of machines eventually *coinheres* with the user, a user who is not left unchanged by his use of technology but instead is molded into its image and likeness. Man uses technology, and man is altered by his use of technology; the effect is bipolar, and from an increase in technocratic use comes a not-so-surprising consequence: an increase in technocratic logic. In this way, we see once again that *how* a person thinks is very much dependent on their relational dimension.

The rate at which this technocratic logic has gained control of the cultural apparatus is helpful to consider. Guardini states,

> During the 19th century technology developed slowly; for that stretch of time it developed only at the hands of a non-technologized mentality. Then at last in the decades just prior to the second World War and in the years of that War, the man motivated by technology broke into the field of history and took possession.[110]

For Guardini, something new happened in the decades just prior to the second war in which the technocratic man emerged and began to "take possession" of so much within the social landscape. In the nineteenth century, technology was being used by a "non-technologized mentality," but

---

108. Guardini, *End of the Modern World*, 181.
109. Guardini, *End of the Modern World*, 187.
110. Guardini, *End of the Modern World*, 55.

as machines assumed more and more responsibility for work and creation, a critical mass was reached, and the man motivated by technology "broke into the field of history." Only with the slow passing of time was a non-technologized mentality replaced by the technocratic logic which dominates today, reminding us how the rational dominance of technocratic logic requires more than the presence of technological gadgetry; it also requires abundance of these gadgets, and only over time can its coinhering logic take deeper root.

Another important dynamic at play is the fact that man controls his surroundings with his machines, but man himself is part of these same surroundings which he seeks to control. He appears to control only one element of nature (such as damming a river with a technical apparatus and sophisticated engineering), but this changes his relationship to this element in nature. To this point, Guardini says the following: "We have today an ever-deeper realization that all existence rests on certain basic forms, and that the individual form is part of a whole, which in turn is affected by the individual. From this springs the awareness that *everything affects everything*."[111] Man finds himself in a web of relationships so intertwined that "everything affects everything," and man is not separate from the system which he tries to control with his technics but is actually part of this same system. This means that, when man builds a dam and changes the flow of a river in order to generate power, he habituates himself to see other rivers as a potential source of power, and this in turn trains his mind to interpret other external objects with a similarly reductive scope. When someone uses their rational faculty to build a dam, the "metaphysical worth" of all rivers is slightly altered and the technocratic vision gains a little more power over the mind, as the river's qualitative dimensions (from the sound of the flowing waters, to the sight of its varied course, to its cleansing effect on those immersed in it) are either neglected or reinterpreted during the scientific analysis requisite for building the dam. The construction of the dam impacts not only the functional rationality of the builder but also of the consumer, for the consumer sees only a calm surface of water within the dammed walls of an uninhabited valley and has literally "forgotten" what the true river looks like; he can be made to appreciate the power generated from the dam, the ability to fish in its waters, and to enjoy both of these things, but he will not be able to "remember" the other qualities which have been lost in the technocratic manipulation. With each passing glance, the consumer "unlearns" the natural relationship with the organic and a more functional relationship takes over, functional relationships which themselves are the

111. Guardini, *End of the Modern World*, 185.

essence of technology.[112] Man is free to exercise his dominion over rivers and build dams, but such dominion has a bipolar effect, and being part of the system which man is trying to control, there is a reciprocal influence of such dominion on his vision of every other river. In this way, technocratic relationships contribute to a technocratic logic, and this logic forms (or re-forms) other natural relationships into a technocratic relationship.

It is tempting to try to establish a first cause in this dynamic interplay between the relational dimension of the human person and the development of the rational faculty, but while establishing such a causal hierarchy is not a primary question of this thesis, we can at least come to see that there is a sort of symbiotic or co-dependent relationship between our rational faculty and relational dimension: what is happening in the relational dimension influences our rational faculty, and the way we think influences our experience of relationship. More and more, we see that the act of reason is not a do-it-yourself project but instead is a consequence of a complex array of relationships; that the human mind is neither autonomous nor self-derived but rather an interactive, relationally-dependent potency; that the human mind operates according to varying types of logic which are received in relationship and not derived from an autonomous subject; that the *ratio* and the *relatio* of the human subject are equally penetrating realities of existence which can be partitioned in theory but not in reality.

---

112. "Thus functional relationships come into being that become progressively independent of direct human participation, relationships to which goals may be prescribed with even greater ease: technology" (Guardini, *End of the Modern World*, 154).

Chapter 4

Ratio in Relatione

Up to this point, we have examined the development of two types of logic which manifest themselves in two distinct cultural conditions. In Tocqueville, we saw the emergence of a "democratic logic" which arises from cultural conditions of equality, and in Guardini and Francis, we saw the emergence of a "technocratic logic" which arises in cultural conditions dominated by the presence of machines. It is now possible to examine what is shared between these two types of logic, considering how they lead to a better understanding of the way the rational faculty of human nature develops in response to the relational dimension of the human person.

THE INFLUENCE OF STRUCTURAL PARADIGMS ON RATIONAL CHOICE

A Crisis of Trust

The point of departure for this thesis was the claim of modern philosophers that man must have the courage to "think for himself," and this claim was rooted in Descartes's idea that "the capacity to judge correctly and to distinguish the true from the false, which is properly what one calls common sense or reason, is naturally equal in all men."[1] By first asserting that every person possesses an equal capacity to reason (defined by Descartes as the ability to judge the true from the false), it necessarily follows that every person is capable of judging for themselves and to "think for himself." But over

---

1. Descartes, *Discourse on the Method*, 27.

the course of this thesis, we have encountered several authors who challenge the assumption that reason itself is an isolated faculty.

First, we encountered Saint Augustine, who greatly desired absolute certainty about the most important truths and dedicated his life to searching for this absolute certainty, but he eventually realized that attaining this certainty was not possible by the power of his own mind. Augustine at one point did possess absolute certainty about the Manichean doctrines, but when he reflects on what undergirded his certainty about these doctrines, it was actually trust and not reason: "You know, Honoratus, that the only reason we fell in with them is because they declared with awesome authority, *quite removed from pure and simple reasoning*, that if any persons chose to listen to them they would lead them to God and free them from all error."[2] Augustine once thought that the Manichean teachings were absolutely certain, but over time, he came to understand that the power of natural reason was only an illusion, for it was his *belief* in their "awesome authority" which was the actual basis of his certitude. What Saint Augustine trusted (or distrusted) had a profound impact on how he could reason, and only after he abandoned his trust in the Manichean system, and learned to trust another authority like Saint Ambrose, did his rationality develop towards certitude of Christian truths. Contrary to the assertion of Descartes, Augustine did not possess an innate ability to distinguish true from false (at least for ultimate matters) but rather learned how to make such distinctions through a network of developing relationships of trust. Likewise, Augustine does not possess a universal rationality which is static and uninfluenced by anything but "facts"; rather, his reason is dynamic and constantly developing according to what he is choosing to trust at a particular period of his intellectual development. He is never "thinking for himself"; he is always deciding who or what he can trust, and these relationships of trust profoundly influence *how* he thinks.

After Augustine, we encountered the writings of Alexis de Tocqueville and Romano Guardini which further illustrate the ideas which the life of Augustine reveal. Like Augustine, they both showed the way in which trust in some authority exerts a profound influence over the way a person exercises their rational faculty, but they deepened our analysis by drawing our attention to some novel sources of trust which we did not see explicitly in the life of Augustine, for while one can readily see the role of *human* relationships in developing Augustine's rationality, Tocqueville and Guardini highlight the influence of *structural* relationships in developing a specific type of rationality.

---

2. Augustine, *Advantage of Believing*, i, 2 (emphasis added).

CHAPTER 4: *RATIO IN RELATIONE* 117

We will first consider the role of structural relationships in the writings of Alexis de Tocqueville. Like other writers, Tocqueville sees how democratic peoples in the modern age are prone to reason in an individualistic manner. This "democratic logic" could be described as an individualistic rationality, and this is striking to many observers because it is characterized by a radical trust in one's own reason to arrive at all truth. But the unique insight of Tocqueville is twofold: first, he shows how it is only an imaginary rationality, for in reality, those who possess such an individualistic rationality are intellectual copies of the majority. In democratic cultures imbued with this democratic logic, it is actually the majority which determines what and how people think, and we addressed this point extensively in the second chapter. Second, Tocqueville shows the way this individualistic logic emerges from a crisis of trust, for he asserts that conditions of equality eliminate the obvious presence of men of "incontestable greatness and superiority," causing people in conditions of equality to be "constantly brought back to their own reason as the most visible and nearest source of truth."[3] Such a crisis of trust is precisely what we find in a democratic mind like Descartes, who wrote,

> I knew of the judgements that the others were making about me; and I saw that one did not think me inferior to my fellow students . . . and finally, our age seemed to me as flourishing and as fertile with good minds as had been any of the preceding ones. This made me take the liberty of judging all others by myself . . .[4]

Descartes was attending one of the finest schools in Europe, so the fact that his intellect is regarded as "not inferior" to his fellow students provides him with confidence to judge everything by himself. Descartes readily acknowledges the presence of "fertile and good minds" among his contemporaries, but he does not find signs of incontestable greatness and superiority among them. For Descartes, the lack of superior minds among his fellows leads to an extreme trust in his own reason, and we saw the extremity of this trust in the first chapter when he stated things like, "My plan has never gone beyond trying to reform my own thoughts and building on a foundation that is *totally my own*."[5] In the social state of aristocracy, superior minds are more obvious and so trust in minds beyond the self is more natural, but in the social state of equality, trust in one's own mind becomes not only the norm, but also reasonable.

---

3. DA, 701.
4. Descartes, *Discourse on the Method*, 18–19.
5. Descartes, *Discourse on the Method*, 31 (emphasis added).

We also saw how this crisis of trust in finding no one of superior intellect leads to another crisis of its own, for while the individual mind is capable of reasoning towards simple truths, it is overwhelmed by the intellectual task of reasoning towards complex truths, and so an individualistic rationality resorts to "commonly held opinions" as the principle source of beliefs. The turn to this source of commonly held opinions is, once again, influenced by the social state of equality, for in finding every mind more or less equal to his own in a structural order of equality, democratic man is led to assume that the majority cannot err. When all minds are more or less the same, the number of people conformed to a certain idea becomes a powerful source of authority, for "it does not seem likely to them that, since all have similar enlightenment, truth is not found on the side of the greatest number."[6] For those immersed in a social state of equality, it is *reasonable* to conclude that the truth is found on the side of the majority, allowing the majority to function like an aristocratic body which sways the mind of the culture in a certain direction. So in both the crisis of trust causing one to turn towards the self, and in the subsequent crisis of trust causing one to turn towards the majority, it is the social state of equality which is *structurally* leading the mind to different sources of trust than those sources which can be found in a social state of aristocracy. Tocqueville asserts that it is the social structure of equality, and not academic discourse, which is the principle source of the rationality which permeates the democratic mind; it is structural relationships, and not specific human relationships, that bend the democratic mind inwards. For Tocqueville, rationality is being shaped by something which cannot be said to be determined by the rational choices of any one individual but rather is inherent to structural dynamics within a democratic culture.

Romano Guardini provides a similar analysis which converges with the thought of Tocqueville, for instead of attributing the development of the technocratic mind to intellectual discourse, the technocratic mind is actually derived from a change in man's structural relationships, primarily with nature but also with others. Guardini spoke about the emergence of this new "structural order" which is characterized by a change in man's relationship with nature, for modern man no longer has an organic encounter with the natural world but instead has seen technocratic relationships dominate the way he interacts with so much of the created world. This new structural order is more of a dissolution than a composition, for it is an order in which "the intimate *relation* of man to his work, in which his eye, hand, will, sense

---

6. DA, 719.

CHAPTER 4: *RATIO IN RELATIONE*

of material, imagination, and general creativeness cooperate, *disappears*."[7] He refers to this disappearance of former ways of relating to nature as "the dissolution of organic creativity," and thus his writing is more focused on the End of the Modern World instead of The Beginning of the Emerging World; he has shown how former relationships have been altered, but he can only partially describe what is emerging.[8] Guardini does not hesitate to offer reasons to explain why he is unable to accurately describe what is emerging after the End of the Modern World: "Because we find ourselves at the center of these changing processes, it has been far from easy to describe changes which occurred in the *relations* between modern man and subjectivity, between modern man and nature."[9] Whereas Tocqueville observed a democratic culture that was relatively fixed in its essential characteristics, Guardini is observing a social state which is still developing and undergoing various "changing processes" that have yet to take on a definitive character, and this significantly impacts his ability to adequately describe what is happening.[10] Despite this inherent instability of observation, Guardini is clear from the beginning to the end of his work that the emergence of this structural order, and its inherent technocratic logic, is derived from these changing dynamics within the relational dimension of the human person and is not the product of any one person's individual decision to embrace a technocratic world; technocratic logic has arisen from structural changes in the relational fabric of the culture and is not a derivative of one person's rational choice.

As man's relations with nature and others change, so too is there a development of trust. To this point, Guardini states,

> The modern age considered every increase in intellectual-technical power an unquestionable gain, fervently believing all such increase to be progress, progress in the direction of a decisive fulfillment of the supreme meaning and value of existence. Today *this belief is growing shaky*, a condition which in itself indicates the beginning of a new epoch.[11]

---

7. Guardini, *End of the Modern World*, 155.
8. Guardini, *End of the Modern World*, 161.
9. Guardini, *End of the Modern World*, 74 (emphasis added).

10. It was for this reason we were required to consider other thinkers besides Guardini on this point, for these thinkers are making observations about technocratic culture which resonate with Guardini but are nonetheless sixty years further into its development and are able to illustrate more clearly what is beginning to emerge from what Guardini could only partially see.

11. Guardini, *End of the Modern World*, 118 (emphasis added).

Modern man had a fideistic trust in the idea that any development of technology was a positive development for human persons, but this belief has entered a moment of crisis and can no longer be presupposed as true, and it is this crisis of trust which in itself indicates the end of the modern world. For Guardini, the cause of this emerging distrust of once-dogmatic belief arises from cultural events in recent centuries, for he states,

> Could the events of the last decades have happened at the peak of a really true culture in Europe? . . . A culture marked by a true ordering could not have invented such incomprehensible systems of degradation and destruction. Monstrosities of such conscious design do not emerge from the calculations of a few degenerate men or of small groups of men; they come from processes of agitation and poisoning which had long been at work. What we call moral standards—responsibility, honor, sensitivity of conscience—do not vanish from humanity at large if men have not already been long debilitated. These degradations could never have happened if its culture had been as supreme as the modern world thought.[12]

After the "incomprehensible systems of degradation and destruction" of the modern age, Guardini thinks that modern man has learned to distrust both himself and his technocratic works. Furthermore, these events are not rooted in "the calculations of a few degenerate men or of small groups of men"; rather, they were the result of "processes of agitation and poisoning" which developed over time; they were structurally imprinted in the culture and not consciously chosen by a few individual men. With such poisoning permeating the very fabric of culture itself, these "monstrosities" of recent centuries show that it is *no longer reasonable to believe* that technocratic advancement is synonymous with human progress, and thus man can no longer trust his technocratic culture as a guide for human activity.[13] He reinforces his point by stating,

> The doubts and criticisms of culture today come from within culture itself, for *we no longer trust it*. We cannot accept culture as it was accepted during the modern age, as a meaningful realm of life or as a dependable rule for action. Culture has lost all kinship with the "objective spirit," with that crucible which contains

---

12. Guardini, *End of the Modern World*, 86.

13. He asserts this view is widely accepted, for "the very fact that we can define these alternatives without seeming utopian or moralistic—because by so doing we but voice something of which the public is more or less aware—is a further indication that the new epoch is overtaking the old" (Guardini, *End of Modern World*, 119).

the truth of existence itself.... No one today can trust the work of man as the modern world trusted it.[14]

For Guardini, the crisis of contemporary man is actually a crisis of trust: the former organic relationships with nature have decayed, and the technocratic relationships which have taken their place are incapable, of themselves, of creating a structural order that naturally leads people to an encounter with the good. What is reasonable for man to trust in such a situation? Guardini is content to leave this question unanswered, and because a resolution falls beyond the immediate scope of this thesis, we will also leave it unanswered. Guardini is simply content to affirm that "(man) no longer controls power" but that "power controls him," and thus "the new epoch's intellectual task will be to integrate power into life in such a way that man can employ power without forfeiting his humanity."[15] That modern man has occasionally had to forfeit his humanity in the exercise of power is clear, but how to control the technocratic power at his disposal (a power which is forming man himself) is an intellectual task that remains unfinished. It is this task which Pope Francis demands of society today, for like Guardini, he sees the way in which power continues to control man by the assault of the technocratic paradigm. For both Francis and Guardini, this technocratic logic is embedded in the culture, thus converging with Tocqueville's assertion that rationality can be significantly shaped by something which is not determined by the rational choices of any one individual but rather is inherent to structural relationships within a culture.

A Reason to Believe

It is appropriate at this point to summarize a few of the essential conclusions that Augustine, Tocqueville, and Guardini highlight for the point of departure of this thesis. From the considerations of these authors, the relational dimension of human reason becomes more apparent, for they all illustrate how human reason should not be considered something which is governed by "reason alone." Parallel to every change in reason is also a change in trust, and as man's relationships of trust (and distrust) develop over time, his rationality develops accordingly. But man's relationships of trust are also influenced by his reasoning about these relations, and so both reason and trust, instead of one being the cause of the other, are actually mutually dependent aspects of the human person.

14. Guardini, *End of the Modern World*, 77.
15. Guardini, *End of the Modern World*, 197, 119.

For example, in Augustine, we saw how his certitude of Manicheanism was rooted in his trust of their "awesome authority," but he began to encounter *reasons* to distrust them, such as their inability to explain complex astronomical realities with the same precision of the astronomers. This distrust increased when the most authoritative teacher of the Manicheans (Faustus) could not explain what everyone else trusted he could explain. Disillusioned by his encounter with Faustus, it is more appropriate to say that Augustine *reasoned away* from Manicheanism because he distrusted both their conclusions and their authoritative teachers who could not explain discrepancies. He no longer had a *good reason* to believe them, and this created a crisis of trust which led him to several months of skepticism before arriving in the diocese of Milan and opening himself to the authority of Ambrose. For Augustine, reason and trust are constantly developing alongside one another, and development (or disintegration) in one of these attributes leads to the development (or disintegration) of the other. He had to learn to distrust many things before he could trust the Christian truths which he once inherited as a child.

Similarly, in Tocqueville, reason and trust are constantly developing in a mutually-dependent way, for the democratic mind learns to distrust the intellectual mediocrity of his fellows which then leads him to trust in himself. A person born in conditions of equality has no *good reason* to trust the minds of men whose intelligences are more or less equal to his own, so trusting his own mind becomes quite reasonable. A person born in conditions of equality also has difficulty believing that a majority opinion can be wrong, so it becomes equally reasonable to trust the majority. Like Augustine, Tocqueville explains that democratic man *reasons away* from trust in other individuals and subsequently is inclined to trust his own self and the majority, creating an almost bi-polar intellectual complex in the mind of democratic man.

As in Augustine and Tocqueville, so too in Guardini: trust in the technocratic culture is faltering, and Guardini hopes that this will allow modern man "to grasp the truth by *breaking away* from the optimisms of the modern mind."[16] Technocratic man has obvious *reasons to distrust* technocratic culture, and so technocratic man is reasoning away from trust in this culture. For Guardini, it is as if modern man is very much like Augustine after his disillusionment with the Manichees, looking for something to trust and yet not finding it immediately. Just as Augustine was a skeptic for several months after his disillusionment with the Manichees, modern man remains skeptical of his activity, and it is this skepticism which Guardini

---

16. Guardini, *End of the Modern World*, 79.

CHAPTER 4: *RATIO IN RELATIONE* 123

interprets as the sign that the Modern World is coming to an end. What will definitively emerge remains elusive, but in this paralysis of skepticism, humanity is being overwhelmed by "power." Guardini asserts that man is being dominated by a "technical-economic-political system" which is holding "all life in thrall," and this is not a power controlled by an individual man but is, at its heart, "autonomous."[17] Guardini thinks that culture itself is being driven by an autonomous power which is *not reasonable* to trust, but what will be trusted in its place remains the fundamental unanswered question constantly reappearing throughout *The End of the Modern World*. For now, technocratic man seems to be content with life as a thrall, and this is discouraging to Guardini because

> In the long run, domination requires not only the passive consent, but also the will to be dominated, a will eager to drop personal responsibility and personal effort. Broadly speaking, the dominated get what they themselves desire; the inner barriers of self-respect and self-defense must fall before power can really violate.[18]

That modern man has sound reasons to no longer blindly trust technocratic culture is self-evident to many within this culture, but whether or not these reasons are enough to move his will against domination remains to be seen. For Guardini, reason alone is not sufficient to move the will in such a way as to avoid domination; man needs something besides good reasons to choose what reason clearly suggests is essential for his freedom.

In summary, neither the mind of Augustine, nor the democratic mind, nor the technocratic mind exhibited the exact same pattern of development, but they did share overlapping tendencies and mutually informative parallels, and what stands out among them all is the drama of the development of trust. We call this development of trust a "drama" because these thinkers reveal how the mind is continually changing allegiances; what is trusted one day is distrusted the next, and what is distrusted can one day have deep reasons to be trusted again. Neither Tocqueville nor Guardini think that a democratic or technocratic logic is inescapable, for we saw at the end of chapter two and chapter three the various ways in which these cultural

---

17. "When we examine the development as a whole, we cannot escape the impression that nature as well as man himself is becoming ever more vulnerable to domination—economic, technical, political, organizational—of power. Ever more distinctly our condition reveals itself as one in which man progressively controls nature, yes, but also men; the state controls the citizens, and an *autonomous* technical-economic-political system holds all life in thrall" (Guardini, *End of the Modern World*, 163–64 [emphasis added]).

18. Guardini, *End of the Modern World*, 165.

logics can be reshaped. By immersion in free associations, or the restoration of a contemplative attitude, new relations can be established which create different bonds of trust and help recover what is lost or limited in the democratic and technocratic structures, keeping the mind from being a slave to a structural logic and allowing it to be permeated by something beyond "reason alone."

So, in dramatic fashion, the human mind is immersed in a complex web of trust and allegiance which undergirds much of the development of the rational faculty, and if the complexity of this web is not yet adequately appreciated, we must note that an individual human mind is capable of many different types of rationality. A person can possess both an individualistic rationality and a technocratic rationality; only for the sake of simplification have our authors isolated these individual rationalities and considered the many sources of trust or distrust influencing their development. When we layer each thinker on top of the other, the profile of any individual mind need not be described as only individualistic or only technocratic; instead, they can co-exist to varying degrees, and there is no reason to suspect that these are the only two types of rationalities capable of emerging from the complex array of relations possible for any given person immersed in a specific culture. In the life of Augustine alone, we can see threads of allegiance to both his father's pagan influence, his mother's Christian teachings, and the Manichean philosophical theories which are interwoven and interacting with one another, pulling his mind in various directions and only over time reaching a settled disposition of trust of truth claims within Christianity. Because there is no such thing as a person who is "technocratic man" but only human persons with traits which can be simplified by the term "technocratic man," we insist that such a label is only an abstraction helpful to rational thought but not an exhaustive description of the breadth of rational potency within a human person. A more fitting word to describe this dynamic potency of human reason is "drama," for the development of each human mind unfolds in a dramatic and unique way.

These are some of the reasons to believe that a statement such as "have courage to use your own reason" is an inadequate description of reason itself because it presupposes a universal rationality which does not exist. Such a statement posits a static form of rationality which is common to all men and assumes that this static rationality is sufficient in and of itself to guide one towards the truth, but these general assumptions about reason do not resonate with the insights of Augustine, Tocqueville, and Guardini, for they highlight the way in which reason itself is dynamic, continually developing in response to relationships of trust which then impact reason itself. Instead of reason being an objective faculty which is inherited in the same way by every member of the human species, it is a subjective faculty which varies according to the subjective experience of various relational dynamics which are not universal across each culture or each person. That all men think is indeed universal to the human species, but *how* men think and how they reason varies so significantly that reason itself ought to be considered dynamic and partially subjective as opposed to static and entirely objective.

Tocqueville and Guardini are not the only people who have noted the plasticity and dynamic nature of human reason. For example, Alasdair MacIntyre says that there are "rationalities rather than rationality . . . and justices rather than justice," and for MacIntyre, these rationalities develop according to intellectual debate and the scholastic development of "traditions of enquiry."[19] Without discounting the real influence of traditions of enquiry on human reason, Tocqueville and Guardini complement the thought of MacIntyre by highlighting the role of structural authorities in forming various rationalities. What is unique about their insights is that these structural authorities are not chosen but received; they are not discovered by debate within a tradition of enquiry but rather inherited through the relational structure of a culture, and in this way, the authors in this paper point to the pre-moral dynamics involved in the development of human reason. Like MacIntyre, both Tocqueville and Guardini recognize the dynamism of human reason, but they distinguish themselves by showing a source of this dynamism which extends into the soil of pre-moral existence. By calling existence "pre-moral," we are referring to the existence of man before making a rational choice, which is recognized in both secular and religious thought.[20] A person living in conditions of equality could not in any way be said to have "chosen" to live in conditions of equality, and yet this social structure shapes their rational faculty in ways which are just as influential as any scholastic encounter with modern philosophers like Descartes. The same could be said for those living in cultural conditions dominated by technics, which is why we assert that the word "choice" is not adequate to describe the role of an individual in deciding whether or not to be part of this structure and thus whether or not they will inherit this structural

---

19. MacIntyre, *Whose Justice? Which Rationality?*, 9.

20. The reason why Catholics do not make their first confession until about eight years old, and why there are no jails for children under the age of ten, is because a moral act is predicated on a person having responsibility for their rational choice, something which is only possible after rudimentary rational development. For both secular and religious traditions, it is acknowledged that it takes time for a person to reach the "age of discretion" (CCC 1457), which is the moment when a person becomes responsible for their moral choices because of the sufficient development of their reason. This sense of "pre-moral" must be distinguished from that which is rejected in *Veritatis Splendor*, where Pope John Paul II rejects the idea of pre-moral *goods* (see VS 48, 73).

logic. How a person thinks is not always dependent on what a person has chosen to read or study; reason itself is significantly influenced by what a person has learned to trust long before it has ever learned to make a rational choice, and what a person has learned to trust becomes an authority over the mind and influences its subsequent rational processes. In this way, these structural developments of trust and distrust are just as authoritative as reason itself, and while they do not develop without reason (we saw how Descartes considered it *reasonable* to trust no one more than himself), neither can the source of trust be said to lie in "reason alone." Long before a person makes their first rational choices, and even after they begin to make rational choices, a person's logic is conditioned by patterns of trust which are structurally received.

Structural Paradigms and Rational Choice

We are now very close to affirming the first claim of this thesis, but before we can do so, we must more precisely understand a word which has already appeared in this thesis but is not yet adequately explained, and that word is "paradigm." This is a word which owes much of its contemporary usage to the thought and writing of Thomas Kuhn, primarily because of the word's novel function within his book *The Structure of Scientific Revolutions*. Articulating a strict definition of the word "paradigm" based on Kuhn's book is difficult, for one critical reader of the text found twenty-one distinct ways in which Kuhn used the word, and Kuhn himself admitted that, in writing the text, he "lost complete control of the word."[21] While an accurate definition is difficult to establish within the text itself, it nonetheless became a hermeneutical lens for understanding his central arguments, especially for his portrayal of the way various intellectual commitments influence the reasonableness of scientific datum. He states,

> the term "paradigm" enters in close proximity, both physically and logical, to the phrase "scientific community." A paradigm is what the members of a scientific community, and they alone, share. Conversely, it is their possession of a common paradigm that constitutes a scientific community of a group of otherwise disparate men.[22]

For Kuhn, a paradigm represents the set of intellectual, mathematical, and logical commitments shared by a scientific group which unites them as

---

21. Kuhn, *Structure of Scientific Revolutions*, xviii.
22. Kuhn, *Structure of Scientific Theories*, 461.

a community and keeps them from being "otherwise disparate men." Such a set of shared commitments is essential to their work because "without a shared commitment to a set of symbolic generalizations, logic and mathematics could not routinely be applied in the community's work."[23] In this way, a paradigm mimics the attributes of language as a set of shared symbols and trusted ideas which are mutually agreed upon and which allow for research to progress in a definitive direction.

Kuhn goes to great lengths to explain the way a paradigm is developed by something other than "reason alone," and this is seen most clearly in his discussion of the various paradigm shifts which accompany scientific revolutions. For example, he says that

> the man who embraces a new paradigm at an early stage must often do so in defiance of the evidence provided by problem solving. He must, that is, have faith that the new paradigm will succeed with the many large problems that confront it, knowing only that the older paradigm has failed with a few. A decision of that kind can only be made on faith.[24]

For Kuhn, faith in a new paradigm is what allows one to "shift" from trust in one paradigm to trust in another, and this decision to make such a paradigm shift is not made by reason alone but instead is a committed act of belief. He describes some of the non-rational characteristics of this act of faith when he states

> There must also be a basis, though it need be neither rational nor ultimately correct, for faith in the particular candidate chosen. Something must make at least a few scientists feel that the new proposal is on the right track, and sometimes it is only personal and inarticulate aesthetic considerations that can do that ... Even today Einstein's general theory attracts men principally on aesthetic grounds, an appeal that few people outside of mathematics have been able to feel.[25]

According to Kuhn, scientists need a *reason to believe* what is offered by a new paradigm, but the reasons to believe this new paradigm are not based on reason alone but instead can include personal or aesthetic reasons, or even just an intuition which makes a scientist feel that the new paradigm is "on the right track." When a scientific community undergoes a paradigm shift, it is not reason alone which is driving its process of acceptance but

23. Kuhn, *Structure of Scientific Revolutions*, 464.
24. Kuhn, *Structure of Scientific Revolutions*, 156–57.
25. Kuhn, *Structure of Scientific Revolutions*, 157.

rather a complex appeal to the aesthetic and personal commitments of various members within the community.[26] This essential connection of paradigms to an act of faith is important for understanding how a paradigm describes those commitments and allegiances which influence reason but clearly do not derive from reason alone.

When we came across the word "paradigm" in the writings of Pope Francis, we saw how he used the word primarily in the sense of a logical framework which conditions what is received within that framework. For both Kuhn and Pope Francis, paradigms do not imply the absence of reason, but they would emphasize that reason is not the primary source of the development of a paradigm and that a paradigm ultimately describes a set of intellectual commitments which dispose a person to think and reason in a certain way. These commitments can come from a great variety of sources.

For Kuhn, a paradigm is created within the mind of a scientist by simply practicing science according to what is presumed by the dominant paradigm of the community. For many scientists, this paradigm is received from the teachers and textbooks which they use in learning science, for "science students accept theories on the authority of teacher and text, not because of evidence ... The applications given in texts are not there as evidence but because learning them is part of learning the paradigm at the base of current practice."[27] So a science student does not actually choose a paradigm; rather, they inherit one from their teachers and their textbooks and thereby learn the paradigm which undergirds current practice. This leads Kuhn to an interesting observation: only those rare scientists who are unfamiliar with the paradigm of current practice are able to create new paradigms that cause science to undergo a revolution.[28]

For Augustine, it seems that his will was the primary source of creating his allegiance to the Manichean paradigm, for it was his desire to believe the

26. This is why Kuhn says, "To discover how scientific revolutions are effected, we shall therefore have to examine not only the impact of nature and of logic, but also the techniques of persuasive argumentation effective within the quite special groups that constitute the community of scientists" (*Structure of Scientific Revolutions*, 94). For Kuhn, scientific revolutions are not just about nature and logic; they are also about persuasion and acts of faith, two things not often associated with the discipline of science. This is what makes Kuhn's claims so challenging to the scientific community, for he exposes the essential role of faith in a discipline which often considers its conclusions based solely on "objective" evidence.

27. Kuhn, *Structure of Scientific Revolutions*, 80–81.

28. "Almost always the men who achieve these fundamental inventions of a new paradigm have been either very young or very new to the field whose paradigm they change ... These are the men who, being little committed by prior practice to the traditional rules of normal science, are particularly likely to see that those rules no longer define the playable game and conceive another set that can replace them" (Kuhn, *Structure of Scientific Revolutions*, 90).

Manichees which provided him with his intellectual commitment to their beliefs. He did not first study their works and then conclude that they were trustworthy; he first encountered their teachers and was moved by their "awesome authority." Like the scientists reading their textbooks, Augustine was not converted by the evidence of the Manichean texts but rather was committed to believing the paradigm which the Manichean texts and teachers assumed.

Francis and Tocqueville differ from Augustine and Kuhn in that they show how a logical framework (or paradigm) can come from being part of a certain structural order which disposes the mind to trust or distrust in a certain way. It is as if the relational structure of a culture is itself a "textbook" which teaches the members of that culture how to think based on their shared commitments, and this then influences so much of their subsequent rational thought. By immersing the human person in a network of relationships which determine specific patterns of trust, a structural order can create paradigmatic assumptions which subsequently influence all rational thought and also rational choice. So despite having varied sources of origin and an admitted ambiguity in the use of the word by various authors, a paradigm can refer to an intellectual "framework" or commitment which then determines what is reasonable for a person operating according to this paradigm, and the reason for this commitment is not always reason alone but also involves personal choice, aesthetics, and even pre-moral forces like equality of conditions or technocratic culture.

We have shown how the structural relationships of a given culture exert an authority over the mind and how this authority is derived from pre-moral relations which then provide a paradigm of thought through established patterns of trust. This is important to consider because, contrary to what is proposed in the Descartian paradigm, the human mind is something much more complex than a simple fact-checking machine; it does not merely distinguish the true from the false but is also concerned with discovering who or what to trust. The human mind is not just looking for reasons *to prove* what is true; it is also looking for reasons *to believe* what is being proposed, and whether or not an idea is reasonable depends in large part on whether or not it is trusted by the operative paradigm of any given person; that which is compatible with the paradigm is reasonable because it is trusted, and that which violates the paradigm is unreasonable simply because it does not fit into the paradigm. Some of these paradigms come from human choice, but others are received from within the culture.

We must consider again Saint Augustine's journey with the Manichees to see this point more clearly. In so far as Augustine's will was committed to believing their teachings, he considered Manicheanism reasonable and Christian teaching to be unreasonable, but then he was immersed in a crisis of trust after reading about the astronomers who had conclusions which were incompatible with the Manichean paradigm. For many within the Manichean tradition, these incompatibilities were not a threat to their commitment to the Manichean paradigm, for although they saw the inconsistencies, they trusted the brilliance of Faustus more than they trusted the inconsistencies. Augustine also trusted in Faustus, until he met him. With his faith in this great authority now diminished, he experienced a crisis of trust in which his intellectual commitments could develop, and a new paradigm could be established which would replace his former allegiance to the Manichean tradition. So long as Augustine was committed to the Manichean paradigm, Christianity remained unreasonable, and Christianity became reasonable only after he had a crisis of trust in his former paradigm, willfully allowing his mind to be built on some other framework.

In this example of Saint Augustine, we can see the influence of a *chosen* paradigm on rational thought, but in Guardini and Tocqueville, we can see the influence of a *received* structural paradigm on rational thought. For Augustine, following the Manichean paradigm was understood as a personal decision, whereas in Tocqueville and Guardini, following the democratic or technocratic paradigm is something which is received by existing in a specific set of pre-moral relationships that are not "chosen." The power of these relationships over rational choice is perhaps greatly underestimated, for they determine not only whether or not someone chooses to follow Catholic morality (an act of the will) but also whether or not someone can rationally understand the moral truths of Catholic morality (an act of the intellect). It has always been difficult for someone who believes in the teachings of Christ to *follow* his teachings, but in so far as a cultural paradigm is incompatible with Christianity, it becomes difficult, if not impossible, for someone to *believe* these teachings. Cardinal Ratzinger once suggested this when he stated that "It becomes difficult, if not altogether impossible, to present Catholic morality as reasonable. It is too distant from what is considered to be obvious, as normal by the majority of persons, conditioned by the dominant culture...."[29] While Catholic morality is deeply allied to human reason and depends for so much of its validity on the inherent reasonableness of her teachings, Ratzinger claims that "the majority" considers these teachings unreasonable and somehow deviant from what is "obviously" true to everyone in the culture. It would seem, then, that cultural paradigms are molding minds in such a way that reason itself is not a sufficient basis for educating a person to believe (let alone follow) Catholic moral truths, for if these truths

---

29. Ratzinger and Messori, *Ratzinger Report*, 83.

CHAPTER 4: *RATIO IN RELATIONE* 131

are presented to a mind conditioned by an incompatible paradigm, they are not capable of being integrated into the person's mind and thus not capable of forming their rational choice.

That some such structural paradigms exist and are influencing rational choice is not just an idea of Cardinal Ratzinger but is increasingly common among recent popes. For example, Pope Francis once commented that he thinks a majority of sacramental marriages are invalid, and he explained his reasoning as follows:

> I heard a bishop say some months ago that he met a boy that had finished his university studies, and said 'I want to become a priest, but only for 10 years.' It's the culture of the provisional. And this happens everywhere, also in priestly life, in religious life ... It's provisional, and because of this the great majority of our sacramental marriages are null. Because they say 'yes, for the rest of my life!' but they don't know what they are saying. Because they have a different culture. They say it, they have good will, but they don't know.[30]

According to Pope Francis, many people who enter into a sacramental marriage come from "a different culture" in which the church's understanding of the words required for the sacrament to be valid are not equivalent to the understanding of the person who is entering into the marriage. Many people live according to a provisional paradigm in which the binding commitment of a promise does not form part of their operative rationality, so while they are ready to say the words "yes, for the rest of my life!," Pope Francis thinks that they "do not know" what they are saying and thus they give these words a meaning which is incompatible with the sacrament. It is as if in the sacramental moment, they are part of two conflicting paradigms: a Catholic paradigm which is permeated by the concept of eternity and understands oaths to be binding, and a provisional paradigm which is ephemeral and understands an oath as something subject to change. They are speaking the words required for the sacrament, but they are not fully integrated into the paradigm required for these words to effect the truth they are meant to communicate, and the provisional rationality which they possess is not in harmony with a rationality required to bind oneself definitively to a person in marriage. In this way, Pope Francis affirms that received cultural paradigms *do* influence the ability of certain people to follow Catholic morality, and this inability to follow Catholic morality does not stem from a weakness of the will but from a weakness of the mind. According to Pope Francis, even sacramental words spoken at a sacramental

---

30. Catholic News Agency, "Most Marriages Today are Invalid," paras. 9–10.

marriage can sometimes be devoid of their sacramental efficacy because of a provisional paradigm which is incompatible with Catholic morality, but unlike Augustine's choice to follow the Manichean paradigm, this "paradigm of the provisional" is not chosen but rather inherited through existence in a cultural structure that conditions the mind to think provisionally.

Although we do not know all the sources influencing the development of a culture of the provisional, Tocqueville would have no difficulty in detecting the influence of equality of conditions. It is precisely in these conditions in which men "change plans and places at every moment," in which they "are always excited, uncertain, breathless, ready to change will and place, thoughts and careers."[31] He further observes,

> A man, in the United States, carefully builds a house in which to spend his old age, and he sells it while the ridgepole is being set; he plants a garden and he rents it as he is about to taste its fruits; he clears a field, and he leaves to others the trouble of gathering the harvest. He embraces a profession, and he leaves it. He settles in a place that he soon leaves in order to carry his changing desires elsewhere. If his private affairs give him some respite, he immediately plunges into the whirl of politics. And when, near the end of a year filled with work, he still has a little leisure, he takes his restless curiosity here and there across the vast limits of the United States.[32]

Tocqueville traces these transitional and provisional habits observed in Americans to the influence of equality of conditions, and to those who are increasingly (and exclusively) exposed to such conditions, it is no surprise to discover the emergence of a culture of the provisional, and neither is it a surprise to observe rational choices increasingly conformed to this provisional logic.

For a person living in a cultural paradigm which influences their rational choice in such a way that Catholic morality is considered unreasonable, it seems as if they possess a sort of epistemological deficit which impairs their ability to actually know what they are doing. As Pope Francis says, these people will say the right words, but "they don't know" what it is that they are actually saying. Such an epistemological deficit recalls the words of Christ who asked the Father to forgive those who crucified him because "they know not what they do." Influenced by a paradigm which inhibited their ability to accept that Jesus was the Son of God, killing this man who claimed to be the Son of God was not only lawful but also reasonable. Only

---

31. DA, 945, 1150.
32. DA, 944.

from the vantage point of another paradigm, one in which the immaterial God can be conceived as being hypostatically united to material flesh, is it then reasonable to accept this claim of a human being who said "the Father and I are one," and the reasonableness of this claim depends in large part on an act of faith. Without a committed act of faith in this theological paradigm shift, those who crucified Jesus could rightly be said to "not know" what they were doing, for their lack of faith influences what is reasonable and thus what is known.

It must immediately be remembered that Christ assigned moral responsibility to many of his contemporaries for this epistemological deficit, for he said, "Why do you not understand what I say? It is because you cannot bear to hear my word. You are of your father the devil, and your will is to do your father's desires."[33] According to Christ, it is not a theological ambiguity which is causing a lack of faith; rather, it is the choice (and thus a moral act) to follow their father's desires which inhibits their act of faith, and no theological understanding is possible so long as they remain attached to this choice. These Jews have chosen to do their own desires and not the desire of Christ, and it is this prior choice (something for which they *do* have responsibility) which leads to the lack of understanding. So in this instance, Christ assigns moral responsibility to an epistemological deficit, and only those who trust him and follow him in faith can actually understand what he is saying.

That being said, we have also seen some instances in which personal responsibility for an epistemological deficit is not derived exclusively from the will of the acting person. To illustrate this, let us return to the example cited in the first chapter of the young woman who wanted advice about whether or not she should have sexual intercourse before marrying the person she is dating. This young woman is an illuminative example of someone who is experiencing an epistemological deficit, for she does not know what to do; she is experiencing a moral conflict between what her parents taught her and what her boyfriend is demanding of her, and so she seeks advice from someone to guide her in this difficulty. In response to this question, the professional author giving her advice asserted "The only orders you should ever heed on personal matters are the ones that come *straight from your own mind*. If you're old enough to get married, you're old enough to know: What do you want? What do you value? What do you think is right?"[34]

We first state the obvious: this is poor advice for someone who does not know what to do. The professional author giving this advice asserts that

---

33. John 8:43–44.
34. Hax, "Premarital Sex isn't the Issue," paras. 2–3.

being old enough to marry necessarily means that someone knows what is right, and yet this is clearly not the case for the young woman asking the question, for she is old enough to get married and yet does *not* know what to do. Furthermore, this situation is helpful for demonstrating the way in which the Descartian paradigm is incapable of being an adequate guide to the rational choices of Catholic morality. This young girl is told to do as Descartes did, which was to seek to "guide myself by myself," and yet her very question shows that she is *not* able to guide herself by herself; the fact that she is seeking advice from someone beyond her thinking self demonstrates a need for her rational choice to be shaped by something beyond her own mind. Yet what is a person like this young woman supposed to do when they inherit a structural paradigm which conditions a person to think that the truth can be found by "searching by oneself and in oneself alone for the reason of all things"? Is it not reasonable for them to search within themselves and come up with their own decision about what is right? Is it not reasonable to stop asking questions of others and seek all answers within one's own mind, whatever the result? For those who have *inherited* a Descartian paradigm, rational choice is always going to be nearly equivalent to personal choice, and the very insufficiency of such a paradigm is shown by those who live by this paradigm and yet ask difficult moral questions about ultimate matters. For those living according to the Descartian paradigm, it can be said that they "do not know what they do," and to the extent that this Descartian paradigm is received through the relational structure of a culture and not rationally chosen, there is a diminishment of personal responsibility for making moral choices which conform to this cultural paradigm.

This same phenomenon manifested itself in various ways throughout chapters two and three, for there were many ways in which rational choices were greatly influenced by paradigms received through the culture and not chosen by individuals. Tocqueville showed how the Descartian paradigm dominates rational thought in democratic cultures, thus making it reasonable to choose to isolate oneself, to reject authority, and to tend towards materialism.[35] Similarly, Guardini and Francis showed how the technocratic paradigm disposes people to rationally choose lives patterned by a violent consumerism, to seek technological advancement regardless of human or environmental costs, to elevate personal interest above communal interest, and to make profits alone the essential factor of development. These thinkers show how paradigms are not merely cognitive structures which

---

35. Regarding materialism specifically, see also DA 957, where Tocqueville calls materialism "a dangerous sickness of the human mind" and yet also "the vice of the heart most familiar to (democratic) people."

condition how people think; they are also cognitive factors which influence how people choose to act. Because human choice is also a *rational* choice, the type of rationality a person receives will influence what their rationality leads them to choose, and part of the novel contribution of the main thinkers within this thesis was to show how such rational choices do not derive exclusively from the will of the acting person but also can be conditioned by structural relationships that provide a distinct paradigm of thought.

By emphasizing the real and decisive role of paradigms in rational choice, there is risk in thinking that we have created a deterministic structure for the human person, enclosing persons within relational structures which completely obstruct their ability to freely choose the good. Of course, such deterministic conclusions are incompatible with Catholic morality, for the very idea of a discipline which examines human choosing and striving is predicated on the idea that humans *can* choose and are not exhaustively determined by something outside of their own choice. While we do not argue that man is completely determined by his culture and thus unable to choose the good, we do wish to better understand the way structural paradigms of a culture influence the way in which a person can know the good and then choose what is known. We are not interested in showing how man is unable to choose, but we are interested in a clearer understanding of how a person's rational choices are shaped by a form of reason which is not a product of their own personal choice.

The non-deterministic understanding of the human person has been present throughout the entirety of this thesis, for all the authors recognized that reason itself, precisely because it is dynamic and malleable, is capable of being "re-engineered" to align with right reason. In Tocqueville, Gaurdini, and Francis, we see a continual emphasis on the way people immersed in a Descartian or technocratic paradigm can escape the epistemological deficit of their received paradigm and learn to live by a new way of thinking, and the way such conversion of thought can be brought about was treated extensively at the end of both chapters two and three.

In summary, we can affirm that structural paradigms influence the exercise of rational choice, for by disposing the mind to specific patterns of trust, structural elements of a culture lead the mind towards specific patterns of choice. Many of these patterns of thought can lead to epistemological deficits which cannot be corrected exclusively by altering the rational choices of individuals but must also consider the rational structure which is conditioning the person to make such choices. This does not eliminate personal responsibility, but it does better identify some of the sources of these "diseases of the mind" which can habituate a person to choose something less than what is proposed by Catholic morality. For persons to choose differently, they must also trust differently, and trust is not derived exclusively from personal relationships but also from structural relationships. To the extent that a paradigm habituates a person to choose wrongly, new structures, and not just discursive teaching, are needed for new choices.

Paradigms and Catholic Morality

In the previous section, we saw how some moral teachings can be perceived as irrational by a person who has been structurally conditioned by a paradigm antithetical to Catholic morality, which suggests that Catholic morality is itself nested within various relational elements which form a paradigm of its own. In this section, we will consider some of these ideas within Catholic morality which, when accepted in faith, provide one with certainty about the church's moral teaching, and when rejected, lead to the conclusion that Catholic morality is unreasonable. As we will shortly see, the source of trust in these ideas does not lie in "reason alone" but rather are received through relations of trust.

To help us with this task, we must rely on some of Kuhn's essential distinctions within the word paradigm. Although he accuses himself of using this term excessively and at times indiscriminantly, he does highlight two distinct versions of paradigm, referring to them as "paradigm$_1$" and "paradigm$_2$."[36] According to Kuhn, paradigm$_1$ describes all the objects of group commitment (such as symbolic generalizations, models, and exemplars) which together make up what he calls the "disciplinary matrix" of the specific community practicing science according to this paradigm. Paradigm$_2$, on the other hand, describes an element within paradigm$_1$, specifically the exemplars, which he defines as the "shared examples of successful practice," and these shared examples are best exemplified by the pre-answered questions found in many scientific textbooks. He regrets that he allowed the paradigmatic behavior of these exemplars to become confused with his description of all the elements within a disciplinary matrix, but he is nonetheless content with their mutually descriptive power for some essential elements within his epistemology.

In this section, we will focus primarily on paradigms as a disciplinary matrix (or "paradigm$_1$") because some of the most essential elements within this matrix are what Kuhn calls "metaphysical commitments." One such metaphysical commitment within the disciplinary matrix of Catholic morality is a firm commitment to certitude in the existence of eternal life, and we can see the consequences of this commitment (or lack thereof) on

---

36. Kuhn, *Structure of Scientific Revolutions*, 462–63.

the reasonableness of moral teachings when we compare the horizon of eternity found in the book of Wisdom and the absence of this horizon of eternity in the book of Ecclesiastes.

The book of Wisdom argues that even if a just man is exposed to a shameful death, following the commandments is nonetheless reasonable, for "though in the sight of men they were punished, *their hope is full of immortality*. Having been disciplined a little, they will receive great good, because God tested them and found them worthy of himself."[37] By placing the sufferings of the just man who follows the law within a framework of eternal life, the author argues that true justice will eventually be realized, for any promises unfulfilled in this world are fulfilled in the hopeful expectation of the next world. In the book of Ecclesiastes, this worldview is not present, and instead of optimism amidst suffering, one encounters a tone of gloom and despair which stem from the belief that human life is *not* immortal:

> Everything before them is vanity, since one fate comes to all, to the righteous and the wicked, to the good and the evil, to the clean and the unclean, to him who sacrifices and him who does not sacrifice . . . The living know that they will die, but the dead know nothing, and they have no more reward; but the memory of them is lost. Their love and their hate and their envy have already perished, and they have no more for ever any share in all that is done under the sun.[38]

The author of Ecclesiastes argues that there is *no good reason* to be faithful to the commandments if "one fate comes to all," this fate being death; if those who die "have no more reward" and all their existence has "already perished," then the author claims that everything done under the sun is useless striving and "vanity." If man's reward is only enjoyed while he exists in this present life, and if this life itself will one day cease to exist, then the author of Ecclesiastes thinks that it is particularly *un*reasonable to strive for living a virtuous life.[39] The existentialists claimed that "If God does not exist, all things are possible," and the author of Ecclesiastes thinks that "If eternity does not exist, all morality is vanity." While there may be logical reasons which suggest that natural life is extended into eternity, there is not rational certainty about such a concept, and thus it is received in trust and forms a metaphysical framework which conditions the "reasonableness" of a moral code which is predicated on rewards which will arrive in eternity.

37. Wis 3:4–5.
38. Eccl 9:1–2, 5–6.
39. St. Paul makes a similar point when he states, "If for this life only we have hoped in Christ, we are of all men most to be pitied" (1 Cor 15:19).

Based on "reason alone," it is more reasonable to conclude with the book of Ecclesiastes that "one fate comes to all," but when reason is penetrated by the light of revelation, there are *reasons to believe* that death is not the end of everything under the sun. Catholic morality is thus predicated on the firm conviction of eternal life, combined with an understanding that one will receive judgement in eternal life for what is done on earth, and the source of trust in this idea is not derived from some self-evident concept but rather is received through one's relationships.

Another metaphysical commitment essential to the reasonableness of Catholic morality is the belief that all of the created world and human nature is "fallen." From purely rational principles, it is not difficult to conclude that something is distorted about human existence, but there are a variety of ways to interpret this distortion, and even within the Jewish and Christian traditions, there is not universal agreement about how to interpret these distortions. That man experiences evil is knowable by reason, but the cause and effect of this evil is much more mysterious and much more dependent on revelation than is often perceived. Is God the one who, as Job said, actually "slashes open my kidneys" and "pours out my gall on the ground" and "runs upon me like a warrior"?[40] When an earthquake ripples through the earth and destroys an entire village, who or what is at fault for this evil? The Christian and Jewish traditions have varying ways to interpret these mysteries, but reason alone is inadequate for providing such an interpretation. Through the hermeneutic of a fallen world, a Christian can learn to interpret the evil he experiences and still find the moral code to be reasonable, but without this paradigmatic assumption, the moral code is quick to fracture under the accusatory weight of an unsolved mystery, leaving one to lament that everything is vanity.

Pope John Paul II would agree that the idea of a fallen world is essential to the reasonableness of Catholic morality, for he notes that this doctrine "has great hermeneutical value insofar as it helps one to understand human reality."[41] He goes on to show how this hermeneutic is integral for understanding the way self-interest can be brought into fruitful harmony with the common good, a harmony that was violently suppressed by various totalitarian regimes which possessed a paradigm that rejected the idea of a fallen world. Without a metaphysical commitment to believing in man's fallen nature, various totalitarian solutions to social evils can become frighteningly reasonable, which is why Pope Benedict XVI said that "ignorance of the fact that man has a wounded nature inclined to evil gives rise to serious

---

40. Job 16:13–14.
41. John Paul II, *Centessimus Annus*, 25.

errors in the areas of education, politics, social action and morals."[42] Without a firm commitment to this idea of fallen human nature, "serious errors" like totalitarian systems arise which deteriorate both morals and the social fabric, but by affirming the man's fallen nature, one is given a different lens through which to understand not only the presence of evil but also the possibility (or impossibility) of uprooting this evil from both individuals and societies. At least on an intellectual level, the rational difference between totalitarianism and Catholic morality is sometimes determined only by the difference of a paradigm, and the source of either paradigm is not "reason alone" but rather a choice to make a metaphysical commitment to believe something which is not self-evident.

A third object within the disciplinary matrix of Catholic morality is the idea of authority, and it has three primary sources which interpenetrate and inform one another: the divine law, the conscience, and the Magisterium. We will explain each of these in brief outline before we can properly orient them within our current discussion.

Pope John Paul II says that "Conscience expresses itself in acts of 'judgement' which reflect the truth about the good, and not in arbitrary 'decisions'. The maturity and responsibility of these judgements are measured by an insistent search for truth and by allowing oneself to be guided by that truth in one's actions."[43] Thus the conscience is a place of *judgement* about the good and not an exclusively rational decision about objective phenomena. The conscience does not decide what it should do by way of rational autonomy; instead, it *judges* what one ought to do by being obedient to a truth which lies beyond the self. This is why the church says that within conscience, there is a "principle of obedience" to something beyond the self-enclosed rationality of the thinking subject, which means that the conscience is not the domain of self-evident truths but is a participation in divine truths which are imprinted on the mind of man.[44] The certitude of the conscience does not come from intellectual investigations that provide calculated decisions on the basis of a strictly autonomous rationality; rather, its certitude comes from this principle of obedience to divine truth which is able to provide absolute certainty of the moral law.

The primary law to which the conscience is made obedient is the divine law, which is why the church says that this divine law forms the "universal and objective norm" of morality, whereas the conscience forms

---

42. Benedict XVI, *Caritas in Veritate*, 34.
43. John Paul II, *Veritatis Splendor*, 61.
44. John Paul II, *Veritatis Splendor*, 60.

the "proximate norm" of morality.[45] The authoritative truths of divine law form the universal and objective norms to guide one's conscience, and the conscience participates in this objective norm by illuminating specific situations with a binding "proximate norm" which renders a rationally-certain judgement about the good or evil of a specific action.[46]

Although the conscience can provide one with a rationally certain judgment, these judgements can sometimes err; therefore, the church teaches that the conscience is meant to be guided not only by divine law but also by a living body of authority, namely the Magisterium. Just as conscience is called to obey the divine law, so too is it called to obey the Magisterium of the church which is considered the rightful interpreter of divine law and which functions as "the teacher of truth."[47] This teacher of truth is rooted in reason, for the Magisterium "does not bring to the Christian conscience truths which are extraneous to it; rather it brings to light the truths which it ought already to possess, developing them from *the starting point of the primordial act of faith*."[48] Thus the Magisterium serves as a guide to reason by appealing to the innate workings of the rational faculty, enlightening reason with truths which "it ought already to possess." These truths can be known with certainty, but they have as their basis the "primordial act of *faith*," and without this act of faith, one will never have certainty in the teachings of the Magisterium; one might be able to discover how certain moral teachings of the Magisterium are in accord with reason (such as teachings about artificial birth control or euthanasia) but such rational alignment is not the basis for rational certainty about these teachings. The "starting point" for such certainty is the primordial act of faith in the authority itself, and without this commitment, Catholic morality quickly becomes unreasonable.

Here we have encountered the fundamental divergent truth claim which separates Descartes and Catholic morality, for both traditions propose that man can know things for certain, and they both acknowledge that authority is needed to arrive at this certainty, but they diverge when articulating the foundation of this authority. According to Descartes, absolute

---

45. John Paul II, *Veritatis Splendor*, 60.

46. "But whereas the natural law discloses the objective and universal demands of the moral good, conscience is the application of the law to a particular case; this application of the law thus becomes an inner dictate for the individual, a summons to do what is good in this particular situation. Conscience thus formulates moral obligation in the light of the natural law: it is the obligation to do what the individual, through the workings of his conscience, knows to be a good he is called to do here and now" (John Paul II, *Veritatis Splendor*, 59).

47. John Paul II, *Veritatis Splendor*, 64.

48. John Paul II, *Veritatis Splendor*, 64 (emphasis added).

rational certainty is possible by the authority of autonomous reason, whereas Catholic morality proposes that absolute rational certainty is rooted in a three-fold expression of authority: the authority of revealed doctrine, the authority of the Magisterium who interprets what has been revealed, and the authority of the conscience which obeys what it has judged. Catholic morality offers certainty to the rational faculty, but it does so in a way which is rejected by Descartes, for it is rooted in an authority which lies beyond the "thinking self" and is known only through a relationship of trust. If we want to find the principle which most significantly divides these two traditions of enquiry, it is the role of authority and where such authority can be found.[49]

Before we move forward, we must note that these statements provide an important illustration of the way in which the essence of Catholic morality is not reason but a relationship of trust. Without a proper understanding of the way the rational faculty of human nature is dependent on the relational dimension of the human person, one can be deceived into thinking that moral truths revealed by the Magisterium can be known by reason alone when in actuality they depend on trust in this authority. Without embracing these sources of authority which lie "outside" of man himself, Catholic morality dissolves into an appeal to autonomous reason. Such a morality might be Catholic in content (such as willing to affirm the evil of abortion or adultery) but it would be a fundamentally non-Catholic morality because its authority is not rooted in something beyond self-evident reason.

This also allows us to see another instance of how reason is a consequence of trust, for erosion in trust is the first stage for reorienting someone's rationality away from the acceptance of moral truth claims based on this trust. The serpent in the garden seemed to understand this very well, for his first tactic with Eve was to present reasons for distrusting God and not with reasons for distrusting his commands. The serpent does not initially contradict God's reasoning; he contradicts God's promise ("you will *not* die"), and succeeding in this latter task, the serpent can easily attack God's reasoning. This is a tactic which seems to repeat itself: convince Eve that God cannot be trusted, and she starts to construct reasons to disobey; convince man that life is not eternal, and all becomes vanity; convince man that he is not fallen, and he will easily construct totalitarian alternatives. The temptation to mistrust a legitimate authority over human reason is a primordial temptation with significant moral implications.

These considerations also highlight that which ultimately gives unity to Catholic moral theology as a discipline, distinct from a discipline like

---

49. Thus Tocqueville could perceive that "Descartes was Catholic by his beliefs and Protestant by his method" (DA, 704).

"philosophical ethics" or "religious studies." Catholic moral theology is not a discipline practiced by a group of autonomous minds who are all united merely because they share the same conclusions; rather, it is a group of related minds who are all united because they share the same source of authority, an authority whose ultimate justification lies beyond reason and above human nature. Man can participate in this authority, he can conform his mind to its dictates and learn its coherence with the natural light of reason, but it is not derived from his "own" natural reason; properly speaking, it comes from something which has been revealed.

We can now return to our subject more explicitly, noting that Catholic morality is received and appropriated by a rational mind only when it has fully committed to the ideas illustrated above, for these ideas form a paradigm which functions as an interpretive lens for understanding and interpreting the reasonableness of moral laws proposed by Catholic morality. A person may know these moral laws as rational concepts, but coming to absolute rational certainty that one should obey these laws is considered either vanity or reasonable, depending on one's trustful acceptance of ideas received through revelation.

This leads to a series of questions whose answers are of considerable import for moral theology: if Catholic morality requires the adherence to specific metaphysical commitments in order for this moral code to be reasonable, to what extent is one responsible for rational choices if one does not possess these necessary ideas as part of their operative paradigm? Are some paradigms so structurally rooted that a person could find themselves inescapably bound to that paradigm, and thus never have a rationality which is compatible with both knowing and following Christian truths? Answers to these questions are not readily apparent, but their answer influences our understanding of sin, human nature, and moral responsibility in such a way that they cannot be readily dismissed.

Some insights into these questions have been articulated by various thinkers within the church. For example, Pope John Paul II says that

> It must certainly be admitted that man always exists in a particular culture, but it must also be admitted that man is not exhaustively defined by that same culture. Moreover, the very progress of cultures demonstrates that there is something in man which transcends those cultures. This "something" is precisely human nature: this nature is itself the measure of culture and the condition ensuring that man does not become the prisoner of any

of his cultures, but asserts his personal dignity by living in accordance with the profound truth of his being.[50]

For Pope John Paul II, "nature" itself is a transcendent and theological category because human nature is permeated by communication with something beyond the collective consciousness of human beings, leading him to suggest that, even if someone is immersed in a democratic or technocratic cultural paradigm which conditions so much of their experience of human freedom and rational choice, man's transcendent human nature can provide a criterion of judgement for any truths received through this culture. According to Pope John Paul II, one need not think of human beings as creatures completely determined by paradigms received through their structural relationships and instead can hope for the ability of a human nature, which is universal in all men, to be the standard by which any culturally-derived logic, which is decidedly not universal in all men, can be evaluated and critiqued.

Such a vision of the dependence-independence of the human person on one's culture is a vision which is shared by both Tocqueville and Guardini. In the closing words of *Democracy in America*, Tocqueville states,

> Providence has created humanity neither entirely independent nor completely slave. It traces around each man, it is true, a fatal circle out of which he cannot go; but within its vast limits, man is powerful and free; so are peoples. The nations of today cannot make conditions among them not be equal; but it depends on them whether equality leads them to servitude or liberty, to enlightenment or barbarism, to prosperity or misery.[51]

Similar to Pope John Paul II, Tocqueville thinks that humanity is curved and molded by its cultural dimensions, and each person is contained within a "fatal circle out of which he cannot go," but within this circle, a person is still powerful and free. For Tocqueville, equality of conditions is a pervasive structural reality which determines many expressions of rational choice, but human freedom is not completely determined by this cultural reality because something beyond the culture can assert itself and help lead a person

---

50. John Paul II, *Veritatis Splendor*, 53. He also says "It cannot be forgotten that the manner in which the individual exercises his freedom is conditioned in innumerable ways. While these certainly have an influence on freedom, they do not determine it; they make the exercise of freedom more difficult or less difficult, but they cannot destroy it. Not only is it wrong from the ethical point of view to disregard human nature, which is made for freedom, but in practice it is impossible to do so" (John Paul II, *Centessimus Annus*, 25).

51. DA, 1285.

to liberty instead of servitude, to prosperity instead of misery. Guardini likewise argues that

> Man may be finite, but he is also a real person—irreplaceable in his unique act of being—one whose dignity cannot be supplanted, whose responsibility cannot be avoided. Moreover, history does not move along its course directed from without by the logic of an absolute spirit which is the very being of the world; it moves forward only as determined by the freedom of man.[52]

Guardini rejects the idea that even something as pervasive as a non-human humanity is capable of reducing humanity to being enslaved entirely by "the logic of an absolute spirit"; rather, the world is still capable of moving forward, and it moves forward as determined by the freedom of man. No logic is so absolute that it completely determines the fate of human freedom and thus completely limits rational choice, for these authors suggest that every culture can be renewed by a transcendent human nature which possesses an ever-present freedom capable of reforming and molding those very forces which have determined so much of who man is and how he thinks. Guardini affirmed above that "Everything affects everything," and just as culture exerts an influence on the rational expression of human nature, so too does human nature exert an influence on culture; the interaction between human nature and human culture is not one-directional but instead is bi-polar; and while a distortion in one leads to a distortion in the other, a purification of one also leads to the purification of the other. This is why minds can think about the very logic which they have received and hope to recalibrate this logic and reorient it towards the truth, for human freedom remains potent enough to correct the lacunas of a cultural logic and provide it with a fuller vision.

THE INFLUENCE OF STRUCTURAL PARADIGMS ON THE SEARCH FOR TRUTH

We have finally achieved a proper grounding of the first half of this thesis, seeing more clearly how the human person is influenced by structural paradigms which then influence their rational choices. We must now articulate more precisely the second half of this thesis, which is the influence of structural paradigms on the search for truth.

The Catholic Church considers the search for truth to be one of the most essential moral obligations of every individual. Pope John Paul II

---

52. Guardini, *End of the Modern World*, 80.

states this explicitly: "Although each individual has a right to be respected in his own journey in search of the truth, there exists a prior moral obligation, and a grave one at that, to seek the truth and to adhere to it once it is known." The pope first asserts the need to respect the exercise of human freedom in each individual's search of truth because "there can be no morality without freedom."[53] Human freedom has a rightful autonomy that must be preserved for a vital moral life, for when this autonomy is breached, we are no longer dealing with moral acts but with forced acts. But he also maintains that freedom itself contains a "prior moral obligation," which is that this freedom is used to "seek the truth and to adhere to it once it is known." For the exercise of human freedom to be authentic, a person is obliged to use their freedom as a means to seek the truth and not as a means to the next emotional or intellectual diversion.

The life of Saint Augustine provides a helpful illustration of this unavoidable tension within freedom. On the one hand, his journey of moral and intellectual development was permeated by complete autonomy, for he freely explored numerous philosophies and moralities, regardless of their compatibility with Christian doctrine. This autonomous freedom allowed him to read any book, speak with any thinker, disagree with any friend, and hear the homilies of any bishop that he so happened to choose. On the other hand, his freedom was closely allied to a deeper search for truth, for all of these books and friends and bishops contributed to his eventual certitude of the Christian faith. There are instances of people like his mother trying to interfere with his rightful autonomy, seeking to impose her personal convictions and restrict his freedom according to what she had come to believe, but finally, his mother was given some helpful advice by a wise bishop: "Leave him alone . . . Just pray to God for him. From his own reading he will discover his mistakes and the depth of his profanity."[54] Instead of demanding immediate intellectual conformity to Christianity, this bishop encouraged Monica to "leave him alone" and respect his rightful autonomy, an autonomy that was all the more necessary because it alone would be the means to discover the truth for himself and therefore allow him to make a moral choice to follow this truth instead of a tame conformity to the dictates of the religious convictions of his mother.

What made autonomous freedom so fruitful in the life of Augustine is that it always respected the deeper moral obligation mentioned by Pope John Paul II, which is the obligation to seek the truth and to adhere to it once it is known. Augustine's autonomy was not exclusively a vain journey

---

53. John Paul II, *Veritatis Splendor*, 34.
54. Augustine, *Confessions*, iii, 12.

from one pleasure to another; it was also a serious search for truth which required a serious encounter with intellectual traditions, even those which he would eventually understand to be in grave error. His ability to distinguish between the truth and a lie, between right religion and harmful heresy, was not learned from blindly following the personal convictions of his mother; it was something he learned from his exercise of an authentic autonomy rooted in a constant pursuit of the truth. Although this autonomy involved him in many years of public and private defense of various heretical doctrines and poor moral choices, it was also a firm foundation for molding him into one of the four original Doctors of the Church. His ability to teach the faith with such conviction and clarity as a Doctor of the Church seems to be partially grounded in his faithful use of freedom and the preservation of this delicate balance between autonomy and authenticity.

This delicate balance is capable of being disturbed not only within individual persons but also within cultures, with the recent encyclicals of the church asserting that the cultural balance is heavily skewed towards an "intoxication with total autonomy."[55] In the eyes of the church, contemporary cultures are more often concerned with the *search* for freedom as an end as opposed to the rightful *use* of freedom as a means to finding and assenting to the truth. In so far as man desires autonomy so that he may search for the truth, the church is careful to protect this autonomy; but when autonomy is desired as an end and is no longer used as a means to the truth, then autonomy itself has become distorted. The remaining task of this thesis is not concerned with reiterating the ways in which modern man has become "intoxicated" with radical freedom; instead, we will illustrate how the two structural paradigms presented in this thesis influence the moral obligation inherent in man's autonomy, which is the search for truth. Man's search for the truth has not disappeared at the End of the Modern World, but we will see the ways in which this search is thwarted and impeded by the democratic and technocratic paradigms. Understanding these cultural impedances can provide richer insight into the possible avenues for restoring the delicate balance which must always be vigilantly guarded by those who love the truth. The church has consistently defended the need for this balance; the remainder of this thesis hopes to better understand some of the structural hindrances to this balance.

---

55. "We must reappropriate the true meaning of freedom, which is not an intoxication with total autonomy, but a response to the call of being, beginning with our own personal being" (Benedict XVI, *Caritas in Veritate*, 70).

The Democratic Paradigm and the Search for Truth

Tocqueville begins his reflections on the search for truth, not by considering the mind of man, but by considering the mind of God. He states,

> God does not consider the human species in general. He sees at a single glance and separately all the beings who make up humanity, and he notices each of them with the similarities that bring each closer to the others and the differences that isolate each other. So God does not need general ideas; that is to say he never feels the necessity to encompass a very great number of analogous objects within the same form in order to think about them more comfortably.[56]

God has no need to think analogically in order to think "more comfortably" but instead can rely on precise knowledge of each individual object; but the mind of man is not the same as the mind of God, for "If the human mind undertook to examine and to judge individually all the particular cases that strike it, it would soon be lost amid the immensity of details and would no longer see anything; in this extremity, (the mind) resorts to an imperfect, but necessary procedure that helps its weakness and proves it."[57] Because the mind is easily "lost amid the immensity of details" which it encounters in various objects of consideration, it must resort to a procedure which is imperfect and yet necessary, a procedure which Tocqueville refers to as the use of general ideas.

The use of general ideas is helpful to thought, but it is also a weakness of the human mind, "for there are no beings exactly the same in nature: no identical facts; no rules applicable indiscriminately and in the same way to several matters at once."[58] According to Tocqueville's epistemology, the natural order is vastly complex and does not admit of "identical facts" or indiscriminate "rules" which can be applied with strict accuracy to several different objects, but precisely because the objects of consideration within nature are so vast, and the detail required for rigorous comprehension so great, the human mind is overwhelmed and resorts to general ideas instead of detailed truth to understand the object in question. So, "after considering a certain number of matters superficially and noticing that they are alike, the human mind gives them all the same name, puts them aside and goes on its way."[59] Tocqueville calls this process "superficial" because, instead of

---

56. DA, 726–27.
57. DA, 727.
58. DA, 728.
59. DA, 728.

providing one with the truth, general ideas only provide one with an approximation: "General ideas are admirable in that they allow the human mind to make rapid judgements about a great number of matters at the same time; but, on the other hand, they never provide it with anything other than incomplete notions, and they always make it lose in exactitude what it gains in breadth."[60] Thus the problem with general ideas is their lack of "exactitude," for while they allow the mind to partially understand many objects, they nonetheless provide only an "incomplete notion" instead of the full truth. The human mind does not appeal to general ideas because the truth can be found within such generalities; instead, it appeals to general ideas because the mind cannot exhaustively descend into the detail necessary for seeing the full truth of every object.

More must be stated about Tocqueville's understanding of the complexity of truth before we can see how the democratic mind interacts with truth. First, it seems that Tocqueville's epistemology despairs of certitude, and this is more than appearance. For example, he states,

> I imagine that after long debating a point with others and with yourself, you reach the *will* to act, but not *certitude*. Discussion can show clearly what must be done, but almost never with utter certainty what must be believed. It always raises more new objections than the old ones it destroys. Only it draws the mind from the fog in which it rested and, allowing it to see different *probabilities* distinctly, forces it to come to a decision.[61]

Man can find enough certainty to act (being confident in the probability of his conclusions), but Tocqueville refuses to equate this confidence in action with certitude of the intellect. Nowhere was this distinction more continuously revealed, and more faithfully maintained, than in his own study of democracy in America, for he states:

> The more I examine this country and everything, the more I see and the more I am frightened by seeing the few certainties that man is able to acquire in this world. There is no subject that does not grow larger as you pursue it, no fact or observation at the bottom of which you do not find a doubt. All the objects of this life appear to us only like certain decorations of the opera that you see only through a curtain that prevents you from discerning the contours with precision. There are men who enjoy living in this perpetual half-light; as for me, it tires me out and drives

---

60. DA, 729.
61. DA, 760 (emphasis in the original).

me to despair. I would like to hold political and moral truths as I hold my pen, and doubt besieges me.[62]

As Tocqueville descended into the details of democracy in America, both the subject matter and the unresolved questions grew, never allowing him to attain the precision with which he desired to understand his subject matter. His analogy to the opera screen is illuminative: detailed study can help the mind see objects more clearly, but there forever remains a veil which partially obscures the complete beholding of an object. For Tocqueville, certitude alone is the secure foundation for truth, and while the mind can reach approximations of the truth, the rigorous precision which he demands of the truth remains elusive. In this way, Tocqueville suggests that the search for truth, even for the truths contained within his subject of *Democracy in America*, is a search which can never be completed within the horizons of time and certainly not by the human mind as it currently operates. For Tocqueville, the very fact that a person is no longer searching for the truth of a matter is a sure sign that they have not attained it.[63]

Tocqueville would find great support for his epistemology both in the Catholic Church and in the modern philosophers. For example, Pope John Paul II states,

> Every truth—if it really is truth—presents itself as universal, even if it is not the whole truth. If something is true, then it must be true for all people and at all times ... Hypotheses may fascinate, but they do not satisfy. Whether we admit it or not, there comes for everyone the moment when personal existence must be anchored to a truth recognized as final, a truth which confers certitude no longer open to doubt.[64]

Tocqueville is an excellent example of someone for whom "hypotheses fascinate but do not satisfy," and Pope John Paul II would agree with him that the truth, to be truth, must be possessed with certitude and no longer open

---

62. DA, 841.

63. Tocqueville says this explicitly and poetically when he writes: "There is no man in the world who has ever found, and it is nearly certain that none will ever be met who will find the central ending point for, I am not saying all the beams of general truth, which are united only in God alone, but even for all the beams of a particular truth. Men grasp fragments of truth, but never truth itself. This admitted, the result would be that every man who presents a complete and absolute system, by the sole fact that his system is complete and absolute, is almost certainly in a state of error or falsehood, and that every man who wants to impose such a system on his fellows by force must *ipso facto* and without preliminary examination of his ideas be considered as a tyrant and an enemy of the human species" (DA, 715).

64. John Paul II, *Fides et Ratio*, 27.

to doubt. Tocqueville mentioned above that he would "like to hold political and moral truths as I hold my pen," and this does not make him a skeptic but rather a realist who demands of truth the same rigor as the Catholic Church. Modern philosophers would take up this same theme, with Descartes resolving "never to include in my judgements nothing more than that which would present itself to my mind so clearly and so distinctly that I were to have no occasion to put it in doubt."[65] For Descartes, as for Tocqueville, the presence of doubt is a sign that one has not arrived at the truth, and if we were to identify a primary idea of unity between Tocqueville, Descartes, and the Catholic Church, it would be the assertion that the truth, to be truth, must be universal and of absolute certitude. For Tocqueville, truth must be as certain as holding a pen, and these intellectual traditions only diverge when someone like Descartes begins to doubt whether or not he is actually holding a pen. It is the criterion for doubt, and not the criterion for truth, which causes these traditions of enquiry to diverge, although the criterion of doubt derivatively influences the criterion of truth.

This larger framework of Tocqueville's epistemology allows us to see how the democratic paradigm influences the search for truth. Tocqueville states, "I showed previously how equality of conditions brought each man to search for truth by himself. It is easy to see that such a method must imperceptibly make the human mind tend toward general ideas."[66] According to Tocqueville, the democratic logic (or "method") which is found in equality of conditions imperceptibly makes the mind lean towards a habitual preference for, and acceptance of, general ideas. He explains how this comes about:

> When I repudiate the traditions of class, of profession and of family, when I escape from the rule of example in order, by the sole effort of my reason, to search for the path to follow, I am inclined to draw the grounds of my opinions from the very nature of man, which brings me necessarily and almost without my knowing, toward a great number of very general notions.[67]

For a person immersed in a democratic logic, the search within oneself is very narrow, for instead of encountering a multitude of diverse subjects, one is left only to contemplate the self. This leads a person to contemplate the nature of man, a subject which "necessarily" brings one to a great number of general ideas, habituating the mind to search for the truth in such

---

65. Descartes, *Discourse on the Method*, 35.
66. DA, 734.
67. DA, 734.

a way that one easily settles for the superficial and incomplete notions of general ideas instead of rigorous truth.

Yet Tocqueville has previously shown how this self-contemplation is only a psuedo-logic, for in reality, the democratic mind is driven towards despair in its need for knowledge about a great many subjects which can never be discovered by the isolated authority of one's own reason. Because of the inherent need to find an intellectual authority which can stabilize the weak and isolated minds of democratic men, combined with the many practical concerns which assault all those democratic persons who must busy themselves with practical affairs, the democratic mind is besieged by another impetus towards the power of general ideas. Tocqueville describes this influence in the following way:

> Men who live in centuries of equality have a great deal of curiosity and little leisure; their life is so practical, so complicated, so agitated, so active, that little time remains for them to think. The men of democratic centuries love general ideas, because they exempt them from studying particular cases; they contain, if I can express myself in this way, many things within a small volume and in little time produce a great result. So when, after an inattentive and short examination, they believe they notice among certain matters a common relationship, they push their research no further, and, without examining in detail how these diverse matters are similar or different, they hasten to arrange them according to the same formula, in order to move on.[68]

This is a deeper influence which increasingly drives the democratic mind towards a habitual preference for general ideas: the need and the desire "to move on" to the many other activities which saturate the interests of democratic men. Because democratic people live a life which is so "practical," "complicated," and "active," little time remains for them to think, and the little thinking they do must prepare them for large amounts of industrial and practical labor, which disposes them to search for general ideas instead of complicated truths. He makes this point in a similar but more insistent way when he states,

> The democratic social state and democratic institutions lead most men to act constantly; now, the habits of mind that are appropriate to action are not always appropriate to thought. The man who acts is often reduced to being content with approximation, because he would never reach the end of his plan if he wanted to perfect each detail. He must rely constantly on ideas

---

68. DA, 736.

> that he has not had the leisure to study in depth, for he is helped much more by the expediency of the idea that he is using than by its *rigorous correctness*; and everything considered, there is less risk for him in making use of a few false principles, than in taking up his time establishing the truth of all his principles ... So in centuries when nearly everyone acts, you are generally led to attach an excessive value to the rapid flights and to the superficial conceptions of the mind, and, on the contrary, to depreciate excessively its profound and slow work.[69]

As Tocqueville noted above, action necessarily contents itself with approximation instead of certitude, building a habitual disregard for attention to that "rigorous correctness" which Tocqueville equates with the truth. For those living in democratic societies, the constant commercial, industrial, and financial activity often leads to the improvement of material well-being, but this gain comes at a cost: it habituates the mind to content itself with superficial conceptions and an irreverence for the profound and slow work of the mind required to understand the true essence of things.

Here we see the layered complexity of the democratic paradigm which has other effects on the democratic mind than merely disposing it to the democratic philosophical method, for there are other realities within the structural dynamics of equality of conditions which push the democratic mind in a certain direction. One of these dynamics is the constant activity and busyness of democratic life, and Tocqueville traces this constant activity to the lack of hereditary wealth: "Among democratic peoples, where there is no hereditary wealth, each man works in order to live, or has worked, or is born from people who have worked. So the idea of work, as the necessary, natural and honest condition of humanity, presents itself on all sides to the human mind."[70] The structural dynamics of equality naturally lead the democratic mind to concern itself with work, and combined with man's natural desire for well-being, the democratic mind soon becomes saturated with concern for large results in little time. This paradigmatic obsession with work is the deeper reason why Tocqueville could state,

> When the inhabitant of democracies is not pressed by his needs, he is at least by his desires; for among all the goods that surround him, he sees that none is entirely out of his reach. So he does everything with haste, contents himself with approximations, and never stops except for a moment to consider each of his actions. His curiosity is at once insatiable and satisfied at

---

69. DA, 780 (emphasis added).
70. DA, 969.

little cost, for he values knowing a lot quickly, rather than knowing anything well.[71]

In an aristocracy, people do not feverishly concern themselves with work because their position in society is relatively fixed, but within democracy, the goods of the world are within reach so long as one is willing to work for them, and so they reach with great effort and hyperactivity, habituating a person (and their mind) to do everything in haste. This is another layer of the structural paradigm which bends the democratic mind towards reductionism for the sake of efficiency, thus hampering the search for truth.

But this structural power which leads to reductionism is not absolute, for Tocqueville thinks that, occasionally, it is possible to pull democratic men out of their habitual preference for general ideas. The only way to do this is by involving them in practical details of a complex question on a daily basis:

> Men who live in democratic countries are very avid for general ideas, because they have little leisure and because these ideas excuse them from wasting their time in examining particular cases; that is true, but it must be extended only to the matters that are not the habitual and necessary object of their thoughts. Tradesmen will grasp eagerly and without looking very closely all the general ideas that are presented to them relative to philosophy, politics, the sciences and the arts; but they will accept only after examination those that have to do with commerce and accept them only with reservation. The same thing happens to statesmen, when it is a matter of general ideas relative to politics.[72]

Thus Tocqueville does not consider general ideas to have an absolute reign on the democratic mind, for they only manifest themselves forcefully in those areas of life in which the practical man must have some basic knowledge and yet cannot become an informed expert because of his constant activity; as soon as they are immersed in a principle which concerns their daily activity and particular field of expertise, they show the doubts and hesitations proper to those who have an in-depth knowledge of a particular topic. This leads Tocqueville to find a novel solution for correcting this democratic tendency to reduce truths to probabilities:

> When there is a subject on which it is particularly dangerous for democratic peoples to give themselves to general ideas blindly

---

71. DA, 1084.
72. DA, 738.

> and beyond measure, the best corrective that you can employ is to make them concern themselves with it every day and in a practical way; then it will be very necessary for them to enter into details, and the details will make them see the weak aspects of the theory.[73]

Once the democratic mind is forced into the daily details of a practical situation which requires their competence and attention, then a healthy doubt introduces itself into their functional probabilities which have mistakenly been confused as indubitable certainties.

It is by way of these structural realities that the democratic paradigm saturates the mind and influences the search for truth. Obsessed with bettering their material advantage, partially because of the real need but also because of the real possibility of doing so, democratic people find it difficult to concentrate on the complex truth of a matter and are more disposed to consider only that which will allow them to act. Democratic people do not inherit the leisure necessary for concentrated thought, and rarely have they even considered the purpose of such concentration. As Tocqueville remarked, such people are made weary by contemplation and meditation, for they are in much haste to "move on" to action, and in a social state where utility, productivity, and activity form the great social event, the search for truth is easily delayed and often abandoned. So while the democratic paradigm does not prevent one from searching for the truth, it does impede this search by habitually disposing the mind to equate probabilities with certainties and to seek meaningful action instead of rigorous coherence. This impedance is not absolute, for as we saw above, it is possible for minds operating according to the democratic paradigm to be seized by a healthy doubt which admits of the incompleteness of their general ideas. Furthermore, Tocqueville thinks that some people possess a grandeur of mind and soul so powerful that no structural influence will be able to completely hamper their unrelenting pursuit of the truth:

> It cannot be believed that, among so great a multitude, there is not born from time to time some speculative genius inflamed by the sole love of truth. You can be sure that the latter will work hard to penetrate the most profound mysteries of nature, whatever the spirit of his country and of his time. There is no need to aid his development; it is enough not to stop it.[74]

---

73. DA, 739.
74. DA, 785.

A "speculative genius" is not hampered by "the spirit of his country and of his time" and thus is not restricted by the structural forces which impede this search for truth. Structural paradigms in a given culture influence the search for truth, but the development and influence of the democratic paradigm is only one of many forces acting within a democratic culture, and our focus on these forces should not be confused as a reverence for their absolute power over the minds of men. Many other forces and causes are mixed within the cultural milieu which allow for man to break through these paradigmatic inhibitions and continue a relentless pursuit of the truth, one of which is the continual recurrence, from time to time, of those speculative geniuses whose love for the truth is greater than any structural inhibition. But there are other forces besides these.

Perhaps the greatest force at work within the minds of democratic people is the continual reemergence of questions. A question reveals a mind that has not yet attained that rigorous certitude which must accompany any truth, for by stating a question, a person is expressing a thirst for greater clarity about what is currently known and thus reveals that the search for the truth is still ongoing. A question, if it is not rhetorical, is itself an indication of a healthy doubt and an unsatisfied mind, but it also indicates the desire to eliminate this doubt and to satisfy the mind with something other than hypothesis and probabilities.

Consider the woman we encountered in the first chapter who was asking for advice about whether or not she should live with a man before marrying him. We do not get the impression that this woman is one of those speculative geniuses who recur from time to time, but by asking the question, she reveals the most essential trait of these speculative geniuses, which is a restless dissatisfaction with what she currently knows, a restlessness that is strong enough to lead her to put her question in words and submit it to a journal for their consideration. This is not someone who is resigned to paradigmatic probabilities, either from her boyfriend or from her parents; instead, this is someone who is searching for the truth, and unable to find the truth within herself or from her closest relationships, she is compelled to ask a question of others. The content of her question can be despairing for someone like Monica who believes with certainty in the rigorous correctness of discouraging cohabitation before marriage, but this young woman's mind is still open to questions about what she has received, and this is a good indication that she is not completely dominated by a cultural logic and instead is on a sincere journey to seek the truth and submit to it once it is known. She has not yet reached the moral conclusion which is in conformity with the Catholic Church, but she is fulfilling her moral obligation to search for the truth, and in this way, she is quite close to being aligned to Catholic morality, not in her ideas, but in her methodology.

This same reliance on unresolved and emerging questions was a methodology essential to the life of Augustine. When one looks at his life, one can notice the many ways his restless heart was leading him down paths which he would later consider gravely immoral and intellectually deficient, but one also notices the ways in which each failed step and erroneous thought was integrated into his search for the truth, for they became pivotal moments of growth and axiomatic points of future reflection and meditation. His ten years immersed in Manicheism was a lengthy amount of time spent in assent to a heretical sect, but one can also see how his mind was continually disturbed by the incomplete truth which he received from this sect, and in the midst of this disturbance, he continued asking questions. Many of his Manichean friends were only annoyed by these questions, so he took these questions to the one Manichean Bishop whom everyone believed could answer them, but Faustus could not answer his questions and thus did not satisfy his mind. So, continuing his methodology which was forever manifesting itself in his Manichean life, he entered a Catholic church in Milan and began listening to Ambrose, where he started finding rigorous answers to his deepest questions. Before he entered Ambrose's church in Milan, Augustine was already aligned to Catholic morality in his methodology, for this heart was possessed by a love for certain truth and would not rest until he found it. The way he manifested this love for the truth was by asking serious questions and not settling for superficial answers, and by filling this deeper moral obligation to search for the truth, he eventually was able to align his mind to the Church's moral truths. The underlying methodology which this speculative genius of the fourth century employed to advance towards the truth was not blind conformity to his mother's beliefs but rather a constant demand for rigorous correctness to the questions he asked.

Ironically, Augustine would eventually find the answers to these questions in the beliefs that his mother tried to impose on him, but this does not mean his journey was in vain. It is hard to imagine Augustine could have been so eloquent a combatant against the Manichees, so persuasive in his defense of marriage, so supremely excellent in his description of truth, if he had not spent so many years familiarizing himself with the lie. If Augustine's testimony is true, then a lie is no permanent threat to someone who continues to ask genuine questions, so long as they continue searching for that rigorous correctness which is not easily attained. Similarly, there is no need to despair of the mind of this young woman asking about cohabitation, so long as she continues to remain dissatisfied with probabilities and allows her questions to be answered only with certitude. This certitude was not provided by the writer who attempted to answer her question, but there is hope that she could find this answer just as unsatisfactory as Augustine found Faustus's answers. So long as there is an unanswered question being pursued, the personal search for truth continues; for those operating according to the democratic paradigm, their greatest risk is that they will readily abandon these questions in order to get on with their lives of activity and utility.

The Technocratic Paradigm and the Search for Truth

In chapter three, we articulated the way in which the technocratic paradigm impedes the search for truth because it is ultimately a blindness to the metaphysical worth of things; it is a habitual failure to see the essence of things and to even know that objects have an essence which can be noticed only with concentrated attention and awareness. The technocratic paradigm often leads to "forgetting the reality in front of us," contenting the mind with a superficial apprehension of objects instead of the deeper reality signified by the exterior appearance.[75] Similar to the democratic paradigm, it leads to a "reductionism which affects every aspect of human and social life."[76] This reductionist tendency of the technocratic paradigm is detrimental to the personal search for truth, for it habituates the mind to reduce the truth to that which is determined only by the methods of science and technology, but science alone does not answer the essential questions of human life, which is why Pope Francis states that "a science which would offer solutions to the great issues would necessarily have to take into account the data generated by other fields of knowledge, including philosophy and social ethics; but this is a difficult habit to acquire today."[77] Instead of habitually considering the multi-variable approach to great issues and questions of the day, the technocratic mind is habitually disposed to consider only the scientific and technocratic perspective. Such a methodology is insufficient to attain the truth of complex matters, but until this habit is broken, the technocratic paradigm leads the mind towards a reductionist and superficial encounter with truth. Both the democratic and technocratic paradigms are reductionist, but they lead to this reductionism in slightly different ways: while the democratic paradigm habituates man to settle for less than the truth because he is often too busy to look, the technocratic paradigm habituates man to be unable to even look at the complex array of truth.

75. Francis, *Laudato Si'*, 106.
76. Francis, *Laudato Si'*, 107.
77. Francis, *Laudato Si'*, 110.

This metaphysical blindness is not the only influence of the technocratic paradigm on man's search for truth, for there are deeper influences of this paradigm on man's freedom. Tocqueville explained above how the democratic method actually leads to a slave-like obedience to a power beyond individual reason, ultimately leading a person to rely on majority opinions as a firm foundation of his firm beliefs. Guardini illustrates something similar: in showing how the technocratic paradigm habituates one to exercise exclusively rational and scientific principles to control an object, man becomes increasingly controlled by an uncontrollable power. By instinctually cooperating with the technocratic paradigm, man becomes uncontrollably dominated by an autonomous power and therefore loses his right to an authentic freedom that operates according to individual autonomy and thus inhibits the search for truth. We must illustrate this point in greater detail.

As the technocratic paradigm saturates the minds of men, it necessarily has consequences for numerous domains of daily life. One example is the modern state, and we will refer to part of a quote which was cited earlier in chapter three to see this example more clearly:

> (The modern state) is losing its organic structure, becoming more and more a complex of all controlling functions. In it the human being steps back, the apparatus forward. Constantly improving techniques of stock-taking, man-power survey, and bureaucratic management—to put it brutally, increasingly effective social engineering—tend to treat people much as the machine treats the raw materials fed into it.[78]

By its increasing application of scientific and technical methods, the modern state increasingly controls and develops the social landscape according to its own pre-determined calculations. When Guardini says that "the human being steps back, the apparatus forward," he is really saying that, as social engineering optimizes the social landscape, the individual human beings within this landscape are diminished in some significant way.

This machine-like manipulation of peoples also manifests itself on the international level, generating increasingly homogenous cultures which have become eerily similar:

> Whereas formerly these ethnic groups showed unmistakable individuality, today they are growing more and more alike. Their mutual economic and political dependence grows constantly greater, their dress and way of life more similar. The nations's

---

78. Guardini, *End of the Modern World*, 162.

political structure and methods of operation are largely interchangeable ... (this) leveling process of the modern age springs
from the rationality of science and functionalism of technology.[79]

As the rationality of science and the functionalism of technology dominate the minds of peoples within formerly dissimilar cultures, these cultures become increasingly interchangeable and similar, and the natural variance that was formerly expected of cultures, not only in language and dress but also in political structure and methods of operation, has greatly diminished. As the machine steps forward, individuality steps backwards.

Guardini also identifies the erosion of ethical norms as another domain which has yielded to technocratic dominion and the increase of power:

> This growing defenselessness against the inroads of power is furthered by the fact that ethical norms have lost much of their influence, hence their ability to curb abuses of power is weakened. (Ethical norms) are replaced—at least temporarily—by formalistic rules and regulations and by the various techniques known as "organization." But organization does not create an ethic.[80]

Ethical norms are meant to restrict power, but as they are replaced by technocratic organization, man is subjected to the dominating power of "organization" and experiences a restriction of his authentic autonomy. This "growing defenselessness against the inroads of power" is Guardini's continual concern, for as man submits to technocratic thinking, he is made subject to autonomous powers, and the loss of ethical norms is one more example of this growing defenselessness which erodes man's ability to exercise his freedom in authentic autonomy. Thus he states, "When man drops the ethical reins, he places himself utterly at the mercy of power," but the "mercy" of the power which has manifested itself is of dubious benefit for human persons.[81]

Where is all this technocratic organization, functional efficiency, and social engineering leading man? Guardini states that the usual answer to this question runs something like this:

> By means of ever more penetrating science and effective techniques, man's power over the world's given conditions steadily mounts. This means increased security, usefulness, well-being, progress. Human life and health will be better protected; people

---

79. Guardini, *End of the Modern World*, 163.
80. Guardini, *End of the Modern World*, 164.
81. Guardini, *End of the Modern World*, 165.

will work less; the living standard will improve; there will be new possibilities for personal and occupational development; man will accomplish greater things with less effort and an even richer life. Taken separately, these claims are obviously true... but what about the picture as a whole?[82]

According to Guardini, technocracy is founded on optimism and hope for the improvement of human life and the growth of both peoples and cultures, but he challenges this optimism by questioning whether or not it has reached its promised goal. He appeals to several examples to illustrate his concern, and we will cite just one:

> When traffic moves more swiftly, smoothly, will people really gain time? They would, if improved transportation meant more rest and leisure. But does it? Aren't people more rushed than ever? Don't they actually stuff more and more into the time they save by getting (to) places faster? And when man does have more leisure, what does he do with it? Does he really break away from the pressures of life, or does he fling himself into more and more crowded pleasures, more exaggerated sports; into reading, hearing, and watching useless stuff; so that in reality, spirit-impoverishing busyness continues, only in other forms, and the beautiful theory of the richer life of leisure proves to be one more self-deception?[83]

When technocratic thinking seeks to improve transportation with its scientific analysis, it is able to reach this goal, for technocratic optimization really has allowed for the swifter movement of persons and goods within numerous transportation systems. But Guardini asks a deeper question which is not even possible for one who operates according to the technocratic paradigm: has this improvement of efficiency been of benefit for the human person as a whole? Has it really provided the optimistic dream of a better life and a richer human experience, or has it only proven to be "one more self-deception"? The technocratic paradigm can only consider an answer to this question in light of science and technology, so Guardini points to these deeper truths, not by way of calculation, but by way of a question. His own answer to these questions is implied in his questions above, and it leads him to the following conclusion:

> No matter where we start from, invariably we arrive at the same fundamental conclusion: the fundamental correction of cultural

---

82. Guardini, *End of the Modern World*, 171.
83. Guardini, *End of the Modern World*, 172.

CHAPTER 4: *RATIO IN RELATIONE* 161

> ills does not lie in the adoption of utilitarian reforms; however great their immediate advantages, *their dangers are greater still.* In the last analysis, the quality of culture is determined by the decisions of the spirit.[84]

Technocratic thought can solve technical problems, but it often does so in such a way that it creates unresolved human problems, and as technical power is used to solve technical problems, the human spirit is still threatened in often unseen but detectable ways.

While Guardini unhesitatingly accepts that technocratic manipulation has led to the completion of its technical goals, these technical results are also supposed to lead to improvements of human existence, and it is this truth claim which Guardini challenges by maintaining that they have actually enclosed the human person within suffocating homogeneity and bleak organizational efficiency. Blindly following the absolute claims of science and technology, man's relationship to the good, the true, and the beautiful begins to decline, and the spirit weakens. This is because

> the health of the spirit depends on its relation to the truth, to the good, and to the holy ... (but) once truth as such loses its significance; once success usurps the place of justice and goodness; once the holy is no longer perceived or even missed, the spirit is stricken indeed. What then occurs is no longer a matter for psychology; then no therapeutical measures can help; the only thing that can save is conversion, *metanoia*.[85]

It is this erosion of the human spirit, and its increasing suffocation by power and subsequent loss of authentic freedom, which forms Guardini's fundamental critique of the technocratic paradigm. We could say that the functional success of technocratic dominion has led, in Guardini's estimation, to spiritual failure, leaving the soul of technocratic man in desperate need of *metanoia* if he is to recover his full health and restore his proper relation to the good, the holy, and the truth.

Before we look at what is involved in this needed *metanoia*, we must pause and consider what this all means for the search for truth. As we mentioned previously, Guardini thinks technocratic man is much like Augustine when he was disillusioned with Faustus: he can see the limitations of his fideistic trust in scientific methodology, but he doesn't quite know where to turn for answers. For Guardini, the presence of many unanswered questions, especially questions which deal with the ultimate destiny of man and

---

84. Guardini, *End of the Modern World*, 172 (emphasis added).
85. Guardini, *End of the Modern World*, 178.

culture and even the world, are the sure sign that the technocratic paradigm has not led to the certitude of truth. Like the democratic paradigm, the technocratic paradigm is comfortable with probabilities instead of certainties, and even these probabilities (such as the probability that increased traffic flow will result in increased well-being for human person) are subject to significant doubt, and the firm foundation of truth proves elusive.

Furthermore, by instinctually yielding to the technocratic paradigm, man becomes uncontrollably dominated by an autonomous power which "moves forward in the final analysis neither for profit nor for the well-being of the human race."[86] This is because power requires direction, but "when power is not determined by freedom—that is to say, by the human will—either nothing happens at all, or there arises a hodgepodge of habits, incoherent impulses, and blind herd-instincts: chaos."[87] Chaos and blind herd-instincts are the result of man's unconscious submission to power as he becomes dominated by the technocratic works which he creates, but such chaotic and instinctual direction is no firm foundation for the good of man because "The unconscious is a chaotic disorder in which the possibilities for destruction are at least as strong as those for healing or consolation."[88] There are no firm *reasons to believe* that man, subject to chaotic power, will be led to authentic flourishing, and there are good reasons to think that these powers are actually destructive in the long run. By gaining control over the world by technocratic manipulation, Guardini thinks that man has lost control of determining his own good, forfeiting it instead to an autonomous, unconscious, and chaotic power which is ultimately detrimental to the well-being of the human person and the human race.

The word Guardini uses most frequently to illustrate how this technocratic submission is detrimental to the human person is "dominion." He states,

> The import of the coming culture is not welfare but dominion, fulfillment of man's God-given assignment to rule over the earth. What is needed is not universal insurance, but the kind of world in which human sovereignty with its greatness can express itself. This is not what the average citizen desired. He feared it, indeed, felt it to be a fundamentally wrong ideal. That is why he exercised the power he did possess with an uneasy conscience, feeling it necessary to justify it with "security," "utility," "welfare." That is why his governing is without a true ethos,

---

86. Guardini, cited in Francis, *Laudato Si'*, 108.
87. Guardini, *End of the Modern World*, 124.
88. Guardini, *End of the Modern World*, 125.

why it has created no genuine government architecture, style, or tradition—because it has taken refuge in anonymity.[89]

For Guardini, rightly exercised dominion is man's first and essential vocation, his "God-given assignment to rule over the earth," and forfeiting this vocation means forfeiting the essence of his human nature. What Guardini demands for the human person is a type of existence in which this greatness of human sovereignty is not only desired, but also possible. At the end of the modern world, neither this desire nor possibility were realized; instead, man feared this dominion and preferred to hide behind the anonymous structures of "security," "utility," and "social engineering." As personal responsibility was replaced by optimization, authentic dominion was replaced by subjection to autonomous power, and the essence of the human person necessarily dwindled.

We stated earlier that the search for truth requires a real autonomy for the human person, but applied technics restrict this autonomy and replaces it with a domineering control over man's encounter with the good, the true, and the holy. However, this control is still only partial and not absolute, for the truth itself continues knocking on the door by way of the unanswered questions which arise from the experience of technocratic absorption. Guardini helps to raise these questions from the unconscious to the conscious by way of his own questions, but they are not merely rhetorical devices used to assert his own opinion; instead, they are the spoken doubts of often unspoken questions, and people like Pope Francis show the ways in which these unanswered questions continue to remain unsolved within the technocratic cultures being assaulted by the technocratic paradigm. Of itself, the technocratic paradigm does not lead the technocratic mind to the firm foundation of universal truth, but the questions it raises can become a way to truth, in much the same way that Augustine's questions with the Manichees became the gateway through which he would find the Christian faith.

For those under the dominion of the technocratic paradigm, what is this gateway to *metanoia* and a renewed relationship to the truth, the good, and the holy? What could allow for true dominion to reestablish itself and the anonymous machine to regress? Guardini is clear about one thing which will not work: the presence of an individual genius. He states,

> In the heyday of the modern age's personality-ideal, hopes would doubtless have been pinned on the great man, the genius with a mastery of power so perfect as to be a model for all men.

89. Guardini, *End of the Modern World*, 199–200.

> We have only to put this idea into words to realize how utterly romantic it would sound today. Present conditions require not the single great genius, but *a whole new human structure*. This is no fantastic dream, but a reality that has recurred time and again in history.[90]

Although a genius with a perfect mastery of power is not a bad start, Guardini does not think that it would not be a solution to the issue at hand, for the chaotic and anonymous powers at work on human persons are so structurally embedded that these very structures themselves must change if man himself is to regain his rightful vocation to dominion and recover his true freedom as a human person. Thus Guardini states,

> Here is the prerequisite for the greatest task (man) faces: that of establishing an *authority* which respects human dignity, of creating *a social order* in which the person can exist. The ability to command and to obey has been lost in the degree that faith and doctrine have disappeared from man's consciousness. As a result, in the place of unconditional truth, we have catchwords; instead of command, compulsion; instead of obedience, self-abandonment. What real command and real obedience are must be rediscovered. This is possible only when absolute sovereignty is recognized, absolute values are accepted; in other words, when God is acknowledged as the living norm and point of reference for all existence.[91]

Man does not need more technical analysis in order to escape his present situation; instead, he needs a "social order" which allows the fullness of the human person to exist, an "authority" which gives human persons their rightful dignity by familiarizing them with authentic obedience, unconditional truth, and real dominion. Until such a social order emerges, the needed *metanoia* (not just of individuals, but of structures) is delayed.

Furthermore, Guardini notes above that such a social order is impossible without the acceptance of absolute values and absolute sovereignty, for human life can only be sustained on absolutes and not on probabilities. This point is similarly expressed by Pope John Paul II when he states, "Life in fact can never be grounded upon doubt, uncertainty, or deceit; such an existence would be threatened constantly by fear and anxiety."[92] Only the certitude of truth is capable of sustaining a social order which is in harmony with the depths of the human person; any other foundation will crumble under

---

90. Guardini, *End of the Modern World*, 198 (emphasis added).
91. Guardini, *End of the Modern World*, 202 (emphasis added).
92. John Paul II, *Fides et Ratio*, 28.

fear and anxiety. The fear and anxiety which Guardini identifies within the technocratic structures of contemporary man is a good sign that these structures have yet to root themselves in the firm foundation of absolute truths which are known with certainty to achieve ends in conformity with the good of human persons.

These concerns for a new structural order are part of the reason why Pope Francis says that, in order to "generate resistance to the assault of the technocratic paradigm," what is needed is "a distinctive way of looking at things, a way of thinking, policies, an educational programme, a lifestyle, and a spirituality."[93] Pope Francis is not proposing a new idea or a holy person as a solution to the debilitations nested within the current technocratic structures; he is proposing a structural reworking of numerous dimensions of daily life which together create a new structural order that can then generate resistance to the "assault" of the embedded paradigm. Like Guardini, Pope Francis does not place his hope exclusively in saints or geniuses (although such people are called for); true cultural *metanoia* which will safeguard the dignity and essence of the human person requires a new structural order which has yet to emerge.

For all the anonymous power working on human persons, Guardini places the possibility of this new structural order firmly within the grasp of human persons, even in their state of significant cultural conditioning. He states,

> There is no help for it; man can only go back—or ahead—to the truth in which the saving *metanoia* may be realized. He cannot retreat behind any system of laws, whether of nature or of history; he himself must be answerable. Herein lies the great opportunity of the future . . . (for) the future will depend on those who know and are ready to accept the all-decisive fact that man himself is responsible for the turn history will take and for whatever becomes of the world and of human existence.[94]

So, while this new structural order has not yet emerged, the unresolved questions nested within the current cultural paradigms have emerged. Whether or not any geniuses or saints will arise who can provide authentic answers to these questions awaits to be seen, but Guardini is firm on this one point: man is answerable for his response. Despite being immersed within paradigms which condition the freedom of man, man is still answerable for his choice to either construct a social order in which true dominion is exercised or to settle for the familiar and habitual control to which he

---

93. Francis, *Laudato Si'*, 111.
94. Guardini, *End of the Modern World*, 192–93.

has become accustomed. *Metanoia* remains within man's reach, but he must exercise his only-partially-conditioned mind and grasp for it voluntarily. It will not be given to him without his active participation, or perhaps, at the very least, without his willful acceptance.

Meeting of the Minds

In the previous sections, there was an intentional separation between the democratic and technocratic paradigms so that they could be considered in isolation from one another, but even in this attempt to isolate them, specific points of similarity began to emerge, and causes and effects began to blend. We must now consider these two paradigms together and investigate the ways each author provides greater insight into the paradigm described by the other and how they mutually influence the search for truth. Because both the democratic and technocratic paradigms are operative within many cultures today, it is helpful to consider their mutual interaction and points of convergence within minds which have inherited both of these paradigms.

When Equality Meets Technology

Tocqueville identifies several ways in which the structural dynamics of equality of conditions influences the emergence of the technocratic paradigm. One of the primary ways it does this is by inhibiting meditation and "profound intellectual synthesis":

> Nothing is more necessary to the cultivation of the advanced sciences, or of the higher portion of the sciences, than meditation; and nothing is less appropriate to meditation than the interior of a democratic society. There you do not find, as among aristocratic peoples, a numerous class that remains at rest because it finds itself well-off, and another that does not stir because it despairs of being better-off. Each man is in motion; some want to attain power, others to take hold of wealth. Amid this universal tumult, this repeated clash of contrary interests, this continual march of men toward fortune, where to find the calm necessary for profound intellectual syntheses? How to fix your thoughts on some point, when around you everything moves, and you yourself are dragged along and tossed about each day by the impetuous current that drives everything?[95]

---

95. DA, 779.

CHAPTER 4: *RATIO IN RELATIONE* 167

As conditions become more equal, Tocqueville thinks that the cultivation of the "advanced sciences" (something he defines elsewhere as the cultivation of theory and first causes) will become more difficult, for the constant agitation and "universal tumult" of democratic life makes the necessary calm for mediation a rare resource. But there are other forces at work on democratic persons that contribute to this universal tumult, especially the desire for well-being. Thus Tocqueville states,

> Most of the men who compose these nations are very greedy for material and present enjoyments; since they are always discontent with the position that they occupy, and always free to leave it, they think only about the means to change their fortune or to increase it. For minds so disposed, every new method that leads to wealth by a shorter road, every machine that shortens work, every instrument that reduces the costs of production, every discovery that facilitates and increases pleasures, seems the most magnificent effort of human intelligence... You can easily imagine that, in a society organized in this manner, the human mind is led imperceptibly to neglect theory and that it must, on the contrary, feel pushed with an unparalleled energy toward application, or at least toward the portion of theory necessary to those who do applications.[96]

This machine-like efficiency of democratic minds, this exaltation of the methods of science and the investigation of applied theory, become those familiar signs of a culture ready to build a structural order dominated by the technocratic paradigm, and all of these habits are something which Tocqueville roots in the emergence of equality of conditions. As the democratic mind is disposed to seek any way to advance his well-being, the mind is bent with "unparalleled energy" toward finding those applications that are immediately useful for this end, and so those machines that shorten work, that reduce costs of production and thereby increase profits of sale, and that provide a "shorter road" to wealth become almost the sole object of contemplation of the democratic mind. As equality of conditions permeate the social fabric, Tocqueville thinks that technocratic dominion will soon permeate the culture.

We saw earlier how Guardini thinks technics were indissolubly united with an economy of greed, and we can now see how Tocqueville roots part of this union in equality of conditions. He stated above that men in these conditions are "very greedy for present enjoyments," and he similarly states that "Greed is always in good condition there, and the human mind,

---

96. DA, 783.

distracted at every moment from the pleasures of the imagination and the works of intelligence, is drawn only into the pursuit of wealth."[97] As conditions grow equal, Tocqueville sees the growth of a greedy restlessness which is so particularly poignant in American culture that it causes him to remark, "It is a strange thing to see with what kind of feverish ardor the Americans pursue well-being, and how they appear tormented constantly by a vague fear of not having chosen the shortest road that can lead to it."[98] Just as egoism was a dominant power in aristocratic cultures, greed is an equally dominant power in democratic cultures and it fuels much of the spiritual drive towards technocratic dominion.

For Tocqueville, the problem with this hyperactive and technocratic focus is not so much about the presence of greed; rather, he thinks that it causes the collective mind to lose sight of the "higher" theories and first causes from which derivative applications can be constructed. Tocqueville is concerned that this focus can become so great that "enlightenment" itself can be extinguished:

> If the light that enlightens us ever happened to go out, it would grow dark little by little and as if by itself. By dint of limiting yourself to application, you would lose sight of principles, and when you had entirely forgotten the principles, you would badly follow the methods that derive from them; no longer able to invent new methods, you would employ without intelligence and without art the learned processes that you no longer understood.[99]

This is one of the principle dangers that Tocqueville sees within conditions of equality, for man can be reduced to slavishly following methods whose principles of origin have been forgotten, and the light of intelligence which makes man capable of innovation and evolution in an ever-changing world would slowly diminish. A culture's situation would only need to change slightly in order for it to require innovation of prior knowledge, but lacking the knowledge of first principles due to an exclusive focus on application, this new situation is now a life-threatening or culture-threatening force which cannot be overcome by the now-stagnant minds of democratic men. Such a situation is not hypothetical, for Tocqueville thinks it already happened in China, so he thinks it can happen again.[100] Thus he says, "you must

---

97. DA, 783.
98. DA, 943.
99. DA, 785.

100. "When the Europeans reached China three hundred years ago, they found all the arts at a certain degree of perfection, and they were astonished that, having arrived

not feel reassured by thinking that the barbarians are still far from us, for if there are some peoples who allow light to be wrested from their hands, there are others who trample it underfoot themselves."[101] Having willfully given up interest in theory and instead feverishly pursuing the immediate benefits of application, man risks subjecting himself to a barbaric invasion of the light of his mind. Thus the technocratic paradigm (and its influence on the search for truth) does not originate solely from the causes identified by Guardini and Francis, for it also has some detectable roots which lie in the structural order of equality of conditions.

But the effect of this interaction between equality and technology is bi-polar, for as Guardini pointed out, the increased application of the scientific method to so many domains of human existence has yielded a very powerful result: increasing equality of conditions. As contemporary minds continue to operate according to the technocratic paradigm, people grow more uniform, their dress and way of life become more similar, they become equal and interchangeable and thus "replaceable to a terrifying degree"; elsewhere, Guardini calls this the "great leveling process" which is the result of a machine-like manipulation of both persons and cultures. So as the technocratic paradigm disposes minds to operate according to its particular logic of scientific and technological thinking, equality of conditions among peoples accelerates, which in turn disposes such peoples to the scientific applications which accelerate the spread of the technocratic paradigm. Thus a positive feedback loop is brought into being which powerfully embeds the technocratic paradigm into minds growing up in a social state with equality of conditions. Both the social state of equality and the social state of technocracy are mutually reinforcing structures which tend towards reciprocal growth, and their derivative logical paradigms intertwine and interpenetrate with mutual efficacy and even dependency.

---

at this point, the Chinese had not advanced more. Later they discovered the vestiges of some advanced knowledge that had been lost. The nation was industrial; most of the scientific methods were preserved within it; but science itself no longer existed. That explained to the Europeans the singular type of immobility in which they found the mind of the people. The Chinese, while following the path of their fathers, had forgotten the reasons that had guided the latter. They still used the formula without looking for the meaning; they kept the instrument and no longer possessed the art of modifying and of reproducing it. So the Chinese could not change anything. They had to give up improvement. They were forced to imitate their fathers always and in all things, in order not to throw themselves into impenetrable shadows, if they diverged for an instant from the road that the latter had marked. The source of human knowledge had nearly dried up; and although the river still flowed, it could no longer swell its waves or change its course" (DA, 786).

101. DA, 786.

One of the best illustrations of this blending of logics can be found in some unique phenomena observed in contemporary usage of the internet, for it is a medium in which the democratic logic and the technocratic logic combine to mold the search for truth in powerful and consequential ways. This will be explained in the following section.

Digital Truth

When a person wants to know what time a movie starts, how to most-efficiently move between two locations, where to find the cheapest flight, or who is the highest paid athlete, they often utilize a search engine on the internet to receive their answer. As a person receives answers to their questions with increasing speed and accuracy, the internet itself grows as a reliable authority which is capable of answering more and more questions, and a bond of trust begins to form between the user and the internet. It has not taken long for this bond of trust to grow and form deep roots in the human users, and while this is not problematic in itself, it has a few potential weaknesses which must be pointed out.

First and foremost, this bond of trust disposes the mind to consider this search engine as an authoritative source of truth and can even diminish a person's ability to see other sources of truth. There are good reasons to believe that this potentiality is already becoming a reality; for example, large signs currently on display in various university libraries in America state, "Future employers want people who know the difference between a web search and research." This advertisement draws the attention of technocratic minds to something which they sometimes do not see, which is that there are other methods besides a web search which lead to the truth. It also argues that some of these other methods (such as "research") are superior to a web search, and the fact that such a statement has to be advertised to students at a contemporary university is a good indication of the growing intellectual authority of the internet over these technocratic minds.[102] Furthermore, it is a good indication that this authority is becoming so strong that other sources of truth are seen only with difficulty, if at all. This supports Tocqueville's claim that the barbarians are not far from us, for man can lose enlightenment through his own habits as much as through a barbaric

---

102. It is also another indication universities are not primarily concerned with enlightenment but with employment, for by warning these students about "future employers," what Tocqueville observed about university education in 1830 is applicable to university life in America today.

invasion, and a habitual trust in web searches as a source of truth is one such habit.

A second weakness is that the internet is filling the role of providing democratic minds with readily-available sources of majority opinions. Disposed to distrust the authority of individual people, the democratic mind is nonetheless powerfully compelled to trust a majority opinion, and such majority opinions abound on the internet. It must be pointed out that a majority opinion does not exclusively refer to an opinion found among the majority of all human persons; it also refers to an opinion found in the majority of a specific group of people that an individual trusts. This group can be numerous or small, local or nation-wide, but its power over the individual mind is not rooted primarily in the group's size but rather in the relationship of trust. This point was argued by Tocqueville in his discussion on free associations, where he shows how they have great power over individual minds, not because of their size or scope, but because of their relationship to the inferior power of the individual. The majority opinion of these free associations, whether they are big or small, become the guide over the mind of each individual person, and Tocqueville sees no reason why a majority opinion in an association with 500 people would necessarily be more authoritative for an individual mind than if this majority opinion arose from an association of five people. For Tocqueville, the free association functions as a sort of "aristocratic person" over the mind of the individual, and regardless of whether an aristocratic person is great or small relative to the greatest aristocrat in the land, they still impose a towering grandeur over the impotence of individual persons. When considering the power of the internet to provide individuals with ready access to majority opinions, it must be remembered that this power depends on the user's trust in a specific group and not the size of that group relative to the entire human population.

It is this easy access to, and continual familiarity with, various circles of trust which allow the internet to become a readily available source of majority opinions which then become a dogmatic authority over the individual mind. These circles of trust take a concrete form in the various blogs, news sites, and even biased internet analytics which present new content according to user preferences. This creates a digital landscape for the individual mind which is vulnerable to habituating the mind to settle for something less than the grandeur of mind envisioned by both Tocqueville and Guardini and easily habituating a person to confuse their *trust* in this aristocratic person with an absolute and certain *truth* which should be known by all.

One such example of this vulnerability is seen by Bishop Robert Barron, someone whom the Wall Street Journal has called "the Bishop of the Internet" and who writes the following words:

> I have used the internet to great positive effect in my evangelical work for many years; so I certainly don't agree with those who denounce it in an unnuanced way. However, there is something about social media comboxes that make them a particularly pernicious breeding-ground for Girardian victimizing. Perhaps it's the anonymity, or the ease with which comments can be made and published, or the prospect of finding a large audience with little effort—but these forums are, increasingly, fever swamps in which hatred and accusation breed. When looking for evidence of the Satanic in our culture, don't waste your time on special effects made popular by all of the exorcism movies. Look no further than your computer and the twisted "communities" that it makes possible and the victims that it regularly casts out.[103]

For Bishop Barron, the internet is not only a source of answers to useful questions such as where to eat or what time a movie starts; instead, it has also become a "pernicious breeding ground" for "twisted communities" that leverage their communal opinion to cast out their victim of choice, and such communities are, in his opinion, increasingly present within the digital landscape.

While Bishop Barron ponders some of the reasons for these twisted communities, Tocqueville and Guardini cast light on their development, for these technocratic minds are also democratic minds, and operating according to the democratic paradigm, many have unknowingly allied themselves to some blogger, news source, or other digital authority, not by an act of the intellect (though the intellect was involved) but by an act of the will. Many have made the choice to ally themselves with a majority opinion which acts as an aristocratic person within their intellectual world, but they mistakenly think that they have arrived at this choice through the effort of their own reason; in actuality, this aristocratic person has become someone they trusted by an extended relationship of digital interaction. Then, when they enter an internet forum, they bring their will as much as their intellect, making such forums a battle ground for a fierce competition between majority opinions held by individuals who follow a different aristocratic person. What makes this competition particularly fierce is that these majority opinions are received as absolute certainties by those who hold them instead of probable conclusions which are permeated by a degree of healthy doubt. Now it

---

103. Barron, "Internet and Satan's Game," para. 5.

is clear that a real dialogue can only happen if a person is open to something new, something unexpected, something *un*certain in the interaction, but when the conversation *begins* with each person holding to their idea with absolute certainty, then no genuine question can be asked. In such a state of inflexible certitude, the only type of question possible is a rhetorical question meant to attack instead of a genuine question seeking the resolution of a healthy doubt, and what is supposedly an exchange of minds becomes in actuality a stubborn clash of wills between those who have chosen to believe the authority of an aristocratic person and someone under the allegiance of a different aristocratic person. This makes an intellectual exchange of first principles impossible and results instead in the willful aggression of personal assertion, and the very fact that the decisive allegiance of the will can hide itself under the veil of discussion and intellectual exchange makes it all the more difficult to achieve intellectual growth and what Tocqueville would call "mutual enlightenment." Just as aristocrats rarely fought hand to hand but relied on their subjects to fight for them, the aristocratic persons within a democracy conduct war-by-proxy, relying on their individual followers to combat with those who follow another aristocratic person, making them intellectual pawns controlled by those aristocratic persons who compete for the intellectual allegiance of a given culture. According to Bishop Barron, such digital deception is a strong sign of the presence of the demonic in the world, for it reveals a power which habituates minds to remain content with partial truths instead of the whole truth, and these partial truths become the insecure foundation for those lies upon which the demonic builds its dominion.[104]

We cannot overstate Tocqueville's insight: democratic men are disposed to an intellectual illusion, thinking that they are following the authority of their own reason when in actuality they are constantly relying on the majority opinion of various groups which then act as an aristocratic authority over their isolated mind. This pattern manifests itself in a wide variety of cultural truths, and it continues to manifest itself in an interesting and important way when it interacts with the digital "search" for truth. Far from seeing the end of this pattern described by Tocqueville, one can see its reemergence in the digital worlds, providing a helpful illustration of how the democratic paradigm interacts and intertwines with the technocratic paradigm in powerful ways in contemporary culture.

---

104. "(The devil) has nothing to do with the truth, because there is no truth in him ... he is a liar and the father of lies" (John 8:44).

Summary of Convergence

In considering the primary point of convergence between Tocqueville and Guardini, one concept which clearly emerges is their mutual concern for the structural sources of power over the human mind and the human person. For these thinkers, power is not just something exerted by one human on another, nor is it something residing only in the forces of nature or the human person; it is also something residing within structural relationships particular to a given culture. These structural powers are so vast that Tocqueville considers them capable of extinguishing the progress of the human mind and Guardini even considers them capable of extinguishing the existence of the human race. Such destructive power originates in the fact that they are often independent of the dominion of man and thus work on the human mind and the human person in a chaotic, unformed, and haphazard way. Similar to Guardini's conception of the chaotic power of the technocratic paradigm, Tocqueville conceives of the majority as "a power that moves in a way haphazardly and can spread successively to everything . . . the omnipotence of the majority is arbitrariness."[105] It is the arbitrary, undirected, and haphazard influence of these structural powers which is their mutual concern, and both consider the blind submission of individuals and cultures to these powers as a forfeiture of their dignity, a loss of true liberty, and ultimately insufficient for guiding rational choice and the search for truth.

Although Tocqueville and Guardini see the detrimental influence of undirected structural powers over human persons, they both hope that man will take control of this power and subject it to his dominion. Just as man is called to exercise dominion over the natural order of creation, so too is man called to exercise dominion over the structural and relational order of human existence, molding these structures and shaping them according to ends which are "suitable for the grandeur and happiness of the human species."[106] Such ends will be beneficial to man only if they are molded by the freedom of human persons whose minds are enlightened by principles in conformity with the certitude of truth; but left to haphazard and undirected chaos, the garden of the human mind (and humanity itself) is threatened to wilt under the suffocating weeds of undirected power. If man will not direct power through an authentic autonomy that is rooted in a rigorous search for truth, then man will be subjected to anonymous powers whose direction affords little hope for grandeur and happiness.

105. DA, 721.
106. DA, 724.

In avoiding their chaotic potential, neither Tocqueville nor Guardini consider the elimination of these powers as either desirable or even helpful. For Tocqueville, the structural order of equality of conditions is inevitable for future societies, and so "It is not a matter of reconstructing an aristocratic society, but of making liberty emerge from within the democratic society in which God makes us live."[107] One essential element for allowing this liberty to emerge from within the current structural order is to love and honor the power of equality instead of treating it like an enemy: "all those among our contemporaries who want to create or to assure the independence and dignity of their fellows must appear as friends of equality; and the only means worthy of them appearing so is to be so."[108] Instead of trying to dethrone equality of conditions and replacing it with an aristocratic society, one must become a friend of equality, and by doing so, one is then capable of serving it well. In performing such a service, Tocqueville would have democratic citizens serve this power "as its counselor, not its courtier," directing it to ends appropriate to the human person and not allowing this power to act haphazardly.[109] Rejecting the flaccid servility of a courtier, but retaining the robust independence of thought appropriate to a counselor, the structural power of the majority can be guided by persons nested within the democratic paradigm to help mold this power in harmony with the authentic good of human persons and the human mind.

Similar to Tocqueville, Guardini states,

> If (man's) decision is essentially romantic, it calls for a return to a relationship with a nature which no longer exists. If his decision is realistic, it points toward an integration with the coming world, an integration through which the "natural" world is saved. Not only must the "natural" be defended against the new world, however, but also it must be regained by forwarding its growth from within that world itself.[110]

For Guardini, a romantic restoration of the "natural" relations between man and nature is futile because these relations no longer exist; the only plausible and "realistic" course of action is to advance the growth of the organic from

---

107. DA, 1264. He also states, "It is no longer a matter of retaining the particular advantages that inequality of conditions gains for men, but of assuring the new advantages that equality can offer them. We must not aim to make ourselves similar to our fathers, but to work hard to attain the type of grandeur and happiness that is appropriate to us" (DA, 1283).

108. DA, 1264.

109. DA, 723.

110. Guardini, *End of the Modern World*, 73.

within the technocratic world which is emerging, of "integrating" the vital form of the natural into the technocratic structural order.

Thus the source of hope for both Tocqueville and Guardini is not the revolutionary replacement of structural power with some prior structure which has been of benefit to human persons; instead, they advocate for these new structural orders to be brought under the dominion of free persons who can integrate what is vital from the past into the otherwise-arbitrary forces at work, to bend them towards the preservation of what is of benefit to human persons and human dignity. This is why Guardini says that "man himself must develop an attitude of greater freedom," for human freedom is being called to exercise dominion over immense powers which call for a deeper level of both freedom and responsibility in order to direct these powers properly.[111] As long as man's freedom remains rooted in an authentic search for truth, and possesses the willingness to follow the truth once it is found, then there is nothing to fear from the responsibility inherent within this "greater freedom," even though it is likely to take many detours along the way.

Such detours in the exercise of this dominion are foreseen by both Tocqueville and Guardini, and they demand patient reverence for this inevitability. Tocqueville says that "There is nothing more fruitful in wonders than the art of being free; but there is nothing harder than apprenticeship in liberty."[112] For man to be free, he must practice the art of liberty by way of an extended and difficult "apprenticeship in liberty," and only over time can his apprenticeship mature into true mastery of this difficult but essential art of democratic peoples. Similarly, Guardini says,

> The true, the good, and the right are realizable only if accepted by living people with inner, genuine conviction, and to bring this about requires reverence, encouragement, patience. He who would be truly effective with men must respect *their* freedom, stir *their* initiatives, awaken *their* creative centers. Working with the impulses of living persons, he must freely accept all their false starts and detours.[113]

For Guardini, aligning the structural order with "the true, the good, and the right" is only possible by allowing for an apprenticeship in freedom, an apprenticeship filled with many false starts and detours which it is tempting to eliminate by force. This is the temptation of Monica, the desire to eliminate the harmful detours of her wayward son by forcing him into

---

111. Guardini, *End of the Modern World*, 189.
112. DA, 393.
113. Guardini, *End of the Modern World*, 179 (emphasis original).

maternal submission, but the greatest fear for Tocqueville and Guardini is not the danger of a wayward detour which exposes a prodigal son to years of dissipation and loose living; their greatest fear is the destruction of authentic freedom which must remain autonomous if it is to serve its noble purpose: being used as a means to search for the truth and to freely assent to this truth once it has been found.

What is true for persons is thus true for cultures, for both personal powers and structural powers are not meant to be buried and "kept safe" but rather used and manipulated by minds undergoing their own apprenticeship in freedom. Tocqueville and Guardini think that the "safe" path of refusing to use these powers, or attempting to shortcut their growth by imposition on the freedom of others, is the most dangerous path of all, for in refusing to use them through conscious choice, man will be dominated by their inevitable and chaotic forces, and in shortcutting their development by imposition, man is denied the ability to exercise the freedom which is essential to his nature. If one agrees with Guardini's statement that "Man cannot be human and, as a kind of addition to his humanity, exercise or fail to exercise power; the exercise of power is essential to his humanity," then the temptation of Monica is understood as a hindrance and not an aid to authentic human growth.[114] One must learn to replace this temptation with a patient reverence towards the unfolding development of the powers of individual men who take many detours in their apprenticeship in freedom, and one should not be surprised to find that man's dominion over structural power is equally exposed to such meandering.

Discipleship in Truth

These points of convergence between Tocqueville and Guardini naturally lead us back to considering a recurring theme, which is the intimate relationship between truth and authority and the role of relationships of trust in establishing such authority.

In writing an apology about the errors of Manicheism, Augustine began his work by asking,

> Where then, shall I begin? From authority or from reason? The natural order is, of course, such that authority precedes reason when we learn something . . . But since we are dealing with people who think, say, and do everything out of order and above all say nothing else but that a reason must be given first, I shall

---

114. Guardini, *End of the Modern World*, 133.

go along with them and undertake what I admit is a defective manner of arguing.[115]

Here and in other passages, Augustine's epistemology is firmly anchored in authority as the basis of knowing and learning, for "authority *precedes* reason when we learn something." Besides stating this point directly, one can also detect in his *Confessions* the power of various authorities over his mind and their continual struggle for his personal allegiance. Augustine was not always aware of the power of these authorities over his mind, but time and reflection allowed them to be seen more clearly and spoken about more cogently.

In the writings of Tocqueville and Guardini, there were two primary sources of trust which emerged as powerful authorities over democratic and technocratic minds: the power of the majority, and the power of technology. The great risk, and current weakness, of these structural powers is the way in which they operate outside the dominion of man, for they habituate the mind to unknowingly trust what Tocqueville calls "arbitrariness" and what Guardini calls "herd instincts"; without even thinking or consciously choosing to do so, acting persons living within cultures dominated by the democratic or technocratic paradigms are subjected to an autonomous authority over their mind which skews both rational choice and the search for truth. The fundamental critique of these powers is not that they exercise authority over human minds (which is unavoidable if a person is to use their rational faculty) but that they do not inherently direct the mind to the firm foundation of certain truth; instead, they lead the human person in an arbitrary and haphazard direction, and such arbitrary wandering is not a foundation for the absolute truth desired by Augustine, Descrates, Tocqueville and Pope John Paul II. Just as Augustine was misled by many years of fidelity to the Manichean authority, both in his personal choices and in his search for the truth, so too do the democratic and technocratic paradigms skew these rational activities and misdirect them in ways which fall short of the full grandeur of the human person. This analogy between Manicheism and the democratic or technocratic paradigms has already been helpful in illustrating a variety of concepts, and we will use it once more to illustrate the fundamental weakness of these paradigms.

From the perspective of Christianity, the most visible error of Manicheism is that it requires a person to assent to ideas which contradict the truths of revelation, and it was on the level of such ideas which many people, including Augustine and Monica, initially tried to learn about, combat against, or assent to Manicheism. Over time, Augustine detected a second

---

115. Augustine, *Catholic Way of Life*, ii, 3.

but more essential error within Manicheism, which was its erroneous methodology.[116] Specifically, Augustine showed how Manicheans proposed to explain everything by way of "reason alone" but could only carry out these explanations by blind trust in some authority like Faustus. Far from eliminating the role of authority in the intellectual life, the Manichean heresy only hid the role of authority and cloaked it in a veil of "universal reason" which nonetheless stood on an indispensable foundation of trust.

Similar to this phenomenon within Manicheism, the democratic and technocratic paradigms easily hide the role of authority in the rational process, habituating minds to trust either their individual reason or the "good" of technology to lead them to the truth. Cloaking authority under ideological veils, these structural powers expose a person, not first and foremost to flawed ideas, but to a flawed methodology, for if it is true that the rational faculty of the human person is dependent on authority in such a way that "authority *precedes* reason," then any structural logic which denies this claim, either implicitly or explicitly, is a flawed methodology. We saw above how the democratic paradigm explicitly denies this methodology and how the technocratic paradigm implicitly denies it, and the power of Tocqueville and Guardini is revealed in their ability to show how such a denial is only theoretical, for in reality, human beings who operate according to these forms of structural logic nonetheless have their human reason molded by a structural authority whose power they cannot control. Far from escaping the power of authority over human reason, these structural logics only hide the source of authority and make it less obvious to see; but that such authority remains irrevocably potent over the human mind, even when operating according a logic that would deny it, has been much of our interest in all that precedes. Thus the democratic and technocratic paradigms expose the mind to a flawed methodology because of their inherent logic which contradicts the objective structure of human reason and proposes something less than what is fitting to the full grandeur of human nature. Simply put, we could say that blind trust in powers that have no good reason to be trusted is a flawed methodology for rational choice and the search for truth.

This objective structure of the rational faculty of human nature implies that the human person truly needs an authority to guide their reason in order for it to attain its most noble purpose, and it would also imply that the human person is ordered to a discipleship in truth. This discipleship would subject man to a power whose true authority is revealed only when it leads man to the satisfactory resolution of the inevitable questions which

---

116. "I was trying to find the origin of evil, but I was quite blind to the evil in my own method of research" (Augustine, *Confessions*, vii, 5).

arise from the truth of his being. The need for such intellectual discipleship is part of the meaning behind Christ's assertion that, "If you continue in my word, you are truly my disciples, and you will know the truth, and the truth will make you free."[117] Like Tocqueville, Jesus proposes a sort of "apprenticeship in liberty" which is rooted in a deeper apprenticeship of trust in his authority, and by remaining in his authority, one participates in a discipleship in truth which sets one free.

We can turn again to Augustine and consider the way in which his *Confessions* reveal the necessity for an ongoing discipleship in truth. Although Augustine attained full rational certitude by the time he wrote the *Confessions*, his book is full of many epistemological and existential questions which remain unresolved. The first chapter is a continued contemplation on how it is that people can pray to God if they do not first know God ("If a man does not know you, how can he pray to you?") and what was happening to him before he was born ("Was I anywhere? Was I anybody?"), and he gives the reasons for asking these questions in a way which reveals his continued dependence on authority: "These are questions I must put to you, for I have no one else to answer them."[118] Unable to find definitive answers to these questions from human authority, Augustine's rationality still appeals to divine authority and asks for guidance on many questions which remain unanswered. His methodology used with Faustus is still being applied to God, and even when he does not get a definitive answer to these questions, Augustine seems much more satisfied in his relationship with God than in his relationship with Faustus. However, having received certain and convincing answers to some ultimate questions, Augustine nonetheless continues his discipleship in truth by asking more unresolved questions, forcing his reason to submit to an authority which lies beyond his individual reason but also enjoying the freedom he experiences while under this authority. Although Augustine has certitude that Jesus Christ is the true authority which he should follow, the full truth contained in this *logos* is only partially obtained; he is no longer in pursuit of a decision about who should have authority over his mind, but he does remain in pursuit of all the truths which this authority has yet to reveal.

Above, Tocqueville explained how every political and moral truth that he wishes to understand remains veiled like objects behind a screen at an opera: he is able to perceive ever greater detail as he applies his rational faculty but still has the experience of a barrier which prevents the complete beholding of the object. Such limited vision is part of what inspires

---

117. John 8:31–32.
118. Augustine, *Confessions*, i, 1; i, 6.

Tocqueville's own discipleship in truth which he never satisfactorily completed in his own studies or in his life, but the ongoing nature of this search for truth was not some sterile academic exercise, for it yielded many fruits which have helped advance the grandeur and happiness of human persons. Like Augustine before him, Tocqueville is frustrated by the partial vision which he beholds, and yet this very frustration stirred his rational faculty and pushed it to greater heights; what he was able to see was only partial, but it was a vision more expansive than many others had seen before him, and this vision generated fruit which still provides insight for many disciplines, including moral theology.

Saint Paul taught something similar to Tocqueville when he stated, "For our knowledge is imperfect and our prophecy is imperfect; but when the perfect comes, the imperfect will pass away . . . now we see in a mirror dimly, but then face to face. Now I know in part; then I shall understand fully, even as I have been fully understood."[119] For Saint Paul, all knowledge is only partial and every idea remains hidden in shadows, reflecting light dimly as in a mirror but still lacking that clear and complete knowledge which comes from seeing face to face. So whether it is the veil of the opera screen or the imperfections of a mirror, whether it is told by a social theorist like Tocqueville or a Christian zealot like Saint Paul, the full truth remains partially inaccessible to the eye of the mind. In this life, these deficiencies of vision are enhanced by various authorities who promise to lead the intellect, in varying degrees, to the resolution of questions which arise. Man can always hope to resolve these questions with a degree of relevant satisfaction, but he can also know that more questions will emerge which expose the incomplete parts of his vision and demand an ongoing discipleship in truth in order to understand fully, "as I have been fully understood." While paradigmatic patterns of thought derived from structural patterns of trust can be reconditioned in this life and aligned more consistently with absolute truth, there will always remain some epistemological deficits which can only be resolved in eternity.

---

119. 1 Cor 13:9–10, 12.

Conclusion

WE HAVE NOW REACHED a height from which we can survey our subject and consider, with a more expansive view, the primary objective of this thesis, which was to demonstrate how the rational faculty of human nature develops according to the relational dimension of the human person. Tocqueville and Guardini demonstrated how a change in structural relationships changes thinking and logic, and the logical framework which results from these various structural relationships was labeled a "paradigm." Referring to these types of logic as a paradigm is both a weakness and a strength. It is a weakness because the term itself is rather plastic and susceptible to abuse, even by someone like Kuhn who is considered one of the most influential contributors to the word's contemporary development. However, the use of the term is also a strength, for it provides a helpful category for conceptualizing how structural relationships contribute to establishing patterns of thought that subsequently condition rational choice and the search for truth. Paradigms first attracted the attention of philosophers, but their presence in contemporary Magisterial writings shows how they are increasingly relevant to theology, including moral theology. This is not the first term to be borrowed from philosophy and then integrated into theology, with terms like *homoousious* and *logos* being some of the most prominent. Perhaps the word "paradigm" will not ever attain such an exalted place in theology as either of these originally philosophical terms, but it seems capable of enriching theology with a valuable conceptual word to help articulate some concepts not explicitly mentioned in the data of revelation.

In this thesis, the word "paradigm" helped describe how the structural order of various relationships in a culture influence not just what someone thinks but also *how* they think. This provided us with a richer epistemology than is found in someone like Descartes, for these structural paradigms demonstrate more clearly how it is that the rational faculty of human nature is influenced by the relational dimension of the human person. In the first chapter, Cardinal Ratzinger stated that "the *relatio* stands beside the substance as an equally primordial form of being," and the structural ordering of *relatio* in a given culture illustrates one way in which the *ratio* of human nature is powerfully influenced by this "primordial form of being." Although we mainly concerned ourselves with the way in which *relatio* influences the *ratio*, man can nonetheless think about his structural relationships and seek to alter them in ways which are more fitting for the grandeur of human persons, which implies that *ratio* can similarly influence *relatio*; far from being two independent dimensions of human existence, the *ratio* and *relatio* are mutually penetrating realities within the human person.

There are some important limits to our investigation, for we did not exhaust all the ways in which human reason is influenced by the relational dimension of the human person, nor did we demonstrate all the ways in which the relational dimension contributes to the establishment of paradigms. As Kuhn has stated elsewhere, the "disciplinary matrix" of a paradigm is vastly complex and is composed of a wide array of objects within this matrix.[1] We did not even attempt to identify all the objects which together generate this matrix, and it would be very interesting to consider the way in which things like language or family of origin, two objects derived from the relational dimension of the human person, contribute to the generation of various paradigms of thought, but that was beyond the scope of this thesis. We chose instead to isolate only one aspect of this relational dimension, focusing specifically on structural paradigms, and we have endeavored to present *good reasons to believe* that this aspect does indeed influence and mold the *ratio* of each human person in a unique and relevant way.

In highlighting this one aspect, we found three words that often intersected and at times interchanged with one another, and those words were "structure," "relation," and "culture." Earlier, we saw how the writing of Tocqueville often resulted in a similar linguistic ambiguity, for "democracy," "America," and "equality" were often interchangeable in a way which could be considered distracting if we demand absolute semantic consistency with each term. Even if such semantic consistency were possible, this interchange of words in the writing of Tocqueville is very valuable for showing how all three words enrich and strengthen one another. We want to suggest something similar here, for the fact that structure, relation, and culture have interchangeable functions at various points in this thesis shows how these terms are vitally important to the generation of paradigms. If we were to speak generically, we could say that a paradigm is generated by the interaction of structure, relation, and culture; if we were to speak more specifically,

---

1. Kuhn, *Structure of Scientific Revolutions*, 462–63.

we could say that the paradigms we identified in this thesis are derivatives of the relational-structural-cultural dynamics of a human person.

There are a few lingering questions which demand comment, and one involves the role of paradigms in Catholic morality. We showed how Catholic morality is nested within a "disciplinary matrix" which has several essential objects for making Catholic morality reasonable, and we are left wondering how exactly one can attain metaphysical commitment and integration with all the elements essential to a paradigm which makes Catholic morality reasonable. What needs to happen on the level of *relatio* to prepare someone for their successful integration of the *ratio* particular to Catholic morality? A strong answer to this question was not given in this thesis, but Pope Francis provides an important suggestion when he says that what is needed to generate a paradigm familiar to Catholic morality is "a distinctive way of looking at things, a way of thinking, policies, an educational programme, a lifestyle, and a spirituality."[2] A wide array of objects must become infused with a Christo-*logos* in order to generate, together, a cultural paradigm which habituates minds to the reasonableness of Catholic morality. It seems that what is demanded is a new cultural structure, and although it is slightly embarrassing to suggest such a seemingly large task, it need not be so overwhelming, for both Tocqueville and Guardini suggest that new cultural structures can be created *within* inherited cultural structures. This would mean that the lifestyle and spirituality and policies envisioned by Pope Francis need not necessarily involve the establishment of a new world order of relations; it may only involve a slight reshaping of the structural relations which have already emerged.

Another question which this thesis provokes is a consideration of the role of paradigms in the discipline of moral theology. If various webs of relations can create specific paradigms, not only in science but also in cultures, we should not be surprised to find them in a discipline like moral theology. To this day, one can trace various paradigms within moral theology which interact and intersect but do not always converge on the same solution. Sometimes, the divergence of a solution comes from a divergence of opinions, but sometimes this difference of opinion comes from a divergence on the level of a paradigm. Possessing different logics and at times a different language (at least on the level of definition), the various paradigms operating within moral theology generate a diversity of responses to very concrete moral questions. These paradigms converge when considering whether or not it is morally licit to kill an innocent human person, but they significantly diverge when considering a moral question of considerable

---

2. Pope Francis, *Laudato Si'*, 111.

complexity, such as deciding whether or not it is morally permissible for a prostitute to use a condom in an epidemiologically high-risk area.[3] For those moral theologians involved in such intricate discussions, it can be helpful to consider how their difference of opinion does not always lie on the level of ideas or even of principles but sometimes lies on the level of a paradigm; sometimes, it is a difference in *how* they think about a particular moral question which leads to a difference in *what* they think is the answer to this question. It would be very interesting to examine the various ways in which the relational dimension of moral theologians generates various paradigms of thought within moral theology, but this was not our primary objective. We only sought to make a general epistemological claim which was relevant to moral theology because it is relevant to many disciplines, and so tracing the specific way in which the *relatio* influences the *ratio* of moral theologians is only an interesting corollary but not the essential content of what we have tried to demonstrate.

A third and final question left unanswered involves the way in which paradigms contribute to the *assent* to truth. Pope John Paul II said that every person has a moral obligation to search for the truth *and* to assent to this truth once it has been found, but we only considered the role of paradigms in the *search* for truth. However, we know from the life of Augustine that finding the truth is not equivalent to assenting to the truth, and this leads us back to questions we encountered in the first chapter. There, we encountered the paradoxical moment in which the will of Augustine was not able to immediately follow his mind; having reached logical certainty about Catholic morality, he still resisted full assent to the truth of these moral teachings. We already saw how the Manichean paradigm inhibited his search for truth, convincing him that "pure reason" was the basis of all authority when in fact divine authority was also a legitimate authority, so could it be that a particular paradigm of thought was also inhibiting his assent to the truth just as it had inhibited his search for the truth?

In reflecting on why he could not assent to the truth of which he was absolutely certain, Augustine said,

> The reason, then, why the command (of the mind) is not obeyed is that it is not given with the full will. For if the will were full, it would not command itself to be full, since it would be so already. It is therefore no strange phenomenon partly to will to

[3]. This was a question considered by Pope Benedict XVI which generated extensive discussion among moral theologians. For an interesting discussion on this question that reveals various paradigms of thought in moral theology today, see the conversation involving Martin Rhonheimer and Janet Smith in *Our Sunday Visitor* referenced in the bibliography.

> do something and partly to will not to do it. It is a disease of the mind, which does not wholly rise to the heights where it is lifted by the truth, because it is weighed down by habit. So there are two wills in us, because neither by itself is the whole will, and each possesses what the other lacks.[4]

Augustine describes this division within his will as a "disease of the mind," for it cannot wholly assent to the truth because it is weighed down by habit. Such habitual "weighing down" of the mind mimics the behavior of a paradigm, for we saw how the democratic paradigm functions as a sort of "disease of the mind" which diverts the mind from the truth because of a habitual preference for general ideas and its habitual (yet blind) obedience to the haphazard variance of the majority. Although Augustine was no longer under the power of the Manichean paradigm, could he have also been under the power of another paradigm which was causing this "disease" of the mind?

Augustine is not the first person to notice this division within the will, for Saint Paul also wrote that "I do not do the good I want, but the evil I do not want is what I do."[5] Like Augustine, Paul is able to find the good and want the good, but he is not always able to assent to this good once it has been found. Like Augustine, Paul reflects on the cause of this division when he states, "I see in my members another law at war with the law of my mind, and making me captive to the law of sin which dwells in my members."[6] For Paul, there is "another principle" at war with his mind, and that is the "law of sin" which habituates him to choose things which his intellect tells him not to choose.

Fortunately, Augustine was not doomed to slavish obedience to this law of sin, for he eventually obtained the inner freedom to assent to the truth and to begin living Catholic morality. As he relates in his *Confessions*, this inner freedom was not gained by the increased exercise of his rational faculty, for he was literally at the terminus of his rational powers; the freedom of his mind came about only through grace received in relationship to a power and a person beyond his self. So, while Augustine's rational faculty was influenced by a relationship to sin, this same faculty was influenced by a relationship to grace, and where sin abounded, grace abounded all the more. Since a superabundance of grace was essential for the cure of the disease of Augustine's mind, it is logical to hope that it can be a pathway for curing the diseases of the democratic and technocratic mind.

4. Augustine, *Confessions*, viii, 9.
5. Rom 7:19–20.
6. Rom 7:23.

Bibliography

Aristotle. *Nicomachean Ethics*. Translated by Robert Bartlett and Susan Collins. Chicago: University of Chicago Press, 2011.
———. *Politics*. Translated by Carnes Lord. Chicago: University of Chicago Press, 2013.
Augustine, Aurelius. *The Advantage of Believing*. In *The Works of Saint Augustine: A Translation for the 21st Century: On Christian Belief*, edited by Boniface Ramsey, translated by Ray Kearney, 105–48. Part I, Books, Volume 8. 43 vols. Hyde Park, NY: New City, 2005.
———. *The Catholic Way of Life and the Manichean Way of Life*. In *The Works of Saint Augustine: A Translation for the 21st Century: The Manichean Debate*, edited by Boniface Ramsey, translated by Roland J. Teske, 15–103. Part I, Books, Volume 19. 43 vols. Hyde Park, NY: New City, 2006.
———. *Confessions*. Translated by R. S. Pine-Coffin. London: Penguin, 1961.
———. *Confessions*. Latin text edited by James O'Donnell. New York: Oxford University Press, 1992.
———. *Confessions*. Translated by Maria Boulding. San Francisco: Ignatius, 2012.
———. *Le Confessioni*. Roma: Città Nuova Editrice, 1975.
———. *The Happy Life*. Translated by Ludwig Schopp. St. Louis: Herder, 1939.
———. *On Free Choice of the Will*. Translated by Anna Benjamin and L.H. Hackstaff. Englewood Cliffs, NJ: Prentice Hall, 1964.
Barron, Robert. "The Internet and Satan's Game." https://www.wordonfire.org/resources/article/the-internet-and-satans-game/.
Batut, Jean-Pierre. "Totalitarian Tendencies and the Perversion of Language." *Communio* (Summer 2015) 192–204.
Benedict XVI, Pope. *Caritas in Veritate*. AAS 101 (2009).
———. "Homily of His Holiness Benedict XVI." https://w2.vatican.va/content/benedict-xvi/en/homilies/2011/documents/hf_ben-xvi_hom_20111009_vespri-serra-san-bruno.html.
———. *Last Testament: In His Own Words*. New York: Bloomsbury, 2016.
———. "New Technologies, New Relationships. Promoting a Culture of Respect, Dialogue and Friendship. World Communications Day Message: May 24, 2009." http://w2.vatican.va/content/benedict-xvi/en/messages/communications/documents/hf_ben-xvi_mes_20090124_43rd-world-communications-day.html.
Brown, Peter. *Augustine of Hippo: A Biography*. Berkeley: University of California Press, 2000.

Carr, Nicholas. *The Glass Cage: Who Needs Humans Anyway?* London: Vintage, 2015.

———. *The Shallows: What the Internet is Doing to Our Brains.* London: W.W. Norton, 2011.

Catholic News Agency. "Most Marriages Today are Invalid, Pope Francis Suggests." https://www.catholicnewsagency.com/news/most-marriages-today-are-invalid-pope-francis-suggests-51752.

Descartes, René. *Discours de la méthode (Discourse on the Method).* Critical edition translated by George Heffernan. Notre Dame, IN: University of Notre Dame Press, 1994.

Feser, Edward. *Scholastic Metaphysics: A Contemporary Introduction.* Piscataway, NJ: Transaction, 2014.

Francis, Pope. *Laudato Si'.* AAS 107 (2015).

Giussani, Luigi. *The Religious Sense.* Montreal: McGill-Queen's University Press, 1997.

Guardini, Romano. *The Conversion of Saint Augustine.* Translated by Elinor Briefs. Westminster, MD: Newman, 1960.

———. *The End of the Modern World.* Translated by Elinor Briefs. Wilmington, DE: ISI, 1998.

———. *Letters from Lake Como: Explorations in Technology and the Human Race.* Translated by Geoffrey Bromiley. Edinburgh: T. & T. Clark, 1994.

Hanby, Michael. "The Gospel of Creation and the Technocratic Paradigm." *Communio* (Winter 2015) 724–47.

Hax, Carolyn. "Premarital Sex Isn't the Issue. A Lack of Self-knowledge Is." *The Washington Post*, August 28, 2018. https://www.washingtonpost.com/lifestyle/style/carolyn-hax-premarital-sex-isnt-the-issue-a-lack-of-self-knowledge-is/2018/08/27/f494091a-a4b0-11e8-a656-943eefab5daf_story.html.

Hildebrand, Alice von. *The Soul of a Lion: Dietrich von Hildebrand.* San Francisco: Ignatius, 2000.

Hildebrand, Dietrich von. *My Battle against Hitler.* Translated and edited by John Henry Crosby with John F. Crosby. New York: Image, 2014.

Hirschfeld, Mary. "Creation Versus the Technocratic Paradigm: The Challenge of Laudato Si'." Koch Chair in Catholic Thought & Culture Lectures. Paper 6, presented at The College of St. Benedict at St. John's University, St. Joseph, MN, February 29, 2016. http://digitalcommons.csbsju.edu/koch_lectures/6.

John Paul II, Pope. *Centessimus Annus.* AAS 83 (1991).

———. *Fides et Ratio.* AAS 91 (1999).

———. *Veritatis Splendor.* AAS 85 (1993).

Kant, Immanuel. *What Is Enlightenment?* Translated by Mary Smith. http://www.columbia.edu/acis/ets/CCREAD/etscc/kant.html

Kuhn, Thomas. *The Structure of Scientific Revolutions.* 50th Anniversary Edition. Chicago: University of Chicago Press, 2012.

Latkovic, Mark. "Thinking about Technology from a Catholic Moral Perspective: A Critical Consideration of Ten Models." *The National Catholic Bioethics Quarterly* 15.4 (2015) 687–99. DOI: 10.5840/ncbq201515470.

Leo XIII, Pope. *Rerum Novarum.* AAS 11 (1982).

MacIntyre, Alasdair. *Whose Justice? Which Rationality?* Notre Dame: University of Notre Dame Press, 1988.

Paul VI, Pope. *Humanae Vitae.* AAS 60 (1968).

———. *Octagesima Adveniens.* AAS 63 (1971).

Pius XII, Pope. *Humani Generis*. AAS 42 (1950).
———. *Miranda Prorsus*. AAS 49 (1957).
Plato. *Republic*. Translated by G. M. A. Grube. Revised by C. D. C. Reeve. Indianapolis: Hackett, 1992.
Pontifical Biblical Commission. *The Bible and Morality: Biblical Roots of Christian Conduct*. Vatican City: Libreria Editrice Vaticana, 2008.
Pontifical Council for Social Communications. *Communio et Progressio*. AAS 63 (1971).
———. *Ethics in Communications*. June 4, 2020. http://www.vatican.va/roman_curia//pontifical_councils/pccs/documents/rc_pc_pccs_doc_20000530_ethics-communications_en.html.
———. *Ethics in Internet*. AAS 94 (2002).
———. *The Church and Internet*. AAS 94 (2002).
Putnam, Robert. *Bowling Alone: The Collapse and Revival of American Community*. New York: Simon & Schuster, 2000.
Putnam, Robert, and Lewis Feldstein. *Better Together: Restoring the American Community*. New York: Simon & Schuster, 2003.
Ratzinger, Joseph. *Called to Communion*. Translated by Adrian Walker. San Francisco: Ignatius, 1991.
———. *Eschatology: Death and Eternal Life*. Translated by Michael Waldstein. Washington, DC: The Catholic University of America Press, 1988.
———. "Foreword." In *The Soul of a Lion: Dietrich von Hildebrand*, by Alice von Hildebrand, 9–12. San Francisco: Ignatius, 2000.
———. *Introduction to Christianity*. Translated by J. R. Foster. San Francisco: Ignatius, 2004.
Ratzinger, Joseph, with Vittorio Messori. *The Ratzinger Report*. Translated by Salvator Attansio and Graham Harrison. San Francisco: Ignatius, 1985.
Rhonheimer, Martin. "Fr. Rhonheimer: A Final Word." *Our Sunday Visitor*. December 19, 2010. https://www.osv.com/OSVNewsweekly/ByIssue/Article/TabId/735/ArtMID/13636/ArticleID/3521/Fr-Rhonheimer-A-final-word.aspx.
Richtel, Matt. "Your Brain on Computers: Outdoor and Out of Reach, Studying the Brain." *New York Times*, August 16, 2010. https://www.nytimes.com/2010/08/16/technology/16brain.html.
Sherman, Lauren E., et al. "The Effects of Text, Audio, Video, and In-Person Communication on Bonding between Friends" *Cyberpsychology* 7.2 (2013) article 3. DOI: 10.5817/CP2013-2-3
Smith, Janet. "A Response to Fr. Rhonheimer on Condoms." https://www.osv.com/OSVNewsweekly/Story/TabId/2672/ArtMID/13567/ArticleID/571/A-response-to-Father-Rhonheimer-on-condoms.aspx.
Tocqueville, Alexis de. *De la democratie en Amerique*. Translated by James Schleifer. Edited by Eduardo Nolla. Indianapolis: The Liberty Fund, 2010.
———. *The Old Regime and the French Revolution*. Translated by John Bonner. Mineola, NY: Dover, 2010.
Turkle, Sherry. *Alone Together: Why We Expect More from Technology and Less from Each Other*. New York: Basic, 2012.
———. "Connected, but Alone?" TED talk, February 2012. https://www.ted.com/talks/sherry_turkle_alone_together?language=en#t-875814.
———. *Reclaiming Conversation: The Power of Talk in a Digital Age*. New York: Penguin, 2015.

Twenge, Jean. *Generation Me.* New York: Simon & Schuster, 2006.
Zizioulas, John. *Being as Communion.* Crestwood, NY: St. Vladimir's Seminary Press, 2002.